Barbara Hansen's
Taste of Southeast Asia

Brunei, Indonesia, Malaysia,
the Philippines, Singapore,
Thailand & Vietnam

Published by HPBooks, A Division of HPBooks, Inc.

P.O. Box 5367, Tucson, AZ 85703   602/888-2150
ISBN 0-89586-419-3
Library of Congress Catalog Card Number 86-45966
©1987 HPBooks, Inc. Printed in the U.S.A.
1st Printing
Food Stylist: Mable Hoffman

Barbara Hansen's
Taste of Southeast Asia

Brunei, Indonesia, Malaysia, the Philippines, Singapore, Thailand & Vietnam

Photography by deGennaro Associates

ACKNOWLEDGEMENTS

The author wishes to thank the following:

Thailand: Hilton International, Regent and Oriental Hotels; restaurants Bussaracum and Djit Pochana in Bangkok; Mae Sa Valley Resort, Chiang Mai.

Malaysia: Kuala Lumpur YWCA, Kuala Lumpur Hilton Hotel and restaurants Shiraz, Omar Khayam, Jothy's and Bilal in Kuala Lumpur; Eastern & Oriental Hotel in Penang.

Singapore: Raffles, Hilton International, Mandarin, Oberoi Imperial and King's Hotels; Luna Coffee Shop of the Apollo Hotel, Singapore Cricket Club, Omar Khayyam and Madras New Woodlands restaurants.

Indonesia: Jakarta Hilton International Hotel in Jakarta; Ramayana Seaside Cottages in Bali.

Brunei: The Istana Nurul Iman (palace of the Sultan) and Sheraton-Utama Hotel in Bandar Seri Begawan.

The Philippines: Manila Peninsula Hotel, Century Park Sheraton and restaurants Ang Bistro Sa Remedios, Aristocrat, Guernica and Kamayan in Manila; Villa Escudero, San Pablo City; Punta Baluarte Resort, Batangas Province.

Los Angeles: Dewi Indonesian Restaurant, Robert's Hollywood Grille and Van Hoa restaurants.

Additional recipes were inspired by dishes served at The Hot Shoppe, My Choice and Toll Gate restaurants in Bangkok; Marco Polo in Kuala Lumpur; Cendol House and Noodle Garden in Singapore; Aling Asiang in Manila. And in Los Angeles, Bussarakum, Indra, Maneeya, Sompun, Sukothai, Sunshine and Taratip, Thai restaurants; Au Fontainebleau, French-Vietnamese restaurant; and Dong Phuong, Hong Phuong, Thanh My and Royal Cuisine (Santa Monica), Vietnamese restaurants.

Thanks also to Rosemarie Wee and Zarina Noordin, Kuala Lumpur; Pat Lee and Cynthia Bushman, Singapore; Ann Soeleiman and Tatie Usman, Yogyakarta; Lina Navarro, Lovelina David, Angelina C. Carranceja and Evelyn Co Chua, Manila, and Minnie Bernardino, Hilde Djie, Mary Djie, Geraldine Kuperus, Tuyen Lecong, Tam Lecong, Chomsri Lewinter, Noi Phanucharas, Lada Pirojboot and Pearl Wong, Los Angeles.

Language consultants were Lada Pirojboot, Thai recipe titles, and Tam Lecong of Van Hoa restaurant, Vietnamese recipe titles.

Contents

INTRODUCTION

In recent years, Southeast Asian cooking has captured the attention of the world. Immigrants and refugees have furthered its spread by opening restaurants and markets in their new homelands. Tourists and business travelers who have tried and enjoyed the food overseas can experience it again by using this book.

Far from being an exotic novelty, Southeast Asian food appeals because it suits contemporary lifestyles. The backyard barbecue chef, the vegetarian, the diet-conscious salad lover and the natural foods advocate can find as much to please them in these intriguing cuisines as the culinary adventurer seeking new horizons.

Aside from being delicious, Southeast Asian cooking is practical. Dishes make the most of whatever nature provides. When meat is scarce, a bit of tofu, a luscious peanut sauce or a wedge of egg supplies protein. Rather than eating the large quantities of meat demanded elsewhere, Asians are content with a small amount added to soup, vegetables, rice or noodles. Fish and shellfish are widely consumed. Fresh vegetables and fruits provide healthful, light eating. Nourishing yogurt appears in curries and other dishes of Indian origin. Resourceful seasoning turns even the most humble ingredients into appetizing fare.

Economy-minded Asian cooks know how to conserve fuel, another trait worth copying. Many dishes are cooked in a wok, which uses heat more efficiently than other pans. Rapid stir-frying in a wok saves fuel. And deep-frying in a wok has a special advantage. Because a wok is narrow at the bottom, it requires less oil than a broad, flat skillet or saucepan. Cutting ingredients into small pieces also helps to reduce the cooking time, as in stir-frying. Another example is satay, which consists of small pieces of meat threaded on sticks and grilled over charcoal.

Practicality puts no damper on imagination, however. The innovative Thais made warm meat and seafood salads long before they were introduced by trend-setting American chefs. Such basic Asian seasonings as lemon grass, tamarind and cilantro (fresh coriander) have been adopted by these same experimental chefs in their ongoing search for new flavors and menus.

On the other hand, Asians do surprising things with common western foods. Corn, regarded as a vegetable in most of the world, is sprinkled over ice cream by the Thais or combined with coconut milk and sugar in a Malaysian porridge. The Thais add sugar to noodles and meats. And the Balinese blend avocados into a sweet drink.

The recipes in this book are drawn from the six countries that compose the Association of Southeast Asian Nations and one additional country, Vietnam. (See map, page 33.) The ASEAN members are Thailand, Malaysia, Singapore, Indonesia, Brunei and the Philippines. Vietnam is included because its cooking has become well known as its inhabitants have spread to other parts of the world.

The region as a whole offers tremendous diversity. China and India have strongly influenced the cuisines. Colonial powers such as Spain, Holland, England and France have left their mark. More recently, expatriate workers from Australia, the United States, Europe, Japan and elsewhere have added to the culinary hodgepodge.

Religion is another important dietary factor. What is eaten varies according to whether the individual is Muslim, Buddhist, Hindu or Christian. Regional variations exist within a single country as do economic variations. The affluent resident of Kuala Lumpur or Jakarta will eat differently from Malays or Javanese living in rural *kampongs* (villages).

In compiling this book, the needs of readers who are unfamiliar with Asian food have been kept in mind. Some recipes require special Asian ingredients, which are increasingly available outside Southeast Asia. However, many dishes require nothing more exotic than soy sauce and can be prepared anywhere. The recipes are not difficult. While a few require a large number of ingredients and several stages of preparation, the steps are not difficult. Other recipes are so simple that a novice can prepare them with ease.

To explore any one Southeast Asian cuisine would require many volumes. This book, therefore, is not a comprehensive study but an introduction. An effort was made to include dishes that have become popular outside the region. Another goal was to document previously unrecorded recipes. Asian cooks pass on their lore informally, by word of mouth or example. Recipes are not standardized but vary from cook to cook and are eventually lost if no attempt is made to preserve them.

The research included talking to Asian immigrants in the United States and recreating the food they cook at home or in their restaurants. Still more recipes were developed from dishes tasted overseas. Restaurants and hotels in Southeast Asia were generous in revealing how their chefs prepare local specialties. Even food stall vendors were willing to demonstrate how their dishes are prepared.

Southeast Asian food is light, healthful and as bright as the sun that warms this part of the world so intensely. Those who try it will agree that its popularity is well deserved.

THE COUNTRIES

THAILAND

Probably no Southeast Asian cuisine has a larger following outside the country than that of Thailand. Responsible for its popularity are Thai immigrants who seem to be born restaurateurs. Wherever they settle, restaurants appear by the score. Thus word has spread that Thai cooking is intriguing, different and very pleasing to western tastes. Like gifted musicians, Thais orchestrate a tantalizing blend of flavors—sweet, sour, salty and spicy—into their cooking, sometimes all of these in a single dish. Curries, salads and soups can be simultaneously refined and blazingly hot with chilies. Elaborate garnishing and carving of fruits and vegetables turn a meal into an artistic experience.

Formerly known as Siam, Thailand today is a constitutional monarchy with some 50 million inhabitants. Buddhism predominates and magnificent temples abound. Unlike other Southeast Asian countries, Thailand has never been colonized by a foreign power. The many influences in its cooking result from its unique location. Bounded by Burma, Laos, Cambodia and Malaysia, it is less than 100 miles from China and Vietnam. For centuries, Thailand flourished as a trade center for Asia and a stop for ships on the way from China to India.

Strong Chinese influence characterizes both the cooking and the population. Approximately one out of six residents of Bangkok is of Chinese ancestry. Cleavers and woks are essential kitchen equipment. Rice is the foundation of a meal, and noodles are prepared in dizzying variety. So close is the link that restaurants outside of Thailand often advertise their food as Thai-Chinese. In Thai hands, dishes that are basically Chinese become transformed; stir-fried dishes can be startlingly spicy. Noodles are seasoned with sugar, chilies and chopped peanuts. And fried rice might be dotted with raisins and pineapple and served in a pineapple shell.

Now that many Thai ingredients are either imported or cultivated abroad, it is possible to prepare Thai dishes that will taste much the same as they do in Bangkok. Asian markets carry curry pastes, fish sauce, canned coconut milk, shrimp paste, chili sauces, canned palm seeds, pandan flavoring and much more. In some areas, it is possible to obtain fresh lemon grass, kaffir lime leaves and Thai eggplants the size of golf balls or even smaller. Laos root, known in Thailand as *kha,* can be purchased dried, frozen and, occasionally, fresh. Thai jasmine rice, prized for its long grain and distinctive fragrance, is exported to a number of countries including the United States.

Today Thailand is a popular destination for tourists, who are attracted by its ancient culture, its beauty and crafts. Since Thais love to eat, food is everywhere. Visitors can sample Thai delicacies not only in restaurants and hotels but in modern supermarkets, which include food stalls that sell savory dishes, and sweet shops that offer tempting confections. Vendors ply the canals of Bangkok in small boats dispensing noodles and other dishes, and snacks of many types are available for a pittance from sidewalk cooks.

MALAYSIA

The Federation of Malaysia is a divided nation. Eleven of its thirteen states and the federal district of Kuala Lumpur occupy the southern portion of the Malay Peninsula and neighboring islands, including Penang. The remaining two states, Sabah and Sarawak, are located on the island of Borneo. These two states are called East Malaysia while the peninsular part of the country, where most of the people live, is West Malaysia.

Rich in tin and rubber, the country was ruled by Great Britain until 1957. The peninsular portion was known as Malaya and

joined with the Borneo states to become Malaysia in 1963.

As might be expected, the population is heavily Malay, but there are also many Chinese and a substantial number of Malaysian Indians. Cultural and regional differences make for an interesting diversity of food. In Kuala Lumpur, the capital city, a typical breakfast consists of *nasi lemak,* which is rice cooked with coconut milk and garnished with a bit of curried chicken, meat or seafood. In Georgetown on the island of Penang, where Chinese influence is more marked, the day might start with a bowl of Chinese-style noodle soup. Cooking in the northern Malaysian state of Kelantan is affected by that of neighboring Thailand. And in Kuala Lumpur, there is a little of everything, including Thai, Chinese, Indian, Pakistani and traditional Malay dishes.

In their early days, Penang, Malacca and Singapore were known as the Straits Settlements. In these settlements flourished the unique cuisine of the Straits Chinese, which is referred to as *nonya* cooking. This cuisine grew out of intermarriage between Malay women and immigrant Chinese workers and is called nonya (or nyonya) because that is the Malay word for a married woman. Nonya dishes combine elements of both cultures. For example, nonya cooks use pork, which is not eaten by Muslim Malays, and prepare curries with coconut milk and seasonings that are not common in China.

In Malaysia, the old custom of eating with the hands is still followed. Some food stalls and small shops provide what looks like a pot of tea on a stand. The pot is actually a container of water to pour over the fingers after eating. The stand is a receptacle for the water.

Newcomers quickly become aware that the official religion of the country is Islam. The bacon or ham served in a hotel coffee shop might be made with beef or turkey because Muslims do not eat pork. A sign outside a hamburger shop guarantees that its burgers are *halal,* which means made according to Islamic dietary rules. During *Ramadan,* the fasting month, Muslims neither eat nor drink from sunrise to sunset. Restaurants are almost vacant during the day, and some close for the duration. Eating places post signs that Muslims will not be served. And those who break the fast publicly are subject to fine.

That may sound grim, but anyone who has been invited to join a family in breaking the fast at nightfall knows there is no ban on bountiful food and pleasant hospitality. Tourists can enjoy the experience, too, for hotels lure customers with elaborate buffets after sundown. Lucky are those who visit Malaysia during *Hari Raya,* the celebration that follows Ramadan. Gifts and greeting cards are exchanged, new clothes are worn, and hospitable Malays hold open house, inviting all to share in the happy occasion.

SINGAPORE

When Sir Stamford Raffles landed on a sparsely populated island at the tip of the Malay Peninsula in 1819, he saw its potential as a trade center. And what foresight that was. Today the island of Singapore is a thriving financial and commercial center, boasting one of the world's leading harbors. Singapore remained under British rule until it joined the Federation of Malaysia in 1963, then it split off from that alliance two years later to become a fully independent republic.

Aside from its commercial importance, Singapore is a favorite stop for tourists. A giant shopping center, it tempts with goods from the western world as well as almost anything made in the Orient. Visitors appreciate the government's promotion of cleanliness, courtesy, safety and civic beauty. The liberal cultivation of tropical greenery has beautified the streets and earned Singapore its reputation as a garden city. Orchids are commonplace and one of them, the Vanda Miss Joaquim, is the national flower.

Modernization has swept the quaint, colorful shops and neighborhoods of the past into high rises and apartment buildings. But one of Singapore's greatest assets will never disappear—and that is food. Concentrated in a small area, the city seems like a food festival with its many places to eat. Singaporeans are discriminating and appreciative customers. They know where to go for the best version of a dish. And they miss their food when away from home.

In the old days, local specialties were readily available at open air street stalls. Now street eating has almost disappeared, and the stalls function in more antiseptic fashion inside orderly centers. The atmosphere may not be the same, but the food is still wonderful—and inexpensive.

The city's diverse population makes for an interesting mix of food. About three-fourths of the population is Chinese. The next largest group is Malay followed by Indians, with a mixture of other groups forming the remainder. Almost every style of Chinese dish is available, from Cantonese dim sum to Taiwanese noodles. Sichuan and other Chinese provinces are represented, but the southern Hokkien (Fukien) Chinese and Teochews (Chiu Chows) have made an especially large contribution. Most Singaporean Indians have emigrated from the South so that spicy southern curries and vegetarian dishes are common, but zesty Indian Muslim dishes and the refined food of the North are also appreciated.

Along with Penang and Malacca, early Singapore was a center of nonya, or Straits Chinese, cooking. Traditionally associated with the home, nonya cooking has become more widely available in restaurants and hotels. The renowned Raffles Hotel offers a nonya buffet and also a curry *tiffin* (lunch) featuring the milder curries popular with the British. Of course, one must start such a meal with a Singapore Gin Sling, the famous cocktail that was created at the Raffles.

As a crossroads of trade and other business, Singapore caters to every taste, whether it be for French, Italian, Japanese, Korean, Thai, Vietnamese, Indonesian, American fast food or local dishes. In this city, culinary boredom is indeed impossible.

INDONESIA

Indonesia consists of 13,677 islands, making it the world's largest archipelago. Some of the islands are tiny, uninhabited atolls. Others, such as Sumatra, Java and Bali, are major centers of population and tourism. Irian Jaya is the western portion of the island of New Guinea, and Kalimantan occupies the bulk of the island of Borneo, where Brunei and the East Malaysian states of Sabah and Sarawak are also located. Madura, Lombok and Sulawesi are other components of the island chain.

With some 150 million inhabitants, Indonesia is the fifth most populated nation in the world. Ninety percent of the people are Muslim except in Bali, where the predominant religion is a form of Hindusim. Since freedom of worship is the national policy, Islam has not been made an official state religion.

In such a diverse land, many languages and dialects are spoken. To ease communication, there is a national language, Bahasa Indonesia, which is derived from Malay. The two languages are similar but deviate in some respects. For example, the Indonesian word for the shrimp paste that is used in cooking is *terasi*. In Malaysia, the paste is known as *belacan*. Candlenuts, which are ground and added to a variety of dishes, are commonly called *kemiri* in Indonesia and *buah keras* in Malaysia. Spellings differ too. *Saté,* the Indonesian word for grilled kabobs, becomes *satay* in Malaysia. The two cuisines resemble each other, but Malaysians say their dishes are hotter.

Indonesia became independent August 17, 1945 after more than 300 years of Dutch domination. Jakarta, the capital, was formerly known as Batavia, and Indonesia was the Netherlands East Indies.

The famous meal of Indonesia is known as *rijsttafel,* a Dutch word meaning rice table. The rice serves as the focal point of a parade of dishes as elaborate as the host is able to provide. Restaurants for everyday eating often simplify this ornate meal to a plate of rice topped with samples of a much smaller assortment of food.

To the foreigner, the most characteristic Indonesian dish is probably saté with peanut sauce, followed by *gado gado,* a salad of vegetables, potatoes and tofu that is also served with peanut sauce. Saté might be made with beef, lamb, chicken, turtle, fish, shrimp, variety meats or pork, the pork eaten only by non-Muslims. Other dishes popular with tourists are *nasi goreng* (fried rice) and *bami goreng* (fried noodles). Rice steamed with coconut milk and tinted yellow with turmeric is served on festive occasions.

In addition to the Dutch, the food has been influenced by Indians, Arabs and Chinese. Common ingredients are shrimp paste, a rich-tasting sweet soy sauce called *kecap,* lemon grass, laos root, candlenuts, coconut milk, chilies, ginger and other spices.

Regional variations add to the richness of Indonesian cookery. In general, Javanese food tends to be sweet, and Sumatran dishes tend to be very spicy. Meals are eaten with a fork and large spoon, but some say the food tastes best when eaten in the traditional way, with the fingers.

BRUNEI

Brunei became independent January 1, 1984 after more than 90 years as a British protectorate. This small country on the northwestern edge of the island of Borneo is a major producer of oil and liquefied natural gas and, as a consequence, has become enormously wealthy. Covering an area of 2,226 square miles, Brunei has only some 200,000 inhabitants, most of them Malays.

Islam is the national religion, and a dominant feature of the capital city, Bandar Seri Begawan, is the golden-domed Omar Ali Saiffudien Mosque. Since the city is very small, one is constantly aware of the *muezzin's* calls to prayer, an exotic sound to those hearing the musical intonations for the first time. A unique subdivision is a water village built on stilts that is said to be the largest such village in the world. The name of the village is Kampong Air, the word *air* meaning water.

Modern and progressive, Brunei offers its citizens free education, free medical care and freedom from income tax as well as other benefits that make it a miniature paradise. It also has its own airline. The country's full name is Negara Brunei Darussalam. *Darussalam* means abode of peace, and Brunei is exactly that, a quiet place where socializing at home is the main form of entertainment.

Malays are hospitable and proud of their houses. Accordingly, Brunei's ruler, His Majesty Sultan Hassanal Bolkiah Mu'izzadin Waddaulah, celebrated independence by building a $300 million palace and by hosting a banquet for 5,000. The palace is called the Istana Nurul Iman. Istana is the Malay word for palace, and Nurul Iman means center of faith. The Istana's vast kitchens are a model of food service efficiency and are supervised by one chef for western cuisine and another for Malay dishes.

The royal dining room, which can hold 300 diners, is fronted with glass. When there are larger events, the door is kept open so that the sultan figuratively dines with the guests massed in the open-air banquet space beyond. No one may eat before the sultan starts, and all must stop when he does. The ordinary citizens of Brunei are able to eat at the Istana, too. During Hari Raya, the festival that ends the fasting month of Ramadan, there is a three-day reception for all who care to come. The visitors are served snacks, cakes and beverages and are greeted personally by the royal family.

The food of Brunei is chiefly Malay, but terminology differs slightly from that used in Malaysia. A curry is called a *gulai*, and the spicing is milder. The country is so small that it cannot raise sufficient food and must rely on imports. Fruits, vegetables and rice are cultivated in small quantity as are beef and poultry. Local seafood is excellent, but the supply is unsteady.

Along with Malay food, Brunei's restaurants serve Chinese, Indian, Indonesian and western dishes. And food from almost anywhere turns up in the homes of an international community of diplomats, bankers, teachers and others who have come to Brunei to work.

A special feature of this book is a selection of recipes from the Istana Nurul Iman. These include several dishes that were served at the independence day banquet. Following Muslim practice, only non-alcoholic drinks are offered at the Istana, among them coffee, tea, juices and local beverages flavored with rose syrup or pandan (see page 22).

THE PHILIPPINES

Geographically, the more than seven thousand islands that make up the Philippines are part of Southeast Asia. The land is lushly tropical, forested with coconut palms and carpeted with rice paddies. *Carabao* (water buffalo) work the paddies and plod along the highways transporting heavy loads. Mangoes, papayas, bananas and other tropical fruits grow profusely in response to the hot, humid climate. Fragrant flowers with exotic names like *ilang-ilang* and *sampaguita* perfume the air. And a Malay-Polynesian heritage, overlaid with other strains, is evident in the people.

Culturally, the islands are very western compared to the rest of Southeast Asia. Spain ruled for more than 300 years, naming the islands for King Philip II and leaving a marked imprint on the language and lifestyle. Roman Catholicism dominates rather than Buddhism or Islam. Spanish surnames like Reyes, Navarro, Gaviola and Romero are prevalent. Towns and barrios celebrate fiestas in honor of their patron saints. And the afternoon snack is called a *merienda*, which is just one of many Spanish words in the vocabulary.

A great number of Filipino dishes originated in Spain, but others stem from Chinese cultural influences that reach back to the early traders. Among these are steamed dumplings, fried noodles, rice dishes and spring rolls, which the Filipinos call *lumpia*.

The first westerner to reach the islands was the Portuguese explorer Ferdinand Magellan, who landed at Samar Island with a Spanish expedition in 1521. Fifty years later, Miguel Lopez de Legazpi, a Spaniard, took possession of Manila, which is located on Luzon, the largest of the islands. Spain retained control until the United States took over in 1898. On July 4, 1946, independence was proclaimed.

Those who have traveled in former Spanish colonies such as Mexico will feel at home in the Philippines. The churches, the towns with their plazas, the lilting traditional songs, the horse-drawn carriages and the generous hospitality extended even to strangers bespeak a common heritage. It is no surprise to learn that the viceroy of New Spain (Mexico) had jurisdiction over the new colony and that early commerce was dominated by the galleon trade with Acapulco.

In keeping with its western ancestry, Filipino food is mildly seasoned. Chilies are used liberally only in Bicol Province in the south of Luzon. Characteristic Filipino ingredients include *bagoong*, which is a strong-tasting shrimp paste, and *patis*, the Filipino name for fish sauce. Garlic, palm vinegar, green tamarind, coconut milk, soy sauce and the *calamansi*, a tiny lime, are other common ingredients.

Fried and barbecued meats and fish are well liked. And in desserts and baked goods, Filipinos have few rivals. Fine European-style cakes, pastries and breads are much admired along with coconut-flavored desserts and distinctive local sweets.

Oddly enough, Filipino food remains largely undiscovered outside the islands. The reason for this is not a communications barrier because English is spoken everywhere along with Pilipino (Tagalog), the national language. It has more to do with Filipino custom, which is to entertain at home. In recent years, creative restaurateurs in Manila have begun to showcase the cuisine, researching traditional dishes and encouraging innovative use of native ingredients. Hopefully, their efforts will bring this entrancing food the attention it rightfully deserves.

VIETNAM

In a small café, customers linger over squat glasses of strong, sweet coffee. The plaintive music in the background calls to mind a Parisian cabaret. A deliveryman carries in a load of crusty baguettes, and sandwiches made with French bread are on the menu. But this is not France. It is one of many small restaurants in Southern California where Vietnamese gather to recall their native land and to savor its food.

The dishes they eat reflect the influence of China, France and Southeast Asia, the result of Vietnam's geographical setting and political history. Ruled by the Chinese for a thousand years, until 939 A.D., the country became part of French Indo-China in the 19th century. It then consisted of Tonkin in the north, Annam in the middle and Cochin-China in the south. Hanoi, located in Tonkin, was the Indo-Chinese capital. Hue reigned over Annam, and Saigon, now Ho Chi Minh City, was the capital of Cochin-China and renowned as the Paris of Southeast Asia. The three parts were united in 1945. Division into North and South Vietnam followed the departure of the French in 1954, and in 1975, the South fell to the Communist North Vietnamese.

War may have shattered Vietnam, but the cuisine thrives, transported to other lands by refugees. Dishes are full of flavor. Although spicy at times, they are not dominated by hot seasoning, which makes them widely acceptable. Most of the food served in Vietnamese restaurants overseas is from the South, which was the richest region and the most developed agriculturally. One exception is the beef-noodle soup, *pho*, which comes from the North but is popular with all Vietnamese.

Eating Vietnamese food often seems like eating a salad, for many dishes are accompanied by platters heaped with lettuce, fresh herbs and raw vegetables, such as carrots, cucumbers and bean sprouts. Portions of crisp-fried spring rolls are wrapped in lettuce and dipped in a mixture of fish sauce, sugar and vinegar that, like the greenery, often goes with Vietnamese food. Grilled meats are folded with lettuce, herbs and vegetables in soft rice wrappers and dipped in the same type of sauce.

In Vietnamese markets, Chinese products share shelf space with Thai ingredients and French imports such as Normandie butter, pâté de foie gras, vanilla sugar and decorative tins of butter cookies. Distinctively Asian staples include fish sauce, which is as basic to the Vietnamese kitchen as soy sauce is to the Chinese; hoisin sauce, lemon grass, fresh red chilies, rice, noodles and parchment-like rice wrappers for spring rolls. Often the shops are perfumed with coffee, which is ground to order.

The Vietnamese recipes in this book were gathered by talking to immigrants and sampling the food served in their restaurants. The restaurants tend to be simple cafés specializing in grilled meats, rich and varied soups and interesting noodle presentations. Popular beverages are lemonade, Chinese tea, soybean milk and French-roast coffee. Dessert plays a minor role, but occasionally menus offer flan (crème caramel), a legacy from the French.

MENUS

The following menus are representative of meals in the various countries. Use them as ideas for a special meal or as an introduction to Southeast Asian dishes. Also feel free to add Southeast Asian dishes and ingredients to menus for Western-style meals as illustrated in the Fiesta Dinner, Easy Dinner and August Dinner.

THAILAND

A Thai Feast

Chicken Satay
(page 42)
Lada's Cucumber Salad
(page 102)
Sweet Sticky Noodles
(page 140)
Hot & Sour Shrimp Soup
(page 51)
Green Chicken Curry
(page 70)
Garlic-Pepper Beef
(page 85)
Basic Steamed Rice
(page 133)
Fried Bananas
(page 162)

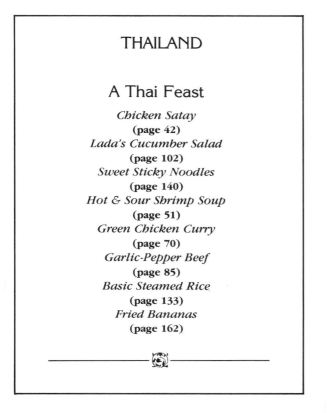

THAILAND

Summer Patio Dinner

Barbecued Chicken
(page 75)
Stir-Fried Rice Noodles
(page 139)
Carrot & Green Bean Relish
(page 101)
Thai Iced Tea
(page 167)
Coconut Ice Cream
(page 154)

MALAYSIA

Foods from India & Pakistan

Beef in Ginger-Tomato Sauce
(page 87)
Chicken with Curry Cream Sauce
(page 73)
Aromatic Rice
(page 137)
Vegetables with Tropical Fruits & Cashews
(page 127)
Rosy Milk
(page 166)
Almond Ice Cream
(page 154)

Hari Raya Buffet

Mr. Lee's Chicken Wings
(page 48)
Beef Satay
(page 44)
Malaysian Lamb Curry
(page 93)
Stir-Fried Cabbage & Eggs
(page 128)
Rice E & O Style
(page 137)
Cucumber Pickles
(page 99)
Corn & Coconut Porridge
(page 156)
Pandan Chiffon Cake
(page 152)

SINGAPORE

Raffles Hotel Curry Tiffin

Singapore Gin Sling
(page 169)
Raffles Lamb Curry
(page 93)
Raffles Fish Curry
(page 62)
Anglo-Indian Chicken Curry
(page 74)
Eggplant Curry
(page 123)
Selection of Curry Condiments:
Diced Pineapple   Sliced Banana
Diced Apple   Diced Cucumber
Diced Tomato   Shredded Coconut
Roasted Peanuts   Mango Chutney
Basic Steamed Rice
(page 133)
Tapioca Pudding with Two Sauces
(page 158)
Sliced Pineapple, Watermelon & Papaya

A Nonya Dinner

Fish with Pineapple & Tamarind
(page 63)
Straits Chinese Pork Satay
(page 95)
Vegetables & Tofu in Coconut Milk
(page 125)
Straits Chinese Pickled Vegetables
(page 98)
Basic Steamed Rice
(page 133)
Black-Rice Porridge
(page 156)

INDONESIA

Rijsttafel

Lamb Satay
(page 42)
Shrimp Satay
(page 43)
Meatballs in Coconut Sauce
(page 92)
Broiled Chicken Dewi
(page 76)
Vegetable Platter with Peanut Sauce
(page 113)
Pickled Green Beans
(page 100)
Sumatra-Style Vegetables in Coconut Milk
(page 124)
Basic Steamed Rice
(page 133)
Shrimp Chips
(page 43)
Coconut Crepes
(page 150)

———————————— ✦ ————————————

A Simple Supper

Ann's Indonesian Meat Loaf
(page 91)
Javanese Eggplant
(page 122)
Basic Steamed Rice
(page 133)
Coconut Pudding
(page 157)

THE PHILIPPINES

Merienda

Cantaloupe Cooler
(page 165)
Noodles with Pork, Shrimp & Vegetables
(page 143)
Cassava Cake with Caramel Topping
(page 160)

———————————— ✦ ————————————

A Filipino Fiesta

Green-Mango Shake
(page 165)
Fried Egg Rolls
(page 46)
Tangy Shrimp Soup
(page 54)
Aristocrat Barbecued Chicken
(page 75)
Pork Adobo
(page 95)
Garlic Rice
(page 133)
Eggplant with Coconut-Vinegar Sauce
(page 122)
Green-Papaya Relish
(page 99)
Le Gâteau Sans Rival
(page 147)

———————————— ✦ ————————————

Springtime Supper

Chicken Adobo
(page 81)
Rice Pilaf
(page 134)
Strawberry Flan
(page 148)

BRUNEI

Dinner at the Istana

Fried Beef Turnovers
(page 48)
Chicken Kapitan
(page 72)
Fish with Spicy Tamarind Sauce
(page 62)
Coconut Beef
(page 84)
Celebration Rice
(page 136)
Fresh Fruit or Ice Cream

VIETNAM

A Vietnamese Lunch

Spring Rolls
(page 45)
Beef & Rice-Noodle Soup
(page 57)
French-Style Filter Coffee
(page 168)

Chicken Dinner

Crab & Asparagus Soup
(page 55)
Lemon Grass Chicken
(page 81)
Shredded Carrot Relish
(page 100)
Basic Steamed Rice
(page 133)
Fruit with Rice Dumplings in Ginger Syrup
(page 162)

Soup & Salad Supper

Shrimp Soup with Pineapple
(page 52)
Hot Beef Salad
(page 114)
Iced Tea

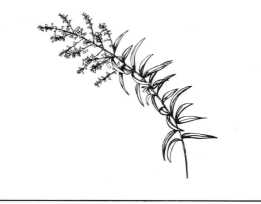

Fiesta Dinner

Steak with Hot Tomato Sauce
(page 83)
Refried Beans
Guacamole
Flan Kamayan Style
(page 148)

Easy Dinner

Broiled Garlic Pork Chops
(page 96)
Scalloped Potatoes
Buttered Green Beans
Cucumber Pickles
(page 99)
Ginger Mousse
(page 149)

August Dinner

Bangkok-Style Steak Salad
(page 117)
Corn-on-the-Cob
Garlic-Cheese Bread
Frozen Lychees
(page 155)

Southeast Asian Buffet

Lime-Marinated Fish
(page 64)
Javenese Stewed Beef
(page 87)
Brunei-Style Chicken Curry
(page 72)
Baked Yellow Rice
(page 139)
Stir-Fried Rice Noodles with Pork
(page 144)
Straits Chinese Pickled Vegetables
(page 98)
Coconut Tarts
(page 149)
Sticky Rice Cake
(page 158)
Pitchers of Pineapple Water
(page 164)

THE INGREDIENTS

Southeast Asian cookery requires surprisingly few ingredients beyond those available in a well-equipped supermarket or Chinese grocery store. Other less common ingredients can be duplicated successfully at home, among them Thai curry pastes and Indonesian-style soy sauce.

The lack of an ingredient is no reason to eliminate a recipe. Some seasonings can be omitted if not available. One of these is the strong-tasting shrimp paste that is used in Indonesia and Malaysia. Even some of the inhabitants of those countries do not like it.

Experimentation will yield satisfactory substitutes for other ingredients. If laos root is not available, try adding a small amount of ground ginger, which is a sharper-flavored member of the same family. Sautéed fresh mushrooms or canned mushrooms can be substituted for Oriental black mushrooms or black fungus. Fresh green chilies can be substituted for red chilies and canned chilies for fresh. Dried hot chilies, red (cayenne) pepper or hot pepper sauce also can provide spicy heat. Adjust amounts to your taste.

Lemon peel is often suggested as an alternative to lemon grass. However, those who grow the herb lemon balm will find its delicate aroma more akin to lemon grass than the acidic fruit.

Substitutions are not advised when an ingredient provides the essential character of a dish. For example, Vietnamese dipping sauce, page 30, would lose its savor without fish sauce, the salty liquid that is basic to Vietnamese cooking and is also used in Thailand and the Philippines. If a recipe specifies only one or two tablespoons of fish sauce, soy sauce can usually be substituted. If soy sauce would discolor the dish, the salt in the recipe can be increased. Experiment with the recipes using the ingredients available in your area. The dishes may not always be authentic, but can still be enjoyed.

Coconut milk is so important to Southeast Asian cookery that a separate discussion and recipes are included in the Basic Sauces, Seasonings & Garnishes chapter.

Annatto seeds	Small, hard orange-red seeds used as a coloring agent in the Philippines, where they are known as *atsuwete*. Look for them in Mexican or Latin markets under the name *achiote*.
Black fungus	A dried product resembling dried mushrooms, black fungus lacks a pronounced flavor but provides color contrast and a crunchy texture. Before it is used, the fungus must be soaked until softened, then well drained. Then it can be sliced or shredded as required.

Candlenuts	These oily raw macadamia nuts are crushed and added to curries and other dishes for flavor and consistency. Asian names are *kemiri* (Indonesia) and *buah keras* (Malaysia). Omit if not available.
Cassava root	Starchy cassava root is white with a rough brown skin. Look for it in Latin markets, where it is called *yuca*, as well as in Asian markets. The sections of root are long and often quite large. Smaller, slimmer pieces are likely to be more tender.
Chayote	A pale-green, pear-shaped squash with a mild flavor. Chayotes are commonly found in Mexican and Latin markets and some supermarkets.
Chilies	Fresh hot red chilies are used in Southeast Asia as an ingredient and a garnish. Since red chilies are not always available, green chilies, such as serranos or jalapeños, may be substituted. The heat of chilies varies. Adjust the amount used according to taste. When it is not important to see chilies in the finished dish, red (cayenne) pepper may be substituted. Another alternative is hot chili powder, provided it contains no additional seasonings. Protect your hands with rubber gloves when peeling or slicing fresh chilies to prevent irritation. Do not rub your eyes after working with chilies.
Chinese grass jelly	A dark brown gelatinous product with little flavor that is used in Southeast Asian drinks and desserts. Grass jelly can be purchased canned in Chinese markets.
Chinese long beans	These slim beans are sometimes called yard beans because of their length. They are similar in taste to fresh green beans with a slightly chewier texture. Substitute fresh green beans.
Chinese preserved plums	Salty plums packed in water. In this book, they are used only in the Vietnamese Preserved Plum Drink, page 166.
Chinese sausage	Firm, dry, reddish-colored, fat-marbled sausages with a sweet flavor. They must be cooked before they are eaten.

Chinese thick sauce	Made with soybeans and molasses, this thick, dark, sweet mixture adds an attractive brown color without the saltiness of regular soy sauce. Other names are thick soy sauce and sweet sauce.
Cilantro	Fresh coriander or Chinese parsley. This herb has a pungent taste. It is also used in Mexican cooking.
Coconut cream	Coconut cream is the thick first squeezing from freshly grated coconut or the top layer in a can of unshaken coconut milk. Cream of coconut is a commercial sweetened drink mix. The two are not interchangeable.
Coconut milk	This is not the water inside the coconut, but the rich white liquid squeezed from the coconut milk after it has been blended with water.
Curry leaves	Small leaves from Indian that give off a curry fragrance when crushed. They are not related to curry powder. The leaves are normally used fresh but are available dried in Indian and Asian markets in areas where the plant cannot be grown.
Curry pastes	The Thais flavor their food with a variety of curry pastes made of ground chilies and other seasonings. These are available canned in many Asian markets. Recipes for two of the most common curry pastes are on pages 29 and 30.
Curry powder	The best curry powder is ground to order from the individual spices and contains no starchy filler. As an alternative, use a good-quality imported Indian curry powder or a domestic Indian-style curry powder.
Fish sauce	A salty, clear, amber-colored liquid made from fish or shrimp and used as a seasoning and table condiment. Asian names are *patis* (the Philippines), *nuoc mam* (Vietnam) and *nam pla* (Thailand).
Garam masala	A blend of ground spices used in Indian cooking. Typical components are coriander, cumin, cloves, cinnamon, cardamom and black pepper.
Ghee	Indian-style clarified butter, available canned in Indian markets.
Golden needles	Dried tiger lily flower buds named for their slim shape and dull golden color. They must be soaked in water about 30 minutes before they are used.

Green cardamom	Cardamom seeds encased in pale green shells that have been oven dried. Most Indian markets carry green cardamom. The pods are added whole to a dish, or the seeds are removed and then added, depending on the recipe.
Hoisin sauce	A dark brown, thick, sweet Chinese condiment made from soybeans.
Jícama	A brown-skinned, juicy, sweet root vegetable that resembles a turnip in texture but is much larger. Jícama is stocked in Mexican markets and many supermarkets. It can be eaten cooked or raw.
Jujubes	Also called Chinese red dates, jujubes are small, wrinkled, dried fruits that add a sweet flavor to curries and other dishes.
Kaffir lime leaves	These are double lime leaves, so called because two leaves grow together on a single stem. Unlike ordinary citrus leaves, kaffir lime leaves have a pronounced flavor and fragrance. The leaves and the peel of the fruit, which is also used in cooking, are sold dried in Asian markets. Regional names for the leaves are *bai magrut* or *makrood* (Thailand) and *daun jeruk purut* or *daun limau purut* (Indonesia and Malaysia).
Kangkong	A long-stemmed green that has various names including water spinach, water convolvulus, and, in Thailand, morning glory vine or *pak bung*. Spinach can often be substituted.
Laos	The Indonesian name of a root that resembles ginger in flavor. The botanical name is *Alpinia galanga*, and the common name in English is *galingal* or *galingale*. Used fresh in Southeast Asia, laos root is available elsewhere frozen, dried or powdered. Other Asian names are *lengkuas* (Malaysia) and *kha* (Thailand).
Lemon grass	A long, thick grass with leaves at the top and a solid portion several inches long at the root end. This lower portion is sliced or pounded and used in cooking. Lemon grass has a light, lemonlike flavor and aroma without the tang or bitterness associated with lemons. It is available fresh, dried and powdered in Southeast Asian markets. Other names are *serai* or *sereh* (Indonesia and Malaysia), *takrai* (Thailand) and *citronella*.

Lotus root	A long, brown-skinned, crisp root that, when sliced, exposes a surface studded with holes. Available fresh in season, it is also sliced and canned in water.
Maggi seasoning	A dark brown, salty, nutty-flavored liquid used as a condiment in Thai and Vietnamese cooking.
Makhua puong	A Thai name for tiny green eggplants the size of a large pea and refreshingly bitter in flavor. Sometimes available fresh in Thai markets, *makua puong* can be replaced with green peas.
Mango powder	Finely ground dried mango is used to add a tartness to some Indian dishes. The Indian name for this product is *amchur.* Lemon juice can be substituted to taste.
Mushrooms	There are special types of mushrooms used in Southeast Asian dishes.
Dried Oriental mushrooms	Dried dark mushrooms that are often called by their Japanese name, *shiitake.* The dried mushrooms must be soaked before they are used. Fresh shiitake are sometimes available.
Straw mushrooms	Frequently used in Chinese cooking, straw mushrooms have a long cap that resembles a partially opened umbrella. Asian markets stock canned ones. Canned whole button mushrooms may be substituted.
Nata de pina	Also called pineapple gel or pineapple gelatin, this translucent, delicately flavored substance resembles colorless gelatin and is a nice addition to desserts and fruit salads. The gel is manufactured in the Philippines from pineapples.
Noodles	Many types of noodles are used in Southeast Asian cookery. There are three varieties that are mainly used in this book.
Bean thread noodles	Also called bean threads, bean vermicelli, cellophane or glass noodles, these dried white noodles resemble rice sticks but are made from mung bean starch. They soften quickly when soaked.
Fresh rice noodles	Available in areas with large Chinese populations, these come in sheets that have been rolled to the proper thickness. Cut into strips of the desired size.

Dried rice noodles	Wiry, thin white rice noodles are also called rice sticks or rice vermicelli; these become puffy and crisp when deep-fried or soft when soaked in water. Other rice noodles are flattened and wider.
Oriental eggplant	Long slim eggplants that are purple or light green. Substitute an equal amount by weight of ordinary eggplant.
Oyster sauce	A thick, brown, salty Chinese seasoning made from oysters and available in Chinese markets.
Pandan	A plant with long, spiky green leaves that are used as a flavoring and a green food coloring. The flavor is reminiscent of butterscotch and new-mown hay and is especially attractive in desserts. Dried pandan leaves can be substituted for fresh. Bottled pandan flavoring is exported from Thailand, where the leaves are called *bai toey,* and from Indonesia, where the name is *daun pandan.*
Rice	When making steamed rice, use long-grain rice rather than converted or instant rice. Special types of rice for Asian cooking include the following:
Basmati rice	A superior grade of rice produced in India and Pakistan. It has a long grain and a nutty flavor.
Glutinous rice	A short-grain rice that becomes very sticky when cooked. Used frequently in desserts, it is sometimes called sticky rice or sweet rice. Glutinous rice is also made into flour. Black glutinous rice is a dark-colored variety.
Jasmine rice	A fine quality Thai rice with a long grain and distinctive fragrance.
Rice wine	Wine made from fermented rice. Examples are Japanese *sake* and Chinese rice wine. Do not use *mirin,* which is sweetened rice wine. A dry sherry can sometimes be substituted.
Rose flavoring	Product of the distillation of rose petals. It is also called rose oil.
Rose syrup	Used in beverages and desserts, the syrup can be found in Indian and Indonesian shops. A recipe is on page 166.
Rose water	Milder flavoring made by blending rose oil with water. It is used in cooking and beverages.

Sambal oelek	A very hot Indonesian seasoning made of ground red chilies. Asian markets carry the commercial product. A homemade version is on page 28.
Shallots	Small, mild members of the onion family frequently used in Southeast Asia. Yellow or white onions may be substituted. One medium onion equals about 12 small shallots.
Shrimp chips	Hard discs of shrimp paste that become puffy when deep fried. Chinese and Indonesian markets carry them. Instructions for frying the chips are on page 43.
Shrimp paste	Malays and Indonesians use this strong smelling paste in many dishes. The flavor in the finished dish is much less intense than the aroma produced while the paste is cooked. The Malay name for the paste is *belacan* or *blachan*. The Indonesian name is *terasi*. A Thai shrimp paste is called *kapi*.
Sichuan peppercorns	These reddish Chinese peppercorns have a distinctive aroma slightly reminiscent of camphor. Other names are wild pepper and *fagara*.
Soybean condiment	A Chinese seasoning made of soybeans. The condiment is a brownish-yellow color and may contain portions of the whole bean.
Soy sauce	There are four special types of soy sauce called for in this book. These are listed below:
Dark soy sauce	Soy sauce with a deeper color and thicker consistency than regular soy sauce.
Indonesian-style soy sauce	A dark, sweet, rich-tasting soy sauce that is used in Indonesian cookery. The Indonesian name is *kecap* (pronounced ketjap) *manis*.
Light soy sauce	Also called thin soy, this sauce is lighter in color than regular soy sauce.
Mushroom-flavored soy sauce	A Chinese product. Substitute regular soy sauce.
Star anise	A hard, dark-brown spice with pointed segments that give it the appearance of a star. The flavor is related to licorice. Look for star anise in Chinese and other Oriental markets.

Tamarind	The pods produced by the tamarind tree contain pulp with a pleasant tart taste. The whole pods are sold in Latin and Asian markets. Blocks of peeled pulp, found in Indian and Asian stores, are more convenient to use. Liquid concentrate and powdered tamarind are also available. In the Philippines, green (unripe) tamarind is used to add tartness. Lemon juice may be substituted.
Thai tea	Orange-red tea leaves processed with vanilla flavoring to give a special flavor and orange hue to the brewed tea.
Toasted rice powder	Thai and other Southeast Asian markets carry this product in small plastic bags. It is easy to make at home according to the method on page 91 in recipe for Spiced Ground Beef.
Vinegars	Palm and sugar-cane vinegars are produced in the Philippines for home use and export. The palm vinegar has a slight winey taste and the cane vinegar a sweeter taste. American distilled white vinegar is substituted in the Filipino dishes in this book. Try using the authentic vinegars if they are available. Rice vinegar is also used in Southeast Asia. Recipes in this book call for plain rice vinegar (not seasoned).
White radish	A large, long radish that is also known by its Japanese name, *daikon*.
Wrappers	A number of recipes call for wrapping the ingredients in pastry. Asian wrappers include the four listed below.
Egg roll wrappers	Sheets of dough, about 7-inches square, that are stocked in the refrigerated section of Chinese markets and some supermarkets.
Lumpia wrappers	Thinner wrappers used for Filipino spring rolls. Chinese spring roll or egg roll wrappers may be substituted.
Rice paper wrappers	Produced in Thailand and used by the Vietnamese, these wrappers are dry and stiff, like heavy, translucent parchment. They are either round or wedge-shaped. The round wrappers are made in several sizes. Brush wrappers with water to soften them before using.
Won-ton wrappers	These miniature versions of Chinese egg roll wrappers come in two shapes, square and round.
Young corn	Canned miniature ears of corn that are stocked in most Chinese markets, many gourmet stores and even the gourmet section of many supermarkets.

THE EQUIPMENT

Asian cooking requires little special equipment. The most important tools are a wok and some means of grinding ingredients. Standard kitchenware can be substituted for specialized and hard-to-find utensils such as Indian *kulfi* molds for ice cream (recipe, page 154), and the Malaysian *roti jala* mold used for making lacy, noodle-like crepes (recipe, page 145).

Woks

The wok is employed in all Southeast Asian countries. The most versatile type for home cooking is a 14-inch model made of heavy steel. A smaller size does not allow enough room for tossing ingredients when stir-frying. Larger woks are unwieldy and also unnecessary because to achieve the best result, only moderate amounts of ingredients should be cooked at one time.

A wok with a flat bottom is best suited to an electric range and may also be used with a gas range rather than the traditional rounded wok that sits on a ring. A long wooden handle on one side prevents burns and makes it easier to hold the wok in place while vigorously stirring. Electric woks are not as efficient for stir-frying but are excellent for deep-frying and steaming.

The procedure for using a wok is to heat the empty pan until it smokes. Next, add the oil called for in the recipe. When the oil is hot, add the ingredients to be cooked. Clean a wok with hot water, using a brush or plastic pad rather than an abrasive metal scrubber. Dry it thoroughly, then coat the interior lightly with oil to prevent rusting. Like an iron skillet, a wok becomes seasoned as it is used. An aged, blackened wok is an asset, not a sign of poor housekeeping.

Grinders

Traditional Asian cooks use stone mortars, either bowl-shaped or flat, to grind ingredients for curries and other dishes. Modern cooks substitute food processors and blenders. However, large processors and blenders will not puree small quantities of ingredients. A compromise is to grind the ingredients as fine as possible, then pound them to a paste in a mortar. A blender will do a better job if a small portion of any liquid specified in the recipe is added to the ingredients to be ground.

The most efficient tool for fine-grinding either moist, or a combination of moist and dry ingredients, is a small food processor or electric mincer. Electric coffee grinders will grind dry spices to a powder, but they must be thoroughly cleaned between uses or reserved only for spices. A mortar is recommended for very small amounts. Thai mortars that are deep and narrow keep the ingredients from flying out. Equipped with lightweight wooden pestles, these inexpensive mortars can be found at Thai and other Asian markets.

Shredders

Some recipes require cutting vegetables into fine shreds. This can be done with the shredding blade of a food processor or a hand shredder. Inexpensive shredding devices imported from the Orient come with interchangeable blades that will produce shreds of varying thickness and will also slice ingredients.

Steamers

A wok or any large pot can be turned into a steamer by adding a rack that will hold the container of food above the water level. Tiered Chinese steamers are especially convenient because the food can be arranged on the tiers and easily placed over and removed from the pot of simmering water.

BASIC SAUCES, SEASONINGS & GARNISHES

Some ingredients that are fundamental to Southeast Asian cooking can be duplicated at home if the commercial product is not available.

It is actually preferable to make your own Thai curry pastes because you can control the heat by adjusting the amount of chilies. Imported canned Thai curry pastes can be very hot. When using the canned product instead of curry pastes made according to the recipes in this chapter, reduce the quantity to about one-third.

Indonesian Ground Red-Chili Paste (sambal oelek) consists of lightly seasoned ground red chilies and is used to add heat to a dish. It is also a handy way for the home cook to preserve fresh red chilies, which are not always available in western markets. Another spicy seasoning is Mr. Lee's Red-Chili Sauce, which can be used in cooking or as a table condiment.

Indonesian-style soy sauce, called kecap or kecap manis, differs from other Oriental soy sauces in that it is sweet. The recipes in this book were prepared with commercial brands produced in Holland and Indonesia. Their flavors can be simulated by adding brown sugar, corn syrup and molasses to any brand of ordinary, all-purpose soy sauce; see recipe, page 31. The base sauce may make homemade kecap saltier than the authentic version. Therefore, when using the homemade product, it may be necessary to reduce or eliminate any salt called for in the recipe.

Sweet-sour Nuoc Mam Sauce is served with many Vietnamese dishes. The recipe combines fish sauce, rice vinegar, sugar, garlic and red chilies. Shredded carrot is usually added for garnish. Some cooks also add shredded white radish or finely chopped roasted peanuts.

Crisp-fried onion or shallot shreds and fried garlic are popular Asian garnishes. Roasted peanuts are also used in many dishes. Prepare these as needed, or make larger batches and store them in airtight containers.

Additional recipes tell how to make Tamarind Liquid, which is used to impart tartness to some dishes; Clarified Butter, which is employed as a substitute for Indian ghee; and Simple Syrup, a sweetener for drinks.

Coconut Milk

Coconut milk is so important to Southeast Asian cookery that a complete discussion is necessary. Coconut milk is not the water inside the coconut but the rich white liquid that is squeezed from the grated coconut meat and water. In Southeast Asia, where coconut milk is used in everything from drinks to desserts, markets sell fresh coconut that is already peeled and grated. This eliminates the laborious task of cracking the hard outer shell, removing the thin brown peel that coats the meat and grating the firm flesh.

In countries where grated fresh coconut is not available, it makes sense to use convenience products, such as canned, frozen or powdered coconut milk or blocks of solid coconut cream. These products are likely to yield better quality milk than old, dry imported coconuts. The powdered milk, which comes in small packets, is especially handy to store and use, and the flavor is very good. Like the powder, the solid coconut cream is dissolved in water to produce coconut milk.

In Southeast Asia, cooks distinguish between coconut cream, which is squeezed from grated coconut without the addition of water, and the thinner milk produced by adding water to subsequent squeezings. These same variations can be achieved by adjusting the amount of water added to powdered or solidified coconut milk. If a can of coconut milk is not shaken, the thick coconut cream can be skimmed off the top when the can is opened.

Instructions follow for those who want to prepare milk from a fresh coconut. In areas where neither fresh coconuts nor the convenience products mentioned are available, it is possible to make perfectly good coconut milk using unsweetened dried coconut.

When substituting homemade coconut milk for the canned coconut milk used in recipes in this book, remember that one 14-ounce can coconut milk equals 1-3/4 cups.

Fresh Coconut Milk

These instructions are for making your own coconut milk using a coconut.

1 coconut

Preheat oven to 350F (175C). Pierce eyes of coconut and drain off water. Place coconut in pie pan. Bake about 30 minutes or until shell cracks. Cool coconut until it can be handled. Tap all over with a hammer to crack shell further. Remove meat from shell. With a sharp knife, peel off brown skin. Cut meat into small dice. Place in a blender in batches; add hot tap water to the level of the coconut. Blend until finely grated, stopping blender occasionally and stirring if necessary. Pour coconut and liquid into a fine sieve placed over a medium-size bowl. Squeeze handfuls of coconut to extract as much liquid as possible. Return coconut to blender, add water to level of coconut and repeat blending and squeezing. Discard coconut. Add a dash of salt, cover and refrigerate until needed. Use within 1 day because fresh coconut milk will sour upon standing or freeze up to 1 month. One coconut yields 2 to 4 cups milk depending upon the richness required.

Coconut Milk with Dried Coconut

Unsweetened dried coconut is usually available in natural food stores. Do not substitute sweetened dried coconut.

Unsweetened dried coconut

Combine equal amounts by cups of dried coconut and very hot tap water in a blender. Blend at high speed 30 seconds, turning blender on and off two or three times. Turn into a fine sieve placed over a medium-size bowl. Squeeze handfuls of coconut to extract as much milk as possible. For thinner milk, use twice as much water as coconut. The quantity of milk will be slightly less than the amount of water added. Use within 1 day.

Rich Coconut Milk for Desserts

Try this method when extra rich, creamy milk is needed.

1 cup unsweetened dried coconut
1 cup water
1 cup evaporated milk

Combine coconut and water in a 1-quart saucepan. Bring to a boil, stirring. Remove from heat; let stand 10 to 15 minutes. Add milk; bring just to a boil. Remove from heat; let stand until cooled to room temperature. Place a fine sieve over a medium-size bowl. Pour mixture into sieve. Squeeze handfuls of coconut to extract as much liquid as possible. Cover and refrigerate if not using immediately. Use within 1 day. Makes 1-1/2 cups.

Ground Red-Chili Paste
Sambal Oelek   (Indonesia)

This homemade version is an alternative to the commercial product, which comes in jars and is stocked in most Asian markets. Use it to add hotness to any dish, not just Southeast Asian food. This can be used immediately or refrigerated for later use.

1/2 lb. fresh hot red chilies, stemmed, seeded
3/4 cup water
1/4 teaspoon salt
1 teaspoon distilled white vinegar

Place chilies in a blender or food processor fitted with the metal blade. Process until chopped but not pureed. Scrape into a small saucepan. Stir in water and salt. Bring to a boil; boil gently, stirring occasionally, until chilies are tender and mixture is reduced to about 1 cup. Stir in vinegar. Turn into a hot clean jar. Cover loosely and cool, then cover tightly and refrigerate. Store in refrigerator 2 to 3 weeks. Freeze for longer storage. Makes 1 cup.

Green Curry Paste

Gaeng Keo Wan

(Thailand)

Fresh chilies are best for curry paste. However, you may also use canned chilies if you rinse them well. Do not use pickled chilies. Wear rubber gloves when peeling fresh chilies.

2 fresh large green mild Anaheim-type chilies (about 1/4 lb.)
3 jalapeño chilies
2 large stalks cilantro, including roots, coarsely chopped (about 1 tablespoon)
3 tablespoons finely sliced lemon grass (1 stalk)
4 shallots, coarsely chopped
4 large garlic cloves
2 teaspoons Thai shrimp paste (kapi)
1 teaspoon black peppercorns
1 teaspoon ground laos
1/2 teaspoon ground cumin
1/2 teaspoon ground turmeric
1/4 teaspoon salt
1 tablespoon vegetable oil

Preheat broiler. Place chilies on a baking sheet; roast under broiler until blistered all over. Place in a paper bag 15 minutes to steam. Peel. Discard stems and seeds. Combine all ingredients except oil in a blender or food processor fitted with the metal blade; process as fine as possible. Pour into a small bowl; stir in oil. Cover and refrigerate at least 1 day before using for flavors to blend. Refrigerate up to 1 week. Freeze for longer storage. Makes 3/4 cup.

Mr. Lee's Red-Chili Sauce

Cili Sos

(Malaysia)

The Chinese proprietor of a food stall in Penang serves this sauce with chicken wings and other snacks. Use it with caution because it is very hot.

1/4 lb. fresh hot red chilies, stemmed, seeded
1/4 medium-size onion
1 (1/4-inch-thick) gingerroot slice
3/4 cup canned tomato sauce
1 tablespoon sugar
1 tablespoon lime juice
1 tablespoon distilled white vinegar
1/2 teaspoon salt

Combine ingredients in a blender or food processor fitted with the metal blade; process until very finely ground. Pour into a jar, cover and refrigerate 1 day before using to blend flavors. Will keep refrigerated at least 1 week. Makes slightly more than 1 cup.

Red Curry Paste
Gaeng Ped

(Thailand)

This zesty seasoning can be added to soups and vegetables as well as to curries.

7 large dried hot red (New
  Mexico-type) chilies
10 small dried chilies
1/4 cup chopped shallots (3 or 4
  large)
3 tablespoons finely sliced lemon
  grass (1 stalk)
1 tablespoon chopped cilantro
  roots and stems
1 tablespoon Thai shrimp paste
  (kapi)
3 large garlic cloves
1 teaspoon ground laos
1/2 teaspoon ground coriander
1/2 teaspoon caraway seeds
1/4 teaspoon black pepper
1/4 teaspoon salt

Place chilies in a large saucepan. Add water to cover, cover pan and bring to a boil. Remove from heat; let stand, covered, about 30 minutes or until chilies are soft. Drain chilies. Remove stems and seeds. Grind very fine in a blender or food processor fitted with the metal blade. Pour into a sieve; force pulp through by pressing with back of a spoon. Peel will remain in sieve; there will be slightly less than 1/2 cup pulp. Return pulp to blender. Add remaining ingredients. Process until pureed. Pour into a small jar, cover and store in refrigerator. Refrigerate at least 1 day before using for flavors to blend. Store in refrigerator up to 2 weeks. Freeze for longer storage. Makes about 3/4 cup.

Variation
For a milder paste, use 8 New Mexico-type chilies and eliminate the small chilies.

Sweet-Sour Dipping Sauce
Nước Mắm (Sauce)

(Vietnam)

This dipping sauce accompanies many Vietnamese dishes. Each restaurant has its own version, some sweeter, some more strongly flavored with fish sauce.

1/2 cup rice vinegar
1/3 cup water
1/3 cup fish sauce
1/3 cup sugar
2 tablespoons fine long carrot
  shreds
1 tablespoon finely chopped fresh
  red chili or 1/2 teaspoon red
  pepper flakes or 1/4 teaspoon
  red (cayenne) pepper
2 garlic cloves, crushed, minced

Combine rice vinegar, water, fish sauce and sugar in a small bowl. Stir until sugar dissolves. Add carrot, chili and garlic. Cover and let stand 1 hour to blend flavors. Serve at room temperature. Makes 1-1/4 cups.

Crisp-Fried Onion Shreds
(Indonesia, Malaysia)

The onion shreds add distinctive flavor when scattered over fried rice, noodles, soups and other dishes.

1 medium-size onion or 6 to 8 shallots
Vegetable oil for deep-frying

Cut onion in half through root end, then cut each half crosswise in very thin slices. If using shallots, peel and cut into thin slices. Heat 2 inches oil in a small saucepan to 360F (180C) or until a 1-inch bread cube turns golden brown in 60 seconds. Add onion slices; fry over medium heat until dry and golden brown. Do not burn. If onion browns too rapidly, reduce heat and cook more slowly. Drain on paper towels. Place in a small container; cover tightly until served. These are best served the same day as made. Exposure to air will cause onion shreds to wilt. Makes about 1 cup.

Indonesian-Style Soy Sauce
Kecap Manis
(Indonesia)

Sweet seasoning is widely used in Indonesia, even for noodles, meats and other savory foods.

1/2 cup soy sauce
1/4 cup packed dark-brown sugar
3 tablespoons dark corn syrup
1 tablespoon molasses

Combine ingredients in a small bowl; stir until sugar dissolves. Pour into a small jar, cover tightly and store at room temperature. This keeps almost indefinitely. Makes 3/4 cup.

Roasted Peanuts

When buying nuts, 2 ounces shelled peanuts equals 1/2 cup. As a shortcut, dry-roasted unsalted peanuts may be substituted. Use a timer when roasting peanuts so you won't forget and let them burn.

Raw, unsalted, shelled peanuts

Preheat oven to 350F (175C). Place peanuts in a single layer in a pie pan or other shallow baking pan. Bake 10 to 12 minutes or until browned. Shake pan occasionally; do not burn. Cool, then chop or grind as directed in recipe.

Tamarind Liquid

Not as sharply sour as lemon juice or vinegar, tamarind liquid seasons many Indonesian, Malay and Straits Chinese dishes.

1 to 2 tablespoons tamarind pulp
1/2 cup warm water

Combine tamarind pulp and water in a small bowl. Knead tamarind to extract color and flavor. Liquid will be cloudy and brown. Strain out seeds. Makes 1/2 cup.

Clarified Butter

This is used as a substitute for ghee.

1 to 2 tablespoons more butter
than the amount specified in
the recipe

Melt butter in a small heavy saucepan over medium heat. Spoon off as much of the white solids as possible. Use only the clear liquid butter.

Simple Syrup

Syrup blends more easily into drinks than granulated sugar.

1 cup sugar
1 cup water

Combine sugar and water in a small saucepan. Stir over medium heat until sugar dissolves. Bring to a full boil. Boil 3 minutes. Let cool. Pour into a small jar, cover and refrigerate. Makes about 1-1/4 cups.

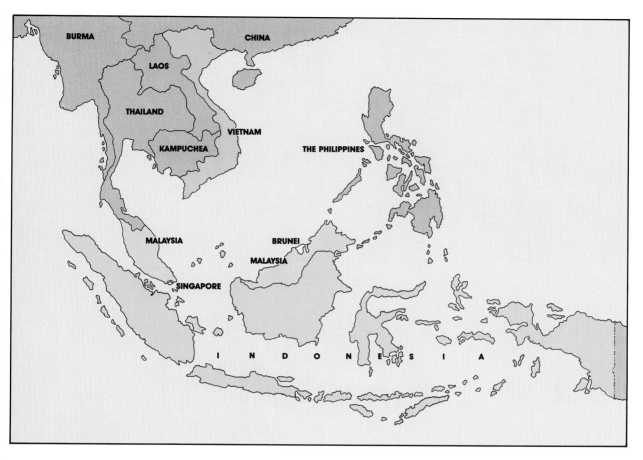

BURMA

CHINA

LAOS

THAILAND

VIETNAM

KAMPUCHEA

THE PHILIPPINES

MALAYSIA

BRUNEI

MALAYSIA

SINGAPORE

I N D O N E S I A

Southeast Asia

Above: 1. Tamarind pulp, 2. Shrimp chips, 3. Bean thread noodles, 4. Rice stick noodles, 5. Rice noodles, 6. Rose syrup, 7. Fish sauce, 8. Indonesian-style soy sauce, 9. Sambal oelek, 10. Powdered coconut milk, 11. Canned coconut milk, 12. Thai shrimp paste, 13. Thai tea, 14. Thai red curry paste, 15. Palm seeds, 16. Black fungus, 17. Candlenuts, 18. Rice paper wrappers, 19. Maggi seasoning, 20. Pandan paste, 21. Pandan flavoring, 22. Garam marsala, 23. Indonesian shrimp paste, 24. Jujubes, 25. Star anise, 26. Laos powder, 27. Annato seeds

Opposite: 1. Kangkong, 2. Lemon grass, 3. Oriental eggplants, 4. Fresh coconut, 5. Coconut grater, 6. Daikon, 7. Green (unripe) papaya, 8. Cassava root, 9. Keffir limes, 10. Keffir lime leaves, 11. Calamansi, 12. Assorted hot chilies, 13. Chinese long beans, 14. Laos root

Previous pages: Clockwise from center left: Basic Steamed Rice, page 133; Shrimp Chips, page 43; Meatballs in Coconut Sauce, page 92; Broiled Chicken Dewi, page 76; Vegetable Platter with Peanut Sauce, page 113; Lamb Satay, page 42; Pickled Green Beans, page 100; Sumatra-Style Vegetables in Coconut Milk, page 124

Above: Clockwise from top left: Yellow Rice, page 135; Noodles with Pork, Shrimp & Vegetables, page 143; Sweet Sticky Noodles, page 140

Opposite: Clockwise from left: Rosy Milk, page 166; Nagasari Avocado Cooler, page 164; Cantaloupe Cooler, page 165; Singapore Cricket Club's Singapore Sling, page 169; Coconut Orchid, page 170

APPETIZERS & SNACKS

Asians love to snack, and much of what they nibble on fits the western concept of appetizers. The same satay that one might buy from an itinerant vendor in Indonesia or a food stall in Singapore makes a sophisticated cocktail snack in other parts of the world. There are four versions of satay in this chapter, one each from Thailand and Malaysia and two from Indonesia, where anything from beef and pork to fish, shrimp and even turtle is cut up and grilled on a stick. Accompanying peanut sauces range from a Thai version made with coconut milk and red curry paste to a Javanese mixture flavored with sweet Indonesian soy sauce.

The Chinese egg roll's influence has spread throughout Southeast Asia. In Vietnam, the filling is enclosed in rice paper wrappers, which look like hard white parchment but soften when they are moistened. If the rice wrappers are not available, Chinese egg roll wrappers can be substituted.

Filipinos call their egg rolls lumpia and use a thin wrapper that they often make themselves. Lumpia wrappers are imported from the Philippines and are also made in the United States but, again, Chinese egg roll wrappers or spring roll wrappers can be substituted. Crisp fried lumpia is delicious with its simple vinegar and garlic dip. No frying is necessary for fresh lumpia, which is rolled and served at once. The filling consists of shredded vegetables enriched with pork and shrimp. A lettuce leaf rolled with the filling makes a pretty green frill that extends through an open end of the roll.

Those who like the Mexican fried pork cracklings called *chicharrones* will enjoy Filipino Fried Chicken Skins. The recipe, from a bistro in Manila, calls for boiling the skins, then frying them slowly until crisp. The skins can be accumulated from chicken parts used in other recipes and frozen until needed.

Chicken wings are handy for parties because they can be marinated well in advance and cooked ahead of time if they are to be served cold. The wings in this chapter reproduce those served at a food stall in Penang, an island off the west coast of Malaysia. Ginger juice, cinnamon, honey, lime juice and soy sauce flavor the marinade.

Additional recipes include spicy Thai corn fritters served with sweet and sour sauce and, fried pastries from Brunei called *Sambosas*. The beef-filled Sambosas are among the snacks offered to guests who visit the sultan's palace during receptions that end the Muslim fasting month of Ramadan.

Ideal for those with no time to cook are Indonesian-style shrimp puffs called *krupuk udang*. These are made from small discs of hardened shrimp paste that puff enormously when fried. In Indonesia, the chips are made from a variety of ingredients, not just shrimp, and are used as a garnish as well as a snack. One advantage is they can be fried in advance and stored for a few days in an airtight container without losing their crispness.

Opposite: Top to bottom: Lada's Cucumber Salad, page 102; Fresh Egg Rolls, page 47; Mr. Lee's Chicken Wings, page 48; Spicy Corn Fritters & Sweet & Sour Red-Chili Sauce, page 49; Shrimp Satay, page 43

Lamb Satay

Saté Kambing

Rich-tasting Indonesian-style soy sauce makes an excellent marinade for meat or chicken. **Photo on pages 36-37.**

2 lbs. trimmed boneless leg of lamb
1/4 cup Indonesian-style soy sauce (kecap)
1/2 medium-size onion, thinly sliced
3 garlic cloves, minced
1/2 teaspoon black pepper
2 tablespoons margarine, softened

Javanese Peanut Sauce:
1/2 medium-size onion, coarsely chopped
2 large garlic cloves
1 small fresh red chili, stemmed, seeded, coarsely chopped
1 tablespoon vegetable oil
3/4 cup water
1/2 cup creamy peanut butter
2 tablespoons Indonesian-style soy sauce (kecap)
2 teaspoons lime juice

Cut lamb into 3/4-inch cubes. Place in a medium-size bowl. Add soy sauce, onion, garlic and pepper. Mix well. Cover and marinate in refrigerator 2 hours or overnight. Bring lamb to room temperature before grilling. Just before serving, make Javanese Peanut Sauce. Prepare barbecue. Coals should be very hot. Set grill close to coals. Divide lamb among 20 skewers. Brush upper sides of meat with margarine; place on grill with margarine-side down. Grill 3 to 5 minutes, or until browned. Turn; brush with margarine; grill 3 to 5 more minutes, or until done as desired. Do not overcook. Serve with peanut sauce for dipping or spoon sauce over meat. Makes 10 appetizer servings.

Javanese Peanut Sauce:
Chop onion, garlic and chili in a blender or food processor fitted with the metal blade. Heat oil in a 1-quart saucepan. Add onion mixture; sauté until onion is tender but not browned. Return to food processor. Add 1/2 cup of the water; process until very finely ground. Return to saucepan. Add remaining 1/4 cup water, peanut butter, soy sauce and lime juice. Bring to a boil, reduce heat and simmer gently, uncovered, 5 minutes, stirring occasionally. Keep warm; pour into a small bowl just before serving. Makes 1 cup.

Chicken Satay

Satay Gai

Curry powder and crushed gingerroot add zesty flavor to the marinade. Cream and butter are ingredients that distinguish this satay from other recipes.

2 whole chicken breasts, boned, skinned
1 teaspoon salt
1/4 teaspoon black pepper
1/2 cup coconut milk
1/2 cup coarsely chopped gingerroot (1/4 lb.)
3 tablespoons whipping cream
2 tablespoons butter, melted
1 teaspoon curry powder
1 teaspoon ground coriander

Cut chicken breasts into long strips 1/2 to 3/4 inch wide. Mix with salt and pepper. Combine remaining ingredients in a medium-size bowl. Stir in chicken. Cover and marinate in refrigerator 4 to 6 hours. Bring to room temperature before grilling. Make Thai Satay Sauce. Prepare barbecue. Coals should be very hot. Set grill close to coals. Remove chicken from marinade; thread onto 16 skewers. Grill chicken 5 to 8 minutes on each side or until cooked through, turning as needed. Do not overcook. Serve with Thai Satay Sauce. Makes 8 appetizer servings.

Thai Satay Sauce:
1 cup coconut milk
1 tablespoon creamy peanut
  butter
2 teaspoons sugar
1 teaspoon Red Curry Paste,
  page 30
1 teaspoon lemon juice
1/4 teaspoon salt

Thai Satay Sauce:
Place coconut milk in a small saucepan. Bring to a boil. Stir in remaining ingredients; boil 1 minute, stirring. Keep warm; pour into a small bowl just before serving. Makes 1 cup.

Shrimp Satay
Saté Udang

(Indonesia)

The simple marinade and short cooking time make this an easy recipe. **Photo on page 40.**

1 lb. medium-size shrimp,
  shelled, deveined
2 tablespoons Indonesian-style
  soy sauce (kecap)

Shrimp Satay Sauce:
1/2 cup unsalted Roasted Peanuts,
  page 31
1 large garlic clove
1 to 2 teaspoons chopped fresh
  red or green hot chili
1/2 cup water
3 tablespoons Indonesian-style
  soy sauce (kecap)
2 teaspoons lime juice
Salt, if desired

Place shrimp in a medium-size bowl; stir in soy sauce. Cover and marinate in refrigerator 1 hour. Bring to room temperature before grilling. Make Shrimp Satay Sauce. Prepare barbecue. Coals should be very hot. Set grill close to coals. Thread 3 to 4 shrimp on each skewer. Grill 2 to 2-1/2 minutes on each side or until shrimp are pink. Do not overcook. Place on a warm platter; coat with Shrimp Satay Sauce. Or serve sauce separately. Makes 6 to 8 appetizers.

Shrimp Satay Sauce:
Process peanuts until finely ground in a blender or food processor fitted with the metal blade. Add garlic, chili and water; process as fine as possible. Pour mixture into a small saucepan. Add soy sauce; bring to a boil. Reduce heat; simmer 3 minutes, stirring. If sauce becomes too thick, thin to desired consistency with 1 to 2 tablespoons additional water. Stir in lime juice. Taste and add salt if desired. Makes about 1 cup.

Shrimp Chips
Krupuk Udang

(Indonesia)

It seems like magic when the small hard chips puff up into large crunchy pieces. Serve them for a snack, like potato chips, or use them to garnish a dish, such as Indonesian Gado Gado, page 113. **Photo on pages 36-37.**

Shrimp-flavored chips
Vegetable oil for deep-frying

Heat 2 inches of oil in a wok or saucepan to 360F (180C) or until a 1-inch bread cube turns golden brown in 60 seconds. Add chips a few at a time. As soon as they puff up, remove and drain on paper towels. Serve immediately or store in an airtight container at room temperature a few days.

Beef Satay
Satay Daging

(Malaysia)

Cucumber wedges and raw onion are traditional accompaniments to satay in Malaysia.

3 lemon grass stalks, sliced
crosswise
1/2 medium-size onion, coarsely
chopped
2 large garlic cloves
1 (1/4-inch-thick) gingerroot slice
1/4 cup light soy sauce
2 teaspoons ground turmeric
1 teaspoon sugar
1/2 teaspoon ground cumin
1/2 teaspoon salt
1/4 to 1/2 teaspoon coarse-grind
black pepper
1 to 1-1/4 lbs. trimmed top sirloin
steak or other tender beef cut
2 medium-size cucumbers,
peeled, cut into wedges
1 medium-size onion, quartered,
sliced

Malaysian Peanut Sauce:
1/2 cup unsalted Roasted Peanuts,
page 31
1 lemon grass stalk, sliced
1/2 medium-size onion, coarsely
chopped
1 large garlic clove
1 tablespoon vegetable oil
1/2 cup coconut milk
1/4 cup water
2 tablespoons sugar
4 teaspoons lime juice
1/2 teaspoon salt
1/4 teaspoon hot chili powder
1/4 teaspoon ground cinnamon

Place all ingredients except steak, cucumbers and sliced onion in a blender or food processor fitted with the metal blade; process as fine as possible. Scrape mixture into a medium-size bowl. Cut meat into 2" x 1/4" strips. Mix with processed mixture. Cover and marinate in refrigerator 2 hours or overnight. Bring meat to room temperature before grilling. Prepare Malaysian Peanut Sauce. Divide meat among about 20 skewers. Prepare barbecue. Coals should be very hot. Set grill close to coals. Lay skewers on grill; cook about 5 minutes on each side or to desired doneness. Serve with Malaysian Peanut Sauce, cucumbers and sliced onion. Makes 10 appetizer servings.

Malaysian Peanut Sauce:
Process peanuts in a nut grinder or food processor fitted with the metal blade until finely ground. Set aside. Combine lemon grass, onion and garlic in a blender or food processor fitted with the metal blade; process as fine as possible. Heat oil in a small saucepan over medium heat. Add lemon grass mixture; cook 5 to 7 minutes or until onion is tender, stirring to keep from burning. Add peanuts and coconut milk. Return to food processor or blender; process as fine as possible. Return mixture to saucepan. Add remaining ingredients. Bring to a boil, reduce heat and simmer gently, uncovered, 5 minutes, stirring often. Pour into a small bowl; serve warm or at room temperature. If sauce thickens upon standing, thin to desired consistency with a little additional water. Makes about 1 cup.

Spring Rolls
Chả Giò

Vietnamese wrap the cut-up rolls in lettuce, then dip them in a tangy sauce. The sugar in the lemon-lime soda, which can be used to soften the rice wrappers, makes them crisp and brown when deep-fried. In Vietnam, where fresh coconuts are readily available, the wrappers are sometimes softened with coconut water. Tap water can also be used.

1 piece dried black fungus
1/4 cup bean thread noodles
1/2 lb. boneless lean pork
1/4 lb. medium-size shrimp, shelled, deveined
1/2 cup drained canned or cooked crabmeat
6 water chestnuts, finely chopped
2 green onions, white part only, finely chopped
1/2 teaspoon salt
1/8 teaspoon white pepper
3/4 cup lemon-lime soda
16 (8-inch) round rice paper wrappers
2 cups vegetable oil
10 to 12 leaves leaf lettuce
1 small cucumber, peeled, sliced
8 mint sprigs
Nuoc Mam Sauce, page 30

Soak black fungus in cold water until softened. Drain and finely chop. There will be about 2 tablespoons; set aside. To measure bean threads, cut from bunch with kitchen scissors; pack into a 1/4-cup measure. Place bean threads in bowl, cover with cold water and let stand about 30 minutes or until softened. Bring 1-1/2 cups water to a boil in a small saucepan. Add drained bean threads, boil 2 minutes, drain and set aside. Grind pork and shrimp in a meat grinder or process in a food processor fitted with the metal blade until finely chopped. Place in a medium-size bowl. Add crabmeat, black fungus, bean threads, water chestnuts, green onions, salt and pepper. Mix thoroughly. Combine soda and 1-1/2 cups water in a small bowl. Place 1 rice paper wrapper on a flat surface. Brush each side lightly with water mixture, using your fingers, a soft brush or moistened paper towel. Or pour enough mixture to form a shallow pool into a large dinner plate; dip wrapper in liquid. When wrapper has softened, place 2 tablespoons filling above bottom edge. Spread slightly, leaving sides clear. Fold bottom of wrapper over filling. Fold sides over filling toward center and roll up to top. Continue until all wrappers are filled. If preparing in advance, place filled wrappers on a platter, cover with plastic wrap and refrigerate. Heat oil in a wok to 360F (180C) or until a 1-inch bread cube turns golden brown in 60 seconds. Add rolls a few at a time; fry about 10 minutes or until golden brown, turning as needed. Drain on paper towels. Keep in a warm oven until ready to serve. If desired, cut rolls in half. Arrange rolls on a serving plate. Arrange lettuce, cucumber and mint on another plate. To eat, tear off a piece of lettuce. Place roll half on lettuce, add a cucumber slice and a leaf or 2 of mint. Wrap, then dip in Nuoc Mam Sauce. Makes 16 rolls.

Variation
If rice paper wrappers are not available, substitute Chinese spring roll skins or egg roll wrappers. One large Oriental dried mushroom, soaked until softened and stem removed, may be substituted for the black fungus.

Fried Egg Rolls
Lumpia

The vinegar-garlic dip distinguishes lumpia from Chinese egg rolls.

1 tablespoon vegetable oil
1 small onion, finely chopped
3 large garlic cloves, crushed,
    then minced
1 lb. boneless lean pork, ground
1/4 lb. green cabbage, shredded
    (1-1/2 cups packed)
1/4 lb. bean sprouts
1 teaspoon salt
16 lumpia or egg roll wrappers
3 cups vegetable oil

Vinegar Dip:
1/2 cup distilled white vinegar
1/4 cup water
2 large garlic cloves, minced
1/2 teaspoon salt

Heat 1 tablespoon oil in a large skillet over medium heat. Add onion and garlic; cook until tender but not browned. Add pork; cook until no longer pink, stirring to break up meat. Add cabbage and bean sprouts; cook until wilted. Stir in salt. Cool thoroughly before filling wrappers. Prepare Vinegar Dip. Place egg roll wrapper with a point at bottom. Place 1/4 cup filling on wrapper above point, spreading filling slightly. Upper edge of filling should be in line with or just below side points. Brush edges from side points to top with water. Fold bottom point over filling. Fold side points to center. Roll up to top. Continue filling wrappers. If preparing in advance, stack on a platter, cover tightly with plastic wrap and refrigerate. Bring to room temperature before frying. Heat remaining 3 cups oil in a wok to 360F (180C) or until a 1-inch bread cube turns golden brown in 60 seconds. Add lumpia 4 at a time; fry 4 to 6 minutes or until golden brown on both sides, turning as needed. Drain excess oil from lumpia over wok, then drain on paper towels. Cut in thirds to serve. Divide Vinegar Dip between 2 small bowls and serve with lumpia. Makes 16 whole lumpia or 48 pieces.

Vinegar Dip:
Combine ingredients. Let stand while preparing rolls to blend flavors.

Fried Chicken Skins
Chicharong Balat Manok

Serve the crisp skins with a vinegar dip, as at Ang Bistro Sa Remedios, a restaurant in Manila. They are also good with spicy brown mustard.

1 lb. chicken skins
3 cups water
1/4 small onion
1 teaspoon salt
1/2 teaspoon black peppercorns
1-1/2 cups vegetable oil

Place chicken skins, water, onion, salt and peppercorns in a large saucepan. Bring to a boil, reduce heat and simmer, covered, 20 minutes. Drain chicken skins; cool. Save broth for another use. Place cooled skins, a few at a time, in paper towels; squeeze as dry as possible. Cut any large pieces into 2- to 3-inch squares or strips. At this point, skins may be refrigerated, covered, for use within a few hours. Bring to room temperature before frying. Prepare Vinegar Dip. Let stand while frying skins to blend flavors. Heat oil in wok to 360F (180C) or until a 1-inch bread cube turns golden

Vinegar Dip:
3 tablespoons distilled white
  vinegar
1 tablespoon water
1 garlic clove, chopped
1/8 teaspoon salt

brown in 60 seconds. Add skins, a few at a time; fry 6 to 8 minutes or until browned and crisp throughout. There should be no soft portions. Drain on paper towels. Serve with Vinegar Dip. These are best immediately after cooking. Makes 2 cups chips.

Vinegar Dip:
Combine ingredients in a small bowl. Let stand to blend flavors. Makes 1/4 cup.

Fresh Egg Rolls
Fresh Lumpia

(The Philippines)

Emphasizing vegetables rather than meat, these lumpia are as light as a salad. Shred vegetables using the shredding blade of a food processor or hand shredder. Eat the lumpia right after they are rolled. **Photo on page 40.**

1/2 cup shredded sweet potato
1/2 cup shredded russet potato
1/2 cup shredded carrot
1/2 cup shredded jícama
1/2 cup shredded chayote
1/2 lb. boneless lean pork
1/4 lb. medium-size shrimp,
  shelled, deveined
2 tablespoons vegetable oil
1/2 medium-size onion, finely
  chopped
3 garlic cloves, minced
1/3 cup chicken broth or water
1-1/4 teaspoons salt
1/8 teaspoon freshly ground black
  pepper
1 cup finely sliced green cabbage
12 small leaf-lettuce leaves
12 lumpia or egg roll wrappers

Sweet Brown Sauce:
1 tablespoon cornstarch
1 cup water
1/4 cup packed light-brown sugar
2 tablespoons soy sauce
1/2 teaspoon salt
1 large garlic clove, minced

Combine potatoes and carrot in a medium-size bowl; cover with cold water until used to prevent discoloration. Set jícama and chayote aside. Cut pork into thin slices, then into fine shreds. Cut shrimp in half crosswise, then cut each piece in half lengthwise. Heat oil in a large skillet. Add onion and garlic; cook until tender but not browned. Add pork and cook, stirring, until no longer pink. Drain potatoes and carrot; add to skillet with jícama and chayote. Add broth, salt and pepper. Cover and cook over medium heat 5 minutes. Stir in cabbage and shrimp. Cover and cook until vegetables are tender, about 5 more minutes. Let cool slightly. Make Sweet Brown Sauce. Wash lettuce leaves; dry thoroughly. For each lumpia, place 1 lettuce leaf on a lumpia or egg roll wrapper parallel to bottom edge. Let leaf extend slightly beyond 1 side. Drain any liquid from lumpia filling. Place about 1/3 cup filling on lettuce. Fold side of egg roll wrapper without lettuce over filling. Leave other side open. Roll up. Arrange on a platter, covering with plastic wrap to keep from drying out until served. Serve at room temperature. To eat, spoon Sweet Brown Sauce into open end. Makes 12 lumpia.

Sweet Brown Sauce:
Blend cornstarch with 2 tablespoons water in a custard cup; set aside. Combine remaining water and other ingredients in a small saucepan. Bring to a boil. Stir cornstarch mixture to blend in cornstarch that has settled; stir into boiling mixture. Cook, stirring, until sauce clears and thickens slightly. Pour into a serving bowl. Serve warm or at room temperature. Makes about 1 cup.

Mr. Lee's Chicken Wings

Kepak Ayam Rekaan Inche Lee

(Malaysia)

A unique blend of seasonings makes these stand out from other chicken wings. Chinese thick sauce is added to the marinade to deepen the color. It may be omitted if it's hard to find. Arrange on lettuce leaves if serving cold. **Photo on page 40.**

2 teaspoons minced gingerroot
2 teaspoons water
1/4 cup soy sauce
3 tablespoons sugar
1 tablespoon honey
4 teaspoons lime juice
1 tablespoon Chinese rice wine or
    dry sherry
1 tablespoon Chinese thick sauce
2-1/2 teaspoons salt
1 teaspoon ground cinnamon
1 teaspoon black pepper
16 chicken wings (about 3 lb.)

Combine gingerroot and water in a small cup. Squeeze gingerroot until water is cloudy. Strain gingerroot juice into a small bowl, discarding gingerroot. Add remaining ingredients except chicken wings; mix well. Cut off chicken wing tips, if desired. Place wings in a shallow baking dish. Add marinade; mix well. Cover and marinate in refrigerator at least 2 hours or overnight, turning wings occasionally. Preheat oven to 350F (175C). Line a 15" x 10" baking pan with foil. Spray foil with non-stick coating. Drain wings, reserving 1/4 cup marinade. Place on prepared pan. Drizzle with reserved marinade. Bake 45 minutes. Place on a heated platter; serve at once, or bake in advance and serve cold. Makes 16 appetizers.

Fried Beef Turnovers

Sambosas

(Brunei)

Brunei is predominantly Malay, but these pastries are Indian in origin.

2 tablespoons vegetable oil
6 shallots, chopped
3 large garlic cloves, minced
1-1/2 lbs. lean ground beef
1-1/2 tablespoons curry powder
1-1/2 teaspoons salt
1/3 cup thawed frozen green peas
4 cups all-purpose flour
6 tablespoons Clarified Butter,
    page 32
1 teaspoon salt
About 1 cup water
Vegetable oil for deep-frying

Heat 2 tablespoons oil in a large skillet. Add shallots and garlic; cook until tender. Add beef; cook until browned, stirring to break up beef. Blend in curry powder and salt. Stir in peas. Set aside until cooled. Place flour in a large bowl. Add butter and salt; stir until combined. Add water as needed to make a dough that is soft but not sticky. Knead until smooth. Divide dough into balls about 1-1/2 inches in diameter. On a lightly floured board, roll each ball into a 6-1/2" x 4" oval about 1/16 inch thick. Cut in half crosswise, making 2 (3-1/2" x 4") pieces. With cut side at bottom, fold dough into a cone, overlapping cut edges and moistening edges with water. Seal overlapped edges tightly. Place rounded teaspoonful of meat inside cone. Moisten inner edge of top, fold over and pinch to seal tightly. Continue until all sambosas are filled. As they are completed, cover with a towel to keep from drying. Heat 1 inch oil in a heavy skillet or 3 cups oil in a wok. Heat to 360F (180C) or until a 1-inch bread cube turns golden brown in 60 seconds. Add sambosas, a few at a time; fry until golden brown, turning as needed. Drain on paper towels. Makes 60.

Spicy Corn Fritters
Khao Pode Thord

These Thai fritters with sweet sauce are not so different in concept from American corn fritters with maple syrup. **Photo on page 40.**

2 tablespoons chopped cilantro
    roots and stems
4 garlic cloves
1/2 teaspoon black pepper
2/3 cup water
1/2 cup rice flour
1/2 cup all-purpose flour
1-1/2 teaspoons sugar
3/4 teaspoon baking powder
1/2 teaspoon salt
1 (8-oz.) can whole-kernel corn,
    drained
1-1/2 cups vegetable oil

Sweet & Sour Red-Chili Sauce:
3/4 cup sugar
3/4 cup distilled white vinegar
1 small fresh red chili, stemmed,
    seeded, finely chopped
1/2 teaspoon salt

Make Sweet & Sour Red-Chili Sauce. Place cilantro, garlic and pepper in a mortar; pound to a paste. Blend paste with water in a small bowl. In a medium-size bowl, combine rice flour and all-purpose flour, sugar, baking powder and salt. Stir in corn. Blend in cilantro-water mixture. Heat oil in wok to 375F (190C) or until a 1-inch bread cubes turns golden brown in 50 seconds. Drop mixture by tablespoons into oil. Fry until golden brown on each side, turning as needed. Drain on paper towels. Keep warm until ready to serve. Serve with Sweet & Sour Red-Chili Sauce. Makes 24 small fritters.

Sweet & Sour Red-Chili Sauce:
Combine all ingredients in a small saucepan. Boil until reduced to 2/3 cup. Pour into a serving bowl; serve warm or at room temperature.

Tip: When handling fresh hot chilies, protect hands by wearing rubber gloves.

SOUPS

Soups with a sour tang are popular in Southeast Asia for the same reason that lemonade is welcome on hot summer days: the sharp flavor is refreshing in steamy weather. In the Philippines, the slightly tart soup called *sinigang* is so loved that it is almost a national dish. Sinigang is made with meat, fish or shellfish and an assortment of vegetables. Green tamarind often supplies the tartness. Overseas, where this ingredient is not available, lemon juice can be substituted. Vinegar is another possibility. And a Filipina living in Japan produced a satisfactory sinigang with the Japanese sour plum.

Eaten Filipino-style, sinigang becomes a hearty meal. The procedure is to spoon some of the meat and vegetables onto a plate of rice, sprinkle this with broth, add a dash of fish sauce and eat everything together.

Sinigang is mildly flavored. In contrast, Thailand's famous sour shrimp soup, Tom Yum Goong, can be incendiary with chilies. In this soup and Tom Kha Gai, made with coconut milk and chicken, the sourness is from lime or lemon juice. Both soups accent the citrus flavor with lemon grass and kaffir lime leaves.

Shrimp Soup with Pineapple (Canh Chua Ca), a Vietnamese variation on Tom Yum Goong, is interesting because the broth is sweet as well as sour. The sweetness comes from pineapple chunks, pineapple juice, tomato wedges and sugar. Vinegar supplies the tang.

Tartness is not always part of the cooked ingredients. Philippine Chicken-Rice Soup (Arroz Caldo) comes with a lemon or lime wedge on the side to sharpen the flavor as desired. Seasoned with gingerroot, this soup is clearly related to Chinese rice gruels.

An example of the latter is Prawn Congee, copied from a Chinese noodle shop in Singapore. Congee is as basic to the Chinese as chicken broth is to western countries. It is also simple to make. The cook prepares a plain rice gruel, then adds any tasty bits of meat, fish or vegetables on hand. Congee can be scaled down to a first-course soup but usually comes in a large bowl and is often eaten in the early hours of the morning after a night on the town.

Vietnamese Pho, a beef-and-rice-noodle soup, is served for breakfast as well as at other meals, and is made in a variety of ways. In the recipe given here, the sliced beef is cooked in the broth. Another way is to place the raw beef in the serving bowl, then pour the hot broth over it. The concentrated broth requires hours of simmering beef bones along with a roasted onion, some gingerroot and a small piece of cinnamon stick. An elaborate version might include both raw and cooked beef slices, beef tendon, brisket and beef tripe.

Vietnam is also the source of delicate Crab & Asparagus Soup laced with egg threads. For a special occasion, the Vietnamese might dress it up with a dash of Cognac. From Indonesia comes Soto, a mildly spiced mixture of chicken broth, coconut milk, shredded chicken, bean sprouts and other vegetables. Sop Kambing, a mutton soup popular in Malaysia, Singapore and Indonesia, can be very spicy. The version in this chapter, made with lamb instead of mutton, is a composite of soups tasted in Penang and in Sumatran and Javanese restaurants in Singapore.

Hot & Sour Shrimp Soup

Tom Yum Goong

(Thailand)

This easy version of the classic Thai soup comes from the Bussaracum restaurant in Bangkok. It takes only a few minutes to prepare.

20 medium-size shrimp with heads, about 1/2 lb.
1 quart water (4 cups)
10 thin gingerroot slices
2 lemon grass stalks, sliced
3 tablespoons lemon juice
3 tablespoons fish sauce
2 to 4 serrano chilies, sliced
4 kaffir lime leaves, coarsely broken
1/2 teaspoon salt
2 tablespoons cilantro leaves

Shell shrimp, leaving on heads. Remove sand veins. Bring water to boil in a 2-quart saucepan. Add gingerroot and lemon grass. Holding each shrimp over saucepan, remove head, allowing juices from head portion to drop into water. Discard head. Add remainder of shrimp to saucepan. Bring to a boil. Add lemon juice, fish sauce, chilies, lime leaves and salt. Boil 2 minutes or just until shrimp turn pink. Ladle into individual bowls. Top each serving with cilantro leaves. Makes 4 servings.

Chicken-Coconut Soup

Tom Kha Gai

(Thailand)

Refined but with a dash of spice, this soup makes an elegant first course. The lime leaves add subtle citrus flavor but can be omitted.

1 large chicken breast half
3 cups water
1 teaspoon salt
1 (14-oz.) can coconut milk (1-3/4 cups)
1/2 cup drained canned straw mushrooms or button mushrooms
1 lemon grass stalk, sliced diagonally into 1-inch pieces
4 kaffir lime leaves, cut into large pieces
1 or 2 fresh red chilies, stemmed, quartered lengthwise, seeded
2 tablespoons fish sauce or additional salt to taste
1 teaspoon ground laos
2 tablespoons lime juice
2 tablespoons fresh basil, cilantro or mint leaves

Place chicken breast, water and salt in large saucepan. Bring to a boil, cover and simmer 30 minutes. Drain chicken; cool slightly. Remove skin and bones; shred meat. Return chicken meat and 2 cups broth to saucepan. Save remaining broth for another use. Add remaining ingredients except lime juice and herb leaves. Bring to a boil. Reduce heat, cover and simmer 30 minutes. Stir in lime juice. Ladle into individual bowls; garnish each serving with a few of the basil, cilantro or mint leaves. Additional lime leaves can also be used for garnish, if desired. Makes 4 servings.

Shrimp Soup with Pineapple
Canh Chua Cá
(Vietnam)

This colorful southern Vietnamese soup is simultaneously sour, sweet and spicy. Green onions and fried garlic sprinkled over the top add still more flavor.

4 very large garlic cloves
1/4 cup vegetable oil
2 tablespoons chopped
   green-onion tops
3 cups beef broth
1 cup water
1/4 cup distilled white vinegar
1 (8-oz.) can pineapple chunks
   (juice pack)
1-1/2 tablespoons sugar
1 tablespoon fish sauce
1 teaspoon salt
1/8 teaspoon red (cayenne)
   pepper
1/4 teaspoon white pepper
1 (4-oz.) can button mushrooms,
   drained
1 small firm tomato, cut into 8
   wedges
24 small to medium-size shrimp
   (about 6 oz.) shelled, deveined
1/4 lb. bean sprouts

Cut garlic into thin slices, then chop; you should have about 3 tablespoons. Heat oil in a small skillet. Add garlic; fry slowly until golden, stirring frequently. Do not burn. Drain on paper towels. Discard oil. Set garlic and green-onion tops aside for garnish. Combine beef broth, water and vinegar in a 3-quart saucepan. Drain juice from pineapple; add to saucepan. Set drained pineapple chunks aside. Add sugar, fish sauce, salt, red pepper and white pepper to saucepan. Bring to a boil. Add pineapple chunks, mushrooms and tomato wedges; bring to a boil again. Add shrimp, reduce heat and simmer 2 minutes or just until shrimp turn pink. Divide bean sprouts among 4 large soup bowls. Ladle soup into bowls. Garnish each serving with some of the reserved fried garlic and green-onion tops. Makes 4 servings.

Pork & Vegetable Soup
Sinigang na Baboy

Served with steamed rice, this soup makes a hearty supper. Any leafy green vegetable may be substituted for the kangkong.

1-1/2 lbs. pork shoulder blade meat or other boneless pork
8 cups water
2 medium-size tomatoes (1/2 lb.), cut into wedges
1 medium-size onion, cut into wedges
1 or 2 jalapeño or serrano chilies
4 teaspoons salt
1/2 lb. white radish (daikon) or turnip, peeled
1/4 lb. Chinese long beans or green beans
1/4 lb. kangkong, tops only, or spinach
1/4 cup lemon juice
Basic Steamed Rice, page 133
Fish sauce

Trim fat from pork; cut pork into 1-1/2-inch chunks. Place in a 4-quart saucepan. Add water; bring to a boil. Skim off foam from surface until clear. Reduce heat. Add tomatoes, onion, chilies and salt. Cover and simmer 45 minutes. Cut radish in half lengthwise, then cut crosswise into 1/2-inch slices. Remove ends of beans. Cut beans into 1-1/2-inch lengths; add to soup with radish. Cover; cook 20 minutes. Add kangkong or spinach. Cook 5 minutes. Stir in lemon juice. Serve soup in large bowls. Accompany with plates of steamed rice. To eat, spoon portions of the soup ingredients and broth over the rice. Season to taste with fish sauce. Eat remaining broth from the bowls. Makes 6 to 8 servings.

Prawn Congee
Ha Tong

This Chinese soup can be prepared with other cooked meat or fish. Green vegetables, such as broccoli or Chinese pea pods, could be added for color.

5 cups water
1/2 cup long-grain rice
1 teaspoon salt
8 small dried Oriental mushrooms
12 medium-size shrimp, shelled, deveined
3 tablespoons chopped green-onion tops
Soy sauce

Combine water, rice and salt in a large saucepan. Bring to a boil. Reduce heat, cover and simmer 1 hour or until rice is very soft. Rice broth can be made up to 4 hours ahead. If rice broth thickens, thin to desired consistency with additional water. Meanwhile, soak mushrooms in cool water about 30 minutes or until softened. Drain, remove and discard stems. Set caps aside. In a medium-size saucepan, add shrimp to about 3 cups (or enough to cover) boiling salted water. Boil 2 minutes or until shrimp turn pink. Drain. Place 3 shrimp and 2 mushrooms in each of 4 soup bowls. Shrimp and mushrooms may be cut into smaller pieces, if desired. Divide rice broth among bowls. Sprinkle with green onions. Season to taste with soy sauce at the table. Makes 4 servings.

Tangy Shrimp Soup
Sinigang na Sugpo

This two-in-one recipe includes a simple version of fish stock that can be used with any seafood soup. Use any inexpensive lean, white fish for the stock.

1/2 lb. medium-size shrimp
3/4 lb. cut-up chowder fish or fish
  scraps
5 cups water
1/4 medium-size onion, sliced
2 parsley sprigs
1 (1/4-inch-thick) gingerroot slice
1 bay leaf
1 teaspoon salt
1/4 teaspoon black peppercorns
1 small onion (1/4 lb.), diced
1 large tomato (1/2 lb.), cut into 8
  to 12 wedges
1 teaspoon fish sauce
Black pepper
1/4 lb. white radish (daikon) or
  turnip
1/4 lb. green beans, ends snapped
  off, cut into 1-inch pieces
1 Oriental eggplant or 1/4 lb.
  regular eggplant, cut into 1-inch
  chunks
1 jalapeño or serrano chili, sliced
  crosswise
1/4 cup lemon juice
Basic Steamed Rice, page 133

Rinse and shell shrimp, reserving shells. Remove sand veins. Cover shrimp and refrigerate until needed. Rinse fish. Combine shrimp shells and fish in a large saucepan. Add 4-3/4 cups of the water, sliced onion, parsley, gingerroot, bay leaf, salt and peppercorns. Bring to a boil. Reduce heat and simmer, uncovered, 30 minutes. Strain through a sieve, pressing to extract liquid from fish and shrimp shells. Add water, if necessary, to make about 1 quart. Rinse saucepan. Return strained stock to saucepan. Bring to a boil. Add diced onion and tomato. Cover and simmer 15 minutes. Stir fish sauce into stock. Taste and add more salt if needed. Add a dash of pepper. Peel radish, cut in half lengthwise, then cut crosswise into 1/2-inch chunks. Add radish, green beans, eggplant and chili to soup. Cover; simmer 15 minutes. Add shrimp. Simmer 5 minutes. Combine lemon juice with remaining 1/4 cup water. Stir into soup; reheat. Serve soup in large bowls. Accompany with plates of rice. To eat, spoon portions of shrimp, vegetables and broth onto rice. Season with additional fish sauce. Eat any remaining broth from bowls. Makes 4 servings.

Crab & Asparagus Soup
Xúp Măng Cua
(Vietnam)

The base of this soup is Oriental-style chicken broth, which is seasoned with gingerroot and green onions. Try using the broth in other soups, too.

1 (6-oz.) can crabmeat
18 spears canned peeled small
　white asparagus
2 eggs, beaten
6 cilantro sprigs

Oriental Chicken Broth:
Carcass portion of 4 chicken
　breast halves or 1 chicken
　carcass or 3 chicken backs
2 green onions, including part of
　the tops, cut into 1-inch lengths
2 (1/4-inch-thick) gingerroot
　slices
6-1/2 cups water
1 tablespoon chicken-bouillon
　granules
3/4 teaspoon salt

Prepare Oriental Chicken Broth. Place in a 3-quart saucepan. Drain crabmeat. Place in a sieve; rinse. Add to broth. Cut asparagus spears into thirds; there will be about 1 cup. Add asparagus to broth. Simmer gently, uncovered, 10 minutes. Beat eggs in a small bowl. Slowly pour eggs into soup, stirring constantly to form egg threads. Spoon into soup bowls. Top each serving with a cilantro sprig. Makes 6 servings.

Oriental Chicken Broth:
Combine all ingredients in a 3-quart saucepan. Bring to a rolling boil. Skim surface. Reduce heat, cover and simmer 1 hour. Strain broth. If desired, make broth ahead, cover and refrigerate until chilled. Remove any fat from surface before using. Makes about 6 cups.

Variation
Add 1 to 2 teaspoons Cognac to each serving.

Chicken-Rice Soup
Arroz Caldo
(The Philippines)

Except for the gingerroot and crisp-fried garlic, this could be American-style chicken and rice soup. In the Philippines, it is also made with tripe.

1 large chicken breast half
5 cups homemade chicken broth
　or 1 (14-1/2-oz.) can condensed
　chicken broth and water to
　make 5 cups
1-1/2 teaspoons salt or to taste
5 large garlic cloves
2 tablespoons vegetable oil
1/4 medium-size onion, thinly
　sliced
1 (1-inch) gingerroot piece, thinly
　sliced
1/2 cup long-grain rice, washed,
　drained
2 large green onions, including
　some of the tops, chopped
4 lemon or lime wedges

Place chicken breast and broth in a 3-quart saucepan. Add salt, adjusting amount according to saltiness of broth. Bring to a boil. Reduce heat, cover and simmer 30 minutes. Remove chicken breast. Strain broth into another container; clean saucepan. Discard chicken skin and bones; shred meat. Cut garlic into thin slices, then chop coarsely. Heat oil in cleaned saucepan over medium heat. Add garlic; cook until lightly browned. Remove garlic with a slotted spoon; drain on paper towels. In remaining oil, fry onion and gingerroot until onion is tender. Drain off excess oil, if desired. Reserve two-thirds of the fried garlic for garnish. Add remaining garlic to the saucepan. Add the broth, rice and shredded chicken. Bring to a boil. Reduce heat, cover and simmer until rice is very soft, 45 minutes. To serve, ladle into 4 large soup bowls. Sprinkle each serving with some of the reserved fried garlic and green onions. Serve with lemon or lime wedges to squeeze into the soup. Makes 4 servings.

Chicken Soup with Bean Sprouts & Coconut Milk
Soto

The broth is poured over the bean sprouts and other ingredients at serving time. This keeps the sprouts crunchy.

1 whole chicken breast
5 cups water
1 lemon grass stalk
1/4 medium-size onion
1 teaspoon salt
1 teaspoon chicken-bouillon
　 granules
1/2 cup coconut milk
1/2 teaspoon ground coriander
1/2 teaspoon ground laos
1/4 teaspoon ground turmeric
1/8 teaspoon white pepper
6 oz. bean sprouts
3 tablespoons diced celery
2 small green onions, including
　 some of the tops, finely
　 chopped
1 hard-cooked egg, cut into 4
　 wedges
Crisp-fried shallots, made as for
　 Crisp-Fried Onions page 31, if
　 desired

Place chicken breast and water in a 3-quart saucepan. Pound lemon grass until crushed. Add lemon grass, onion, salt and bouillon granules to saucepan. Bring to a boil. Reduce heat, cover and simmer 30 minutes. Remove chicken breast. Strain broth into another container; rinse saucepan. Discard chicken skin and bones. Shred meat; set aside. Return broth to rinsed saucepan. Add coconut milk. Combine coriander, laos, turmeric and white pepper in a custard cup. Blend a small amount of broth with spices, then add to saucepan. Taste and add more salt, if desired. Reheat broth. Divide chicken, bean sprouts, celery and green onions among 4 large soup bowls. Add an egg wedge to each. Divide broth among the bowls. Sprinkle with Crisp Fried Shallots, if desired. Makes 4 servings.

Beef & Rice-Noodle Soup
Phở

(Vietnam)

Make the stock the day before, then it takes only a few minutes to prepare this hearty main-dish soup. Part of the fun is adding seasonings to taste at the table. The beef slices easier if it is partially frozen.

1 large onion, unpeeled
1 (3- to 4-lb.) beef shank bone, cut into several large pieces
Water to cover beef
11 cups water
1 (1-inch) gingerroot piece, sliced
1 (1-inch) cinnamon stick
1 tablespoon salt
1/4 teaspoon black peppercorns
1/4 lb. rice stick noodles
3/4 lb. beef eye of the round, partially frozen
1/2 lb. bean sprouts
1 or 2 jalapeño chilies, sliced crosswise
1 lemon, cut into 4 wedges
Hoisin sauce
Fish sauce, if desired
1 small onion, quartered, thinly sliced
1/4 cup chopped green onions, including some of the tops

Preheat oven to 350F (175C). Place unpeeled onion in a pie pan. Bake 45 minutes. Place beef bones in a 6-quart Dutch oven. Cover with water; bring to a full boil. Pour off water. Rinse pan and bones. Return bones to pan. Add the 11 cups water, the roasted onion, gingerroot, cinnamon stick, salt and peppercorns. Bring to a boil. Reduce heat and simmer, uncovered, 3 hours. Remove bones. Strain broth. There should be about 6 cups; if not, add water to make 6 cups. Place in a large jar or bowl, cover and refrigerate overnight. The next day, remove solid layer of fat at the top. About 1 hour before serving, soak rice sticks in cold water to cover about 30 minutes or until soft. Cut beef across grain into paper-thin slices; set aside. Arrange bean sprouts, chilies and lemon wedges on a serving plate. Pour hoisin sauce into a small bowl. Just before serving, bring 2 quarts water to a boil in a large saucepan. Add rice sticks, boil 2 minutes and drain. Divide among 4 heated large soup bowls; bowls should hold at least 3 cups. Meanwhile, bring chilled broth to a boil in a large saucepan. Add beef and sliced onion; boil until beef is no longer pink, 1-1/2 to 2 minutes. Divide broth, beef and onion among soup bowls. Sprinkle 1 tablespoon chopped green onion over each serving. At the table, add bean sprouts and chili slices as desired. Squeeze in lemon juice; add 1 to 2 tablespoons hoisin sauce. Serve with soup spoons for the broth and chopsticks to pick out the meat, vegetables and noodles. Makes 4 large servings.

Spicy Lamb Soup

Sop Kambing

(Malaysia, Singapore, Indonesia)

For Asian-style spiciness, increase the number of dried hot chilies, or substitute a liberal dash of red (cayenne) pepper.

3/4 lb. lamb bones, with some meat attached
6 cups water
1 medium-size onion, quartered
3 medium-size garlic cloves
2 (1/4-inch-thick) gingerroot slices
1 small dried hot chili
1 (3-inch) cinnamon stick
3 whole star anise
6 whole cloves
1-1/2 teaspoons salt
1/4 teaspoon black peppercorns
1 cup coconut milk
1 (6- to 8-oz.) russet potato
1 small carrot
1/2 lb. boneless lean lamb, cut into 1/2-inch chunks
1 medium-size tomato, cut into thin wedges
2 large green onions, including tops, finely chopped

Place lamb bones in a 3-quart saucepan. Add water; bring to a boil. Skim foam off surface until clear. Add onion, garlic, gingerroot, chili, cinnamon, star anise, cloves, salt and peppercorns. Bring to a boil. Reduce heat and simmer, uncovered, 2 hours, stirring occasionally. Strain broth into another container, reserving bones. Add water, if necessary, to make about 3 cups broth. Rinse saucepan; return broth to saucepan. Stir in coconut milk. Peel potato; cut into 1/2-inch pieces. Cut carrot into 1/2-inch pieces. Cut off any usable meat from bones; add to broth with lamb chunks, potato and carrot. Bring to a boil. Reduce heat, cover and simmer 30 minutes. Cut tomato into wedges; add to soup. Simmer 10 minutes. Ladle soup into 4 large bowls; sprinkle with green onions. Makes 4 servings.

Fresh Gingerroot

Fresh gingerroot varies in size so it is difficult to be precise with measurements. The larger body of the root, as opposed to the outer knobs, usually measures about 1 to 1-1/2 inches across. A 1/4-inch-thick slice of gingerroot weighs about 1/3 ounce or slightly more, but less than 1/2 ounce, and yields about 1-1/2 teaspoons when chopped. One ounce, finely chopped and packed into a measuring spoon, yields about 2 tablespoons. Exact quantities are not crucial: If you like the flavor of ginger, use more; if you aren't sure, start with less.

SEAFOOD

Fundamental to the Southeast Asian diet, seafood is prepared in a multitude of ways and is even used as a condiment. All countries season with either amber-colored, salty fish sauce or strong-tasting shrimp paste or both. For snacks, there is krupuk, the deep-fried Indonesian chips that taste delicately of shrimp. Tiny dried fish appear as a drink accompaniment in luxury hotels in Singapore and Malaysia or as a side dish with rice at humble food stalls. Larger dried fish are a breakfast favorite in the Philippines.

Thrifty Asian cooks add small quantities of fish and shellfish to noodles, rice and soups and create great dishes around parts that might not be valued elsewhere. Fish maw is the primary ingredient of one Straits Chinese soup. And Singaporeans relish fish-head curry, a startling dish to those gazing for the first time into the eyes of this ingredient in a bowl of steaming, rich curry sauce.

Other dishes, while thoroughly Asian, are easier to make outside the region and please a wide range of tastes. A steamed whole fish flooded with coconut-milk sauce is a handsome entree from Brunei. This same small country is the source of an unusual sweet-sour combination of fried fish and vegetables. The independence celebration that drew heads of state from around the world to the palace of Brunei's sultan was highlighted by a banquet of western and Malay foods that included Ikan Sambal, fish seasoned with turmeric and topped with tamarind sauce.

The Raffles Hotel in Singapore serves fish in a coconut milk sauce as part of its curry tiffin buffets, which recapture the meals once served to British colonials. Its traditional *tok panjang* (long table) buffets of Straits Chinese food might include fish and pineapple in a sauce enhanced with tamarind and shrimp paste. From Thailand comes a luscious fish curry that is sweet, spicy and rich at the same time, blending coconut milk with red curry paste and the wrinkly red dates called jujubes.

Easy dishes for shrimp fanciers include Malaysian Shrimp in Tomato Sauce and Thai Shrimp with Mint & Chilies. In Java, shrimp might be bathed in coconut milk seasoned with tamarind and hot chilies, and a salad-like Thai dish tosses the cooked crustaceans with lemon grass and lemon juice.

Reminiscent of a quiche except that it is steamed, not baked, is a Vietnamese cake that includes crabmeat, pork and bean thread noodles. Egg yolk brushed over the top and a sprinkle of paprika give it appetizing color. The Vietnamese serve the cake alongside rice topped with pork shreds, but it would be equally at home at a western-style luncheon, served with a green salad and croissants.

Additional recipes that include seafood either as a main or supplementary ingredient appear in chapters on appetizers, soups, salads, vegetables, rice and noodles, indicating how basic the products of the sea are to Southeast Asian cookery.

Steamed Fish with Coconut Sauce

Ikan Masak Molek

(Brunei)

A beautiful dish to present at a dinner party, and surprisingly easy to prepare.
Photo on page 111.

1 (1-3/4-lb.) whole rock cod, red
  snapper or other lean fish
1/2 teaspoon salt
1/8 teaspoon white pepper
2 lemon grass stalks, cut into
  1-inch lengths, or 4 large strips
  lemon peel, yellow portion only
1 cup coconut milk
8 shallots, finely chopped
1-1/2 tablespoons minced
  gingerroot
1/2 to 1 fresh red chili, finely
  chopped
1 teaspoon grated lemon peel
1/2 teaspoon salt
1/4 teaspoon white pepper
1 teaspoon chopped fresh parsley

Place fish on a platter. Season with 1/2 teaspoon salt and 1/8 teaspoon white pepper. Arrange lemon grass or lemon peel over top. Place on a rack in a large steamer over simmering water. Cover and steam until fish has turned from translucent to opaque when tested with a fork, about 25 minutes. Meanwhile, combine coconut milk, shallots, gingerroot, chili, lemon peel, 1/2 teaspoon salt and 1/2 teaspoon white pepper in a small heavy saucepan. Bring to a boil. Reduce heat; simmer, uncovered, 20 minutes, stirring occasionally. With aid of 2 large spatulas, transfer cooked fish to a heated large platter, discarding liquid. Pour coconut sauce over fish; garnish with parsley. Makes 4 servings.

Sweet & Sour Pickled Fish

Acar Ikan

(Brunei)

The fish can be served hot as a main dish or at room temperature as a salad.

1 (1-1/2-lb.) cleaned whole red
  snapper, excluding head and
  tail, or thick-cut fish steaks
2 teaspoons salt
1 teaspoon ground turmeric
2 small cucumbers (1 lb.)
2/3 cup distilled white vinegar
1/4 cup sugar
1/2 teaspoon ground turmeric
1/4 teaspoon salt
2 cups vegetable oil
2 small onions, halved lengthwise,
  thinly sliced
2 (1/2-inch-thick) gingerroot
  slices, cut into thin strips 1/2
  inch wide
1 small fresh red chili, sliced
  lengthwise
1 serrano chili, sliced lengthwise
2 large garlic cloves, chopped

Cut whole fish into small individual portions; if using large fish steaks, cut into smaller portions. Season fish all over with 2 teaspoons salt and 1 teaspoon turmeric. Let stand at room temperature 1 hour. Peel cucumbers. Cut in half lengthwise; scoop out seeds with a sharp spoon. Cut cucumbers crosswise into 1-1/2-inch lengths, then cut lengthwise into thin slices. Set aside. Mix vinegar, sugar, remaining 1/2 teaspoon turmeric and salt in a small bowl until sugar dissolves; set aside. Heat oil in a wok to 360F (180C) or until a 1-inch bread cube turns golden brown in 60 seconds. Add fish pieces, a few at a time; fry until fish has turned from translucent to opaque when tested with a fork and is lightly browned, 4 to 8 minutes depending upon thickness of fish. Drain on paper towels; keep warm. When all fish is cooked, drain off oil, reserving 2 tablespoons. Clean wok. Reheat reserved oil in wok. Add cucumbers, onions, gingerroot, chilies and garlic; stir-fry 1 minute. Add vinegar mixture. Boil, uncovered, 5 minutes. Place fish portions on a heated large platter. Top with vegetable mixture, including any liquid in wok. Makes 4 servings.

Fried Fish Cakes

Tod Mun Pla

*The chewy fish cakes are always served with a sweet and sour cucumber relish,
here dressed up with the addition of carrots, red onion and cilantro. Red curry
paste seasons the fish mixture, but the cakes can also be made without it.* **Photo
on page 111.**

1 lb. lean white fish fillets
1/2 teaspoon salt
1 tablespoon water
1 egg
1 tablespoon Red Curry Paste,
    page 30
4 slender young green beans,
    thinly sliced crosswise (1/4 cup
    slices)
1 cup vegetable oil

Cucumber Relish:
1/3 cup distilled white vinegar
2 tablespoons sugar
1 teaspoon salt
1 small fresh red hot chili or
    serrano chili, thinly sliced
1 small, slender, tender-skinned
    cucumber (1/4 lb.)
1/4 cup thinly sliced red onion,
    cut into small pieces
2 tablespoons cilantro leaves
4 teaspoons finely shredded carrot

Process fish and salt in a food processor fitted with the metal
blade until finely ground. While motor is running, gradually
pour in water through feed tube. Add egg and curry paste;
process until thoroughly mixed. Pour mixture into a
medium-size bowl. Stir in green beans. Cover and refrigerate
until chilled. Prepare Cucumber Relish. When ready to
cook, form fish mixture into 12 small flat patties, about 2
inches in diameter; mixture will be sticky. Heat oil in a large
skillet—oil should be at least 1/2 inch deep—to 360F
(180C) or until a 1-inch bread cube turns golden brown in
60 seconds. With a spatula, place half the patties in the oil.
Fry 5 minutes or until bottom sides are golden brown. Turn
and fry 5 more minutes. Drain on paper towels; keep warm.
Repeat with remaining patties. Serve with Cucumber Relish
to spoon over the patties. Makes 4 servings.

Cucumber Relish:
Combine vinegar, sugar and salt in a medium-size bowl; stir
until sugar and salt dissolve. Add chili. Cut unpeeled cucumber lengthwise into halves. Cut crosswise into thin slices.
Add to vinegar mixture. Just before serving, divide relish
among 4 small bowls. Divide red onion, cilantro and carrot
among the bowls; spoon some of the liquid from relish over
them.

Tip: Deep-frying in an electric wok conserves oil and makes it easy to control the temperature.

Fish with Spicy Tamarind Sauce
Ikan Sambal

(Brunei)

The sauce can be prepared in advance and reheated, reducing last minute work to the frying of the fish.

1 lb. lean white fish fillets
1 teaspoon ground turmeric
1/4 teaspoon salt
3 tablespoons vegetable oil
1 thin slice from a medium-size onion, separated into rings

Tamarind Sauce:
8 shallots or 1/2 medium-size onion
2 large garlic cloves
1 small fresh red chili, chopped
1/2 teaspoon shrimp paste (terasi), if desired
1 tablespoon vegetable oil
1/2 cup Tamarind Liquid, page 32
1-1/2 teaspoons sugar
1/2 teaspoon salt

Cut fish into 4 portions. Rub turmeric over both sides of each fillet. Sprinkle with salt. Cover and refrigerate. Make Tamarind Sauce. Heat oil in a skillet large enough to hold fish in a single layer. Add fish; fry 2-1/2 to 3 minutes on each side, depending upon thickness, or until fish has turned from translucent to opaque when tested with a fork. Place fish on a heated platter. Spoon sauce over fish. Garnish with onion rings; keep warm. Makes 4 servings.

Tamarind Sauce:
Combine shallots, garlic, chili, and shrimp paste if desired, in a blender or food processor fitted with the metal blade; process until very fine. Heat oil in a small saucepan. Add ground mixture; sauté gently 3 minutes. Add tamarind liquid, sugar and salt. Bring to a boil. Reduce heat; simmer gently, uncovered, 5 minutes or until thickened, stirring frequently; keep warm. Makes 1/2 cup.

Raffles Fish Curry
Kari Ikan

(Singapore)

Curries served to English colonials were generally milder than those eaten by native inhabitants.

1/2 medium-size onion
2 large garlic cloves
1 (1-inch) gingerroot piece
1 or 2 serrano chilies, seeded
2 tablespoons curry powder
2 tablespoons water
2 tablespoons vegetable oil
1 (14-oz.) can coconut milk (1-3/4 cups)
1/3 cup Tamarind Liquid, page 32
1 teaspoon salt
1/2 teaspoon sugar
1-1/2 to 1-3/4 lbs. red snapper fillets, cut into 12 portions
Basic Steamed Rice, page 133

Process onion, garlic, gingerroot and chilies as fine as possible in a blender or food processor fitted with the metal blade. Blend curry powder and water into a paste in a custard cup. Heat oil in a Dutch oven over medium heat. Add ground mixture; fry, stirring often, about 3 minutes. Add curry paste; cook, stirring often, 2 minutes. Add coconut milk, tamarind liquid, salt and sugar. Bring to a boil. Add fish. Reduce heat, cover and simmer gently 15 minutes or until fish has turned from translucent to opaque when tested with a fork. Serve with rice. Makes 4 to 6 servings.

Fish with Pineapple & Tamarind
Ikan Asam
(Singapore)

Distinctive Straits Chinese seasonings blend in this dish. The pineapple should be very sweet to give the proper flavor. For spicy authenticity, double the amount of chilies.

1 small dried chili
2 rounded tablespoons tamarind
   pulp
1-1/2 cups warm water
1 serrano chili, sliced
1/2 lb. shallots or 2 small onions
6 candlenuts
1 teaspoon shrimp paste (terasi)
1 teaspoon ground laos
1/2 teaspoon ground turmeric
2 tablespoons vegetable oil
1-1/2 cups warm water
2-1/2 tablespoons sugar
2 teaspoons salt
1 lemon grass stalk, pounded
1 cup fresh pineapple chunks (1/4
   medium-size pineapple)
1-1/2 lbs. red snapper fillets
Basic Steamed Rice or Coconut
   Rice, page 133

Soak dried chili in warm water in a custard cup until softened; drain. Discard stem and seeds. Combine tamarind and 1-1/2 cups warm water in a medium-size bowl. Knead tamarind to extract flavor and color. Strain liquid into a small bowl, discarding pulp; set aside. Combine dried and serrano chilies, shallots, candlenuts, shrimp paste, laos and turmeric in a blender or food processor fitted with the metal blade; process to a paste. Heat oil in a large skillet over medium heat. Add ground mixture; sauté 5 minutes, stirring to prevent burning. Add tamarind liquid, remaining 1-1/2 cups water, sugar, salt, lemon grass and pineapple. Bring to a boil, reduce heat and simmer 3 minutes. If desired, prepare in advance to this point, then reheat before adding fish. Lay fish fillets in sauce. Bring to a boil again. Reduce heat; simmer, uncovered, 10 minutes, or until fish has turned from translucent to opaque when tested with a fork. Remove lemon grass. Serve with rice to soak up the sauce. Makes 4 servings.

Fish Curry with Jujubes
Choo Chee Pla Sawai
(Thailand)

Jujubes, also known as Chinese red dates, add an interesting sweet taste to the sauce.

12 jujubes
1-1/2 cups coconut milk
2 tablespoons Red Curry Paste,
   page 30
2 tablespoons fish sauce
1-1/2 teaspoons sugar
1/4 cup canned straw mushrooms,
   sliced if large
1-1/4 lbs. lean fish fillets, cut into
   3-inch portions
Peel of 1 large lime, cut into fine
   slivers

Place jujubes in a small saucepan. Add 1 cup water. Cover and bring to a boil. Remove from heat; let stand until jujubes are softened. Drain, discarding liquid. Heat 1/4 cup of the coconut milk in a medium-size skillet. Add curry paste; cook, stirring, 1 minute. Add remaining 1-1/4 cups coconut milk, fish sauce, sugar, mushrooms and drained jujubes. Bring to a boil. Lay fish pieces in sauce. Cover and simmer 6 to 8 minutes or until fish has turned from translucent to opaque when tested with a fork. Arrange on a heated serving dish; garnish with lime peel. Makes 4 servings.

Fish with Spicy Tomato Sauce
Ca Hap Ca Chua

(Vietnam)

A French-Vietnamese chef from Paris created the dish that inspired this recipe. The sauce is sweet, sour and spiced with red pepper.

2 tablespoons vegetable oil
1 small onion, cut into
　1/2-inch pieces
1 garlic clove, crushed, minced
1-1/2 lbs. tomatoes, peeled,
　seeded, chopped
3 tablespoons fish sauce
3 tablespoons distilled white
　vinegar
1 tablespoon sugar
1/2 teaspoon paprika
1/8 teaspoon red (cayenne)
　pepper
1-1/2 lbs. sole or other white
　fish fillets
1/2 teaspoon salt
2 tablespoons vegetable oil
2 garlic cloves, cut into tiny dice
1/3 cup lightly packed cilantro
　sprigs

Heat 2 tablespoons oil in a 2-quart saucepan over medium heat. Add onion and minced garlic; cook until onion is tender but not browned. Add tomatoes, fish sauce, vinegar, sugar, paprika and red pepper. Bring to a boil. Reduce heat; simmer, uncovered, about 15 minutes or until sauce is reduced to 2 cups, stirring occasionally. Keep sauce warm. Season fish fillets with salt. Heat remaining 2 tablespoons oil in a large skillet. Place half of fish fillets in skillet in a single layer; cook 2 minutes. Turn with a spatula; cook 2 more minutes or until fish has turned from translucent to opaque when tested with a fork. Remove fish, place on platter and keep warm. Add remaining fish to juices in pan; cook 2 minutes on each side. Divide fish among 4 heated dinner plates. Spoon 1/2 cup tomato sauce over each serving. Sprinkle with diced garlic; arrange a few cilantro sprigs on top. Makes 4 servings.

Lime-Marinated Fish
Kilawin Isda

(The Philippines)

The fish is "cooked" with lime juice rather than heat, which is the same technique employed in Mexican ceviche. *The difference is the seasoning—fresh ginger— which is not used in Mexico.*

1 lb. red snapper fillets or any
　white fish fillets
3/4 cup lime juice
1/4 medium-size onion, finely
　chopped (about 1/4 cup)
2 tablespoons lime juice
1-1/2 tablespoons finely chopped
　gingerroot
1/2 teaspoon salt
1/8 teaspoon white pepper
1 large green onion, including
　some of the top, chopped

Rinse fish; pat dry with paper towels. Discard any bones and traces of skin. Cut fish into cubes measuring 1/2 inch or slightly less. Place in a medium-size bowl. Stir in 3/4 cup lime juice. Cover and refrigerate overnight or at least 6 hours or until fish becomes opaque, which indicates it is "cooked," stirring occasionally. Turn fish into a colander. Rinse with cold water. Drain well, pressing against colander to squeeze out excess liquid. Place fish in a clean bowl. Stir in remaining ingredients except green onion. Cover and marinate in refrigerator 1 to 2 hours. Just before serving, sprinkle with green onion. Makes 6 to 8 servings.

Shrimp in Tomato Sauce
Sambal Udang

(Malaysia)

This shrimp dish from Kuala Lumpur would be one of several dishes served with rice at a Malay meal. A dash of red pepper may be substituted for the sambal oelek, if desired, and the small quantity of shrimp paste may be omitted. **Photo on page 111.**

2 tablespoons vegetable oil
1/2 medium-size onion, finely
   chopped
2 shallots, finely chopped
2 garlic cloves, minced
1-1/2 teaspoons minced gingerroot
1/2 teaspoon sambal oelek
2 tablespoons tomato sauce
1 tablespoon tomato paste
1 teaspoon sugar
3/4 teaspoon salt
1/8 teaspoon shrimp paste (terasi),
   if desired
1/4 cup water
1 lb. medium-size shrimp,
   shelled, deveined
4 cilantro sprigs

Heat oil in a medium-size skillet. Add onion, shallots, garlic, gingerroot and sambal oelek; cook, stirring, until onion is tender. Stir in tomato sauce, tomato paste, sugar, salt, shrimp paste and water; simmer until shrimp paste is dissolved and mixture is hot. Add shrimp; cook over medium-high heat 4 minutes or just until shrimp turn pink, stirring often. Spoon into a serving dish; garnish with cilantro sprigs. Makes 4 servings.

Lemony Shrimp
Goong Pla

(Thailand)

The shrimp are cooked separately, then tossed with shallots, lemon grass, onions and a lemony dressing.

2 garlic cloves
2 serrano chilies, sliced
3 tablespoons lemon juice
1 tablespoon fish sauce
1 tablespoon soy sauce
1 teaspoon Maggi seasoning
1 lb. medium-size shrimp
6 large shallots, thinly sliced, or 1
   small onion, halved, thinly
   sliced (about 1 cup)
4 green onions, white part only,
   thinly sliced
2 lemon grass stalks, thinly sliced

Pound garlic and chilies in a mortar until crushed to a paste. Place in a small bowl. Stir in lemon juice, fish sauce, soy sauce and Maggi seasoning. Let stand until serving time. Shell shrimp, retaining tail and small portion of shell attached to shrimp at tail end. Remove sand veins. Preheat broiler. Place shrimp in a single layer in a shallow baking pan. Do not crowd; if necessary, broil in 2 batches. Place shrimp under broiler 3 inches from heat source. Broil 2 minutes or until shrimp are pink throughout; do not overcook. Place shrimp in a large serving bowl. Stir in shallots, green onions and lemon grass. Add lemon-juice mixture; toss to combine. Makes 4 servings.

Shrimp in Hot Coconut Sauce
Sambal Goreng Udang
(Indonesia)

This dish is very spicy. To reduce the intensity, eliminate the ground chili and add only the sliced chili, which gives a decorative finish.

1 teaspoon tamarind pulp
3 tablespoons hot water
1 tablespoon vegetable oil
1/2 small onion, finely chopped
4 garlic cloves, minced
1/2 teaspoon shrimp paste (terasi)
1 small fresh red chili, ground or
  minced
1 cup coconut milk
1 teaspoon ground laos
1 teaspoon brown sugar
1 teaspoon salt
2 bay leaves
1 lb. medium or large shrimp,
  shelled, deveined
1 fresh red chili, cut diagonally
  into thin slices
Basic Steamed Rice, page 133

Combine tamarind pulp and hot water in a small cup. Knead tamarind to extract flavor and color. Strain liquid into another small cup; discard pulp. Set liquid aside. Heat oil in a large saucepan. Add onion, garlic, shrimp paste and ground chili; sauté until onion is tender. Add coconut milk, tamarind liquid, laos, brown sugar, salt and bay leaves. Bring to a boil. Add shrimp; bring to a boil again. Reduce heat, cover and simmer 4 minutes or just until shrimp are pink. Add sliced chili during last minute of cooking time. Remove bay leaves. Serve with steamed rice. Makes 4 servings.

Shrimp with Mint & Chilies
Goong Bai Kaprow
(Thailand)

Chicken may also be prepared in this fashion.

3 serrano chilies, sliced
2 large garlic cloves
2/3 cup chicken broth
1 teaspoon sugar
1/2 teaspoon salt
2 tablespoons vegetable oil
1 lb. medium-size shrimp,
  shelled, deveined
1/2 cup lightly packed mint leaves

Pound chilies and garlic in a mortar until well crushed. Spoon into a small cup; set aside. Combine chicken broth, sugar and salt in a small bowl; set aside. Heat wok over high heat. Add oil and heat. Stir in chili mixture. Immediately add broth mixture; bring to a boil. Add shrimp; cook, stirring, about 2 minutes or just until shrimp turn pink. Stir in mint leaves; cook until wilted, about 30 seconds. Spoon onto a heated platter. Makes 4 servings.

Crab & Pork Cake with Noodles
Chã Trửng
(Vietnam)

Similar to a crustless quiche, the cake shows Asian influence in the addition of bean threads and dried black fungus. Sliced canned mushrooms or sautéed fresh mushrooms could be substituted for the black fungus.

1/2 cup bean thread noodles
(about 1/2 oz.)
1 piece large dried black fungus,
soaked until softened
4 eggs
1/4 cup water
1 teaspoon salt
1/8 teaspoon white pepper
1 (6-oz.) can crabmeat, drained, or
1 cup shredded cooked fresh
crabmeat
6 oz. lean pork, ground (1 cup)
2 large green onions, white part
only, chopped
1/4 teaspoon paprika

To measure bean threads, cut from bunch with kitchen scissors and pack into measuring cup. Soak in cold water to cover about 30 minutes or until softened; drain. Bring a small saucepan of water to a boil. Add bean threads, boil 2 minutes and drain. Drain and chop black fungus; there should be about 1/4 cup. Separate 1 egg. Place yolk in a custard cup, cover and refrigerate until needed. Place egg white in a medium-size bowl. Add remaining 3 eggs, water, salt and white pepper; beat until combined. Stir in crabmeat, pork, bean threads, black fungus and onions. Oil a round 8-inch cake pan. Turn crab mixture into pan. Place on rack in a steamer over simmering water. Cover and steam 30 minutes. Beat reserved egg yolk with 1 teaspoon water. Brush over top of cake. Cover and steam 2 more minutes. Remove cake from steamer; sprinkle with paprika. Cut into wedges to serve. Makes 4 to 6 servings.

Ginger Squid
Mửc Xào Gửng
(Vietnam)

If using squid that have already been cleaned, you will need about 1 pound.

2 lbs. small squid (3 to 4 inches
long)
1 (1/2-inch-thick) gingerroot piece
1/2 cup chicken broth
1 tablespoon light soy sauce
2 teaspoons oyster sauce
1 teaspoon fish sauce
1 teaspoon sugar
1/8 teaspoon coarsely ground
black pepper
1-1/2 teaspoons cornstarch
1 tablespoon water
1 tablespoon vegetable oil
1 serrano chili, cut crosswise into
thin slices
1 large garlic clove, crushed,
minced
1/4 cup sliced green-onion tops
(1/2-inch slices)

Clean squid. Pull out and discard all contents of the hood; rinse well. Discard tentacles. Under running water, pull off the thin speckled skin that coats the hood. Slit squid lengthwise down 1 side; open flat. Make diagonal slashes across squid, in 1 direction, about 1/2 inch apart, then in opposite direction, forming diamonds. Do not cut through squid. Squid may be prepared in advance to this stage and covered and refrigerated a few hours. Bring to room temperature before cooking. Peel gingerroot. Cut lengthwise into thin slices, then cut slices into thin strips; there will be about 1/4 cup strips. Combine chicken broth, soy sauce, oyster sauce, fish sauce, sugar and pepper in a small bowl. Combine cornstarch and water in a custard cup. Heat wok over high heat. Add oil and heat. Add chili, garlic and ginger strips; stir-fry 30 seconds. Add broth mixture; bring to a boil. Add squid and green-onion tops. Boil, uncovered, 3 minutes. Stir cornstarch mixture to blend in cornstarch that has settled. Pour gradually into wok; boil, stirring, until sauce thickens. Spoon into a serving container. Serve with rice. Makes 4 servings.

Squid with Hot Wine Sauce
Pla Mueg Pad Prik

(Thailand)

Do not overcook squid or it will become chewy and tough. In this recipe, tender small squid are scored Chinese style, sliced and cooked just 3 minutes. The recipe, from Bangkok, is an interesting blend of Asian ingredients including Chinese oyster sauce, Thai fish sauce and Chinese or Japanese rice wine.

2 lbs. small squid (3 to 4 inches long)
1/3 cup rice wine
2 tablespoons fish sauce
1 tablespoon oyster sauce
1/2 teaspoon sugar
Dash white pepper
3 tablespoons vegetable oil
8 shallots, sliced
3 large garlic cloves, sliced
4 green onions, white part only, sliced
2 fresh hot red chilies, sliced
1/4 cup lightly packed cilantro leaves, coarsely chopped

Clean squid. Pull out and discard all contents of the hood; rinse well. Discard tentacles. Under running water, pull off the thin speckled peel that coats the hood. Slit each squid lengthwise down 1 side and open flat. Make diagonal slashes across squid in 1 direction about 1/2 inch apart, being careful not to cut through squid. Now make diagonal slashes in opposite direction, forming diamonds. Squid may be prepared in advance to this stage, then covered and refrigerated a few hours. Combine rice wine, fish sauce, oyster sauce, sugar and pepper. Heat wok over high heat. Add oil and heat. Add shallots and garlic; cook until lightly browned. Add squid, green onions, chilies and wine mixture. Cook, stirring often, 3 minutes. Stir in chopped cilantro. Serve at once. Makes 4 servings.

Tip: Removing seeds from chilies will reduce the spiciness of any dish to which they are added. For hotter flavor, do not remove seeds.

POULTRY

Cooks the world over think along the same lines, so it is not surprising that some Asian chicken dishes resemble those popular in the West. Chicken Pasanda, which is Pakistani in origin, comes reasonably close to creamed chicken. Representing chicken and rice casseroles is Chicken Bukhara Briani, a Sunday specialty at an Indian restaurant in Kuala Lumpur. Barbecued chicken is popular everywhere. One example is from Thailand; another is from the venerable Aristocrat restaurant in Manila. The Philippine dish borrows from Indonesia by adding a peanut sauce. Broiled chicken from Java foregoes the peanut sauce in favor of a crackly, sweet finish.

Cooks also share an interest in economy and practicality. And nothing could be more practical than Singaporean Chicken-Rice, a three-course meal prepared from a single chicken. The broth produced by simmering the chicken is used to cook the rice that accompanies it. Still more of the broth goes into soup.

Other recipes range from Vietnamese Lemon Grass Chicken to Philippine *adobo*, one of the most popular dishes of that country. Two versions of adobo appear in this chapter. A third, made with pork, is in the chapter on meats. All are flavored with vinegar and garlic, which are typical seasonings not only for adobo but for many other Filipino dishes.

Curry to some means meat, poultry or seafood in a sauce flavored with pre-mixed curry powder from the supermarket. That, however, is only one interpretation, and a limited one. In Asia, where curries are regular fare, cooks prefer to blend their own seasonings rather than use a commercial mix. As a result, the flavors differ radically. The six curries in this chapter serve as illustration. Each is distinct from the others. Their only common ground is that all involve a sauce.

Instead of curry powder Thais flavor their dishes with curry pastes, which come in a variety of colors and flavors. These would not be used in Indian or Malay curries. The Thai chicken curry in this chapter is made with green curry paste, so named because it is based on green chilies. A duck curry from Bangkok switches to red chilies. A *gulai,* the term used in Brunei for curries, resembles the Thai dishes in its use of coconut milk but is seasoned differently. Chicken Pasanda, from Kuala Lumpur, has a creamy sauce flavored with curry gravy that is made separately. Brunei's Chicken Kapitan is linked in name to chicken country captain, an old-time American dish. But there the resemblance ends. The tomatoes, raisins and curry powder of the American recipe change to lemon grass, chilies, shrimp paste and coconut milk in Brunei. The closest to the popular concept of curry would be an Anglo-Indian dish from Singapore that involves spices similar to those used in prepared curry powders. Still more curries appear in chapters on meat, seafood and vegetables.

Green Chicken Curry
Gaeng Keo Wan Gai

(Thailand)

Miniature Thai eggplants add a touch of bitterness that contrasts well with the rich sweetness of coconut milk. Green peas, suggested as a substitute, are not bitter but provide color appropriate to a "green" curry. As is typical of many curries, this dish includes a great deal of sauce to eat with rice. This recipe works well with canned coconut milk.

4 chicken-breast halves, boned, skinned
3 (14-oz.) cans coconut milk
1/3 cup Green Curry Paste, page 29
3/4 cup tiny Thai eggplant (makhua puong) or 1/2 cup thawed frozen green peas
2 tablespoons fish sauce
1 teaspoon salt
1 teaspoon sugar
1 cup lightly packed basil leaves
6 kaffir lime leaves, finely shredded, if desired
1 jalapeño chili, if desired, cut into strips lengthwise
1 small fresh red chili, if desired, cut into strips lengthwise
Basic Steamed Rice, page 133

Cut chicken breasts into 1/2-inch-wide strips or bite-size pieces; set aside. Spoon 1/2 cup of the thickest milk from top of a can of coconut milk that has not been shaken into a Dutch oven. Measure 3-1/2 cups of remaining coconut milk for recipe; freeze remaining coconut milk for another use. Heat thick coconut milk over medium heat. Add curry paste; cook, stirring constantly, until clear oil separates from the mixture. Stir in remaining coconut milk; bring to a boil. Add chicken, eggplant, fish sauce, salt and sugar. Bring to a boil. Reduce heat, cover and simmer 30 minutes. (If using green peas, add during last 5 minutes of cooking time.) Add basil leaves and lime leaves; cook 1 minute. Stir in chilies, if desired. Spoon into a serving bowl. Serve with steamed rice. Makes 4 to 6 servings.

Tip: Leftover canned coconut milk can be frozen up to 1 month. Shake before using.

Roast Duck Curry
Gaeng Ped Ped Yang

(Thailand)

For a shortcut, use a roast duck from a Chinese market rather than preparing the duck yourself. Notice that this recipe includes its own red curry paste, which is seasoned differently from that on page 30.

1 (4-lb.) duckling
5 cilantro sprigs
1/2 teaspoon black peppercorns
1/4 cup soy sauce
1 tablespoon dry sherry
1 tablespoon brown sugar
4 (14-oz.) cans coconut milk
2 tablespoons vegetable oil
3 tablespoons fish sauce
Salt, if desired
20 cherry tomatoes
1 cup firmly packed basil leaves
Basic Steamed Rice, page 133

Red Curry Paste:
1 teaspoon dried
   kaffir-lime-peel-strips or 1
   teaspoon minced fresh lime
   peel, green part only
1 lemon grass stalk, cut crosswise
   in 1/4-inch-thick slices
7 shallots, sliced
2 small fresh red chilies, seeded
2 tablespoons cilantro leaves
2 large garlic cloves
1 teaspoon ground laos
1 teaspoon coriander seeds
1/4 teaspoon cumin seeds

Remove duckling giblets and neck; save for another use. Wash duckling; pat dry. Place in an 11" x 7" baking dish. Combine cilantro sprigs, including stems, and peppercorns in a mortar; pound to a paste. In a small bowl, mix pounded ingredients with soy sauce, sherry and brown sugar. Pour over duckling, inside and out. Cover and marinate in refrigerator 2 hours, turning occasionally. Bring to room temperature before roasting. Preheat oven to 325F (165C). Drain marinade from duckling. Place on a rack in a 13" x 9" baking pan. Pierce skin with a fork to allow fat to drain off. Roast 2 hours or until juices run clear when duck is pierced between breast and thigh. Remove from pan; let stand until cool enough to handle. Remove meat from carcass; cut into bite-size pieces. Set aside. Skin may be used or discarded, as preferred. Make Red Curry Paste. Open cans of coconut milk without shaking. Spoon off 1 cup of the thickest milk from top of cans. Measure 5 additional cups coconut milk. Freeze remaining 1 cup milk for another use. Heat oil in a Dutch oven over medium heat. Add curry paste; fry 5 minutes, stirring constantly to keep from burning. Add thick coconut milk; cook until oil separates from milk, about 2-1/2 minutes. Add remaining 5 cups coconut milk and fish sauce. Bring to a boil. Reduce heat. Add duckling meat; simmer, uncovered, 10 to 15 minutes or until heated through, stirring. Taste and add salt, if needed. Add cherry tomatoes and basil leaves; cook about 3 minutes or until tomatoes are heated through. Spoon into a heated large bowl. Serve with rice. Makes 6 to 8 servings.

Red Curry Paste:
If using dried kaffir lime peel, rehydrate in warm water; drain. Combine lime peel and remaining ingredients in a blender or food processor fitted with the metal blade; process as fine as possible, stopping occasionally to push mixture down from side of container. Transfer half of mixture to mortar; pound until finely crushed. Repeat with remaining half.

Brunei-Style Chicken Curry
Gulai Ayam

(Brunei)

This Malay dish from the sultan's palace is seasoned mildly, as inhabitants of Brunei prefer.

1 (3-1/2-lb.) chicken
2 russet potatoes (3/4 lb.)
3 tablespoons vegetable oil
1 medium-size onion, finely chopped
1 (1-inch-thick) gingerroot piece, finely chopped
4 large garlic cloves, finely chopped
3 tablespoons curry powder
1 (1-inch) cinnamon stick
2 whole cloves
1 whole star anise
1 cardamom pod
1 qt. coconut milk (4 cups)
1-1/2 teaspoons salt
2 tomatoes, each cut into 8 wedges
Basic Steamed Rice, page 133

Cut up chicken. Cut off wing tips and reserve for another use; separate remaining wing joints. Separate thighs from drumsticks. Cut breast in half lengthwise and crosswise. Peel potatoes; cut each into 8 chunks and place in bowl of cold water to cover until needed. Heat oil in a Dutch oven. Add onion, gingerroot, garlic, curry powder, cinnamon stick, cloves, star anise and cardamom pod. Sauté over medium heat 5 minutes, stirring frequently to keep from burning. Drain potatoes. Add chicken and potatoes; mix with spices. Stir in coconut milk and salt. Bring to a boil. Reduce heat; simmer 45 minutes, uncovered, stirring frequently and pushing chicken pieces down into coconut milk. Add tomato wedges; cook 15 more minutes. Serve with rice. Makes 4 to 6 servings.

Chicken Kapitan
Ayam Kapitan

(Brunei)

Another curry recipe from the Istana Nurul Iman, the sultan's palace in Brunei.

1 (3-1/2-lb.) chicken
8 shallots, coarsely chopped
6 lemon grass stalks, sliced
6 garlic cloves
2 to 4 small fresh red chilies, seeded
1/3 cup candlenuts
1 (1/4-inch-thick) gingerroot slice
3/4 teaspoon shrimp paste (terasi)
2 cups coconut milk
1/2 teaspoon ground turmeric
2-1/2 tablespoons vegetable oil
1 tablespoon sugar
1-1/2 teaspoons salt
Basic Steamed Rice, page 133

Cut up chicken. Separate thighs from drumsticks. Cut breast in half crosswise. Remove wing tips; save wing tips and backs for broth. Rinse and drain remaining chicken pieces. Combine shallots, lemon grass, garlic, chilies, candlenuts, gingerroot and shrimp paste in a blender or food processor fitted with the metal blade; process as fine as possible. Add up to 1/4 cup of the coconut milk to facilitate processing. Stir in turmeric. Heat oil in a Dutch oven over medium heat. Add pureed mixture; fry, stirring frequently, 5 minutes. Add chicken pieces; coat with seasonings. Cook, stirring, 5 minutes. Stir in coconut milk, sugar and salt. Bring to a boil. Reduce heat, cover and simmer until chicken is tender, about 45 minutes, stirring occasionally. Serve with rice. Makes 4 servings.

Chicken with Curry Cream Sauce
Chicken Pasanda

This spicy version of creamed chicken is a Pakistani recipe from Omar Khayam, a restaurant in Kuala Lumpur. Serve it with Basic Steamed Rice, page 133, or Aromatic Rice, page 137.

2 large whole chicken breasts
   (about 2-1/4 lbs. total)
3 cups water
1 teaspoon salt
1 tablespoon vegetable oil
1 small red onion (4 oz.), halved
   lengthwise, sliced
1/2 lb. tomatoes (2 medium),
   unpeeled, sliced
1/2 cup undiluted canned
   condensed tomato soup
1/2 cup evaporated milk
1/2 teaspoon garam masala
1/2 teaspoon salt
1 small jalapeño chili, if desired,
   stemmed, seeded, slivered
Basic Steamed Rice, page 133

Curry Gravy:
1/2 small onion
2 large garlic cloves
1 (1/4-inch-thick) gingerroot slice
1 tablespoon vegetable oil
3/4 teaspoon ground coriander
3/4 teaspoon garam masala
1/2 teaspoon ground cumin
1/2 teaspoon ground turmeric
1/8 teaspoon hot chili powder or
   red (cayenne) pepper
2 small tomatoes (6 oz.), peeled,
   finely chopped
1-1/2 cups chicken broth
1/2 teaspoon salt

Place chicken breasts in a 3-quart saucepan. Add water and 1 teaspoon salt. Bring to a boil. Reduce heat, cover and simmer 30 minutes. Cool chicken in broth. Drain, reserving 2 cups broth for Curry Gravy. Save remainder for another use. Remove and discard chicken skin and bones. Tear meat into thick shreds; set aside. Make Curry Gravy. Heat oil in a large skillet. Add onion; cook until soft. Add tomato slices; cook 1 minute. Add chicken; cook 2 minutes, stirring gently. Add Curry Gravy, tomato soup, evaporated milk, garam masala and 1/2 teaspoon salt; cook until heated through, stirring gently to blend. Stir in jalapeño chili, if desired. Spoon into a heated serving bowl. Serve with rice. Makes 4 servings.

Curry Gravy:
Combine onion, garlic and gingerroot in a blender or food processor fitted with the metal blade; process as fine as possible. Heat oil in a 1-quart saucepan over medium heat. Add onion mixture; cook about 5 minutes or until tender, stirring frequently. Stir in coriander, garam masala, cumin, turmeric and chili powder. Add tomatoes; cook about 3 minutes or until softened. Add chicken broth and salt. Bring to a boil. Reduce heat, cover and simmer 15 minutes, stirring occasionally. Makes 2 cups.

Variation
If garam masala is not available, add an additional 1/4 teaspoon each of coriander, cumin and turmeric to Curry Gravy. Eliminate garam masala from chicken mixture.

Anglo-Indian Chicken Curry
Kari Ayam

This is a two-in-one recipe. Part of the resulting sauce is used to make Eggplant Curry, page 123. **Photo on pages 108-109.**

1 (3-1/2- to 4-lb.) chicken
2-1/2 cups water
1 thin wedge onion (1/8 small onion)
1/4 teaspoon salt
1/4 teaspoon black peppercorns
1 (1-inch-thick) gingerroot piece, coarsely chopped, about 1/4 cup
5 garlic cloves
2 tablespoons vegetable oil
1 large onion, chopped
1 large tomato, seeded, chopped
1 teaspoon ground coriander
1 teaspoon ground cumin
1 teaspoon ground turmeric
1/4 teaspoon red (cayenne) pepper
2 bay leaves
2 cardamom pods, crushed
1-1/2 teaspoons salt
2 tablespoons plain yogurt
2 tablespoons whipping cream
1/2 teaspoon garam masala
1/4 cup lightly packed cilantro leaves, chopped
Basic Steamed Rice, page 133

Cut up chicken. Separate thighs from drumsticks. Cut breast in half crosswise. Cut off wing tips and reserve. Cut back in half crosswise. Remove and discard any excess chicken skin. Place back pieces, wing tips and neck in a large saucepan. Add water, onion wedge, 1/4 teaspoon salt and the peppercorns. Bring to a boil. Reduce heat, cover and simmer 45 minutes. Strain broth and skim off fat; add water, if necessary, to make 2-1/2 cups broth. Set aside. In a food processor fitted with the metal blade, process gingerroot and garlic as fine as possible, or pound in a mortar. Heat oil in a Dutch oven. Add chopped onion; cook, stirring frequently, until lightly browned. Add gingerroot mixture; cook gently 3 minutes, stirring often. Add tomato; cook 3 minutes. Mix in coriander, cumin, turmeric and red pepper. Add chicken pieces; cook until meat becomes firm, about 8 minutes, stirring to mix with spices. If making Eggplant Curry, add 2-1/2 cups reserved broth to chicken; if not, add 2 cups broth. Add bay leaves, cardamom pods and salt. Bring to a boil. Reduce heat, cover and simmer 30 minutes. If making Eggplant Curry, ladle out 1 cup sauce. To continue chicken curry, spoon yogurt and cream into a small cup. Gradually stir some of curry sauce into yogurt mixture, then add to chicken. Stir in garam masala and bring to a boil. Stir in cilantro. Serve at once with rice. Makes 4 servings.

Tip: Imported mango chutney from India is usually found in the specialty food section of supermarkets.

Barbecued Chicken

Gai Yang

(Thailand)

Accompany the chicken with Lada's Cucumber Salad, page 102.

1 (3-lb.) chicken
3 to 4 garlic cloves
1 teaspoon salt
1/4 cup soy sauce
1 tablespoon water
Sweet & Sour Red Chili Sauce, in
   recipe for Spicy Corn Fritters,
   page 49

Cut up chicken. Separate thighs from drumsticks. Cut breast in half crosswise. Place in a shallow pan or glass dish. Pound garlic with salt in a mortar until reduced to a paste. Blend in soy sauce. Turn mixture into a small cup. Rinse out mortar with the water; add to mixture. Rub evenly over chicken pieces. Cover and marinate in refrigerator 2 hours. Bring to room temperature before grilling. Prepare barbecue. Place chicken skin-side down on grill over hot coals; cook, turning to brown evenly, 30 to 40 minutes, depending upon size of pieces, or until juices run clear when meat is pierced. Serve with individual bowls of Sweet & Sour Red Chili Sauce for dipping or to spoon over chicken. Makes 4 servings.

Aristocrat Barbecued Chicken

(The Philippines)

A recipe from one of Manila's oldest and most popular restaurants, the Aristocrat. Serve the chicken and its peanut sauce with Java Rice, page 134, for a memorable summer dinner. **Photo on page 107.**

1/2 cup plus 2 tablespoons dark
   soy sauce
2 tablespoons light soy sauce
2 tablespoons lime juice
1/2 cup sugar
1 large or 2 medium garlic cloves,
   crushed, minced
1/4 teaspoon black pepper
1 (3-1/2- to 4-lb.) chicken
1 recipe Java Rice, page 134

Java Sauce:
1/4 lb. Roasted Peanuts (about 1
   cup), page 31
3/4 cup water
1/4 cup soy sauce
1/4 cup sugar

Stir together soy sauces, lime juice, sugar, garlic and pepper. Cut chicken into serving pieces. Cut breast in half lengthwise. Leave drumsticks attached to thighs. Place chicken pieces in a 13" x 9" baking dish. Add marinade; turn to coat completely. Cover with plastic wrap; marinate in refrigerator 2 days. Bring to room temperature before grilling. Make Java Sauce. Prepare barbecue. Drain chicken pieces. Place skin-side down on grill over hot coals; cook, turning and basting with marinade every 10 minutes, 30 to 40 minutes, depending upon size of pieces, or until juices run clear when meat is pierced. Chicken will brown quickly because of the sugar in the marinade; do not burn. Serve with Java Sauce and Java Rice. Makes 4 servings.

Java Sauce:
In a food processor fitted with the metal blade or in a nut grinder, grind nuts as fine as possible. Place in a small saucepan. Stir in water, soy sauce and sugar. Boil 4 minutes, stirring occasionally; sauce should thicken slightly but still be fluid; keep warm. If it becomes too thick while standing, dilute to desired consistency with additional water. Serve warm. Makes 1-1/4 cups.

Broiled Chicken Dewi

Ayam Panggang Dewi

(Indonesia)

Indonesian-style soy sauce adds a sweet flavor and rich dark color to the chicken in this Javanese recipe. **Photo on pages 36-37.**

1 small onion or 1/2 medium
    onion, coarsely chopped
4 garlic cloves
6 candlenuts
1 cup Indonesian-style soy sauce
    (kecap)
1 teaspoon ground coriander
3/4 teaspoon salt
1/8 teaspoon black pepper
1 (3-1/2-to 4-lb.) chicken,
    quartered

Combine onion, garlic and candlenuts in a blender or food processor fitted with the metal blade; process as fine as possible. Place in a medium bowl. Stir in soy sauce, coriander, salt and pepper until blended. Place chicken in a 13" x 9" glass baking dish. Add marinade; turn chicken pieces to coat thoroughly. Cover with plastic wrap; refrigerate overnight. Bring to room temperature before cooking. Preheat broiler. Remove chicken from marinade; reserve marinade. Place chicken, skin-side down, on a rack in a broiler pan. Broil 15 minutes. Turn chicken. Spoon marinade over generously. Broil 10 to 15 more minutes or until juices run clear when chicken is pierced. Makes 4 servings.

Ginger Chicken

Pad Khing

(Thailand)

This dish shows the Chinese influence in Thai cooking. Soybean condiment, packed in jars, is stocked in most Chinese markets. Maggi seasoning is a more recent addition to the Thai larder.

2 whole chicken breasts, boned,
    skinned
2 medium-size onions
1 tablespoon Chinese soybean
    condiment
1 tablespoon Maggi seasoning
3 tablespoons water
1 piece dried black fungus,
    soaked until softened
2 tablespoons vegetable oil
1 (1-inch-thick) gingerroot piece,
    shredded (1/4 cup)
3 large garlic cloves, minced
Tops of 3 large green onions, cut
    into 1-inch lengths

Cut chicken into thin strips about 1/2-inch wide; set aside. Cut onions in half lengthwise. Cut each half into 6 wedges; set aside. Combine soybean condiment, Maggi seasoning and water in a small cup; set aside. Cut black fungus into shreds; there will be about 2 tablespoons. Heat a wok over medium-high heat. Add oil and heat. Add gingerroot and garlic; stir-fry 30 seconds. Increase heat, add chicken and stir-fry 3 minutes or until no longer pink. Add onion wedges and black fungus; stir-fry 1 minute. Add soybean-condiment mixture; cook 1 minute. Add green-onion tops; cook, stirring, 30 seconds. Spoon onto a heated platter. Makes 4 to 6 servings.

Bilal's Chicken-Rice Casserole
Chicken Bukhara Briani

(Malaysia)

This North Indian dish from Kuala Lumpur has been adapted to South Indian tastes by the addition of coconut and hot chili powder.

2 cups basmati rice
6 tablespoons ghee, vegetable oil
    or Clarified Butter, page 32
2 small onions, halved, sliced
2 (3-inch) cinnamon sticks
3 cups water
1/2 cup plain yogurt
2 tablespoons evaporated milk
2 teaspoons salt
1 (3-1/2-lb.) chicken
1 (1-inch-thick) gingerroot piece
4 large garlic cloves
1 teaspoon poppy seeds, if desired
8 whole cloves
2/3 cup finely ground fresh
    coconut or 1/2 cup
    unsweetened dried coconut,
    rehydrated in warm water,
    drained
3 medium-size tomatoes (3/4 lb.),
    cut into 4 slices each
1/4 cup canned tomato sauce
1-1/2 teaspoons ground turmeric
1/2 teaspoon hot chili powder
1-1/2 teaspoons salt
1/4 teaspoon black pepper

Wash rice thoroughly. Drain well; set aside. Heat 3 tablespoons ghee in a Dutch oven. Add 1 onion and cinnamon sticks; sauté until onion is tender. Stir in rice. Stir in water, yogurt, evaporated milk and 2 teaspoons salt. Bring to a boil. Cover; boil 5 minutes or until most of liquid is absorbed. Steam, covered, over very low heat 20 minutes, using a heat diffuser if necessary to prevent rice from sticking and burning. Uncover and let rice dry slightly while preparing chicken. Discard cinnamon sticks. Cut up chicken. Cut off wing tips and reserve for another use. Separate thighs from drumsticks. Cut breast in half crosswise. Discard excess chicken skin and as much fat as possible. In a food processor fitted with the metal blade, process gingerroot and garlic as fine as possible, or mince by hand. If using, grind poppy seeds in an electric spice grinder; set aside. Heat remaining 3 tablespoons ghee in a large skillet. Add remaining onion; fry until tender. Add gingerroot mixture and cloves; cook 2 minutes, stirring to keep from burning. Add chicken pieces; cook 5 minutes, stirring to mix with seasonings. Add coconut, tomatoes, tomato sauce, ground poppy seeds, turmeric, chili powder, 1-1/2 teaspoons salt and pepper. Simmer, uncovered, 20 minutes, turning chicken pieces as needed to cook evenly. Preheat oven to 350F (175C). Remove chicken pieces from skillet. Add cooking liquid to rice; toss gently to mix. Spoon 1/3 of the rice into a 5-quart casserole. Top with 1/2 of the chicken pieces. Add another 1/3 of the rice. Top with remaining chicken pieces. Cover with remaining rice. Bake, covered, 30 minutes. Makes 6 servings.

Tip: A heat diffuser, often made of cast iron, serves as a buffer between the burner and saucepan and can be used on either gas or electric ranges. It spreads heat evenly and reduces the risk of burning or sticking for more delicate or temperamental foods, such as rice.

Singaporean Chicken-Rice
Hai Nan Jī Fàn

(Singapore)

This recipe originated with the Chinese who came to Singapore from Hainan Island and who obviously knew how to get the most from a single bird. Chicken-rice, with its accompanying soup and sauces, is served at restaurants ranging from food stalls to luxury hotels. This version is from the Mandarin.

1 (3-1/2-to 4-lb.) chicken
2 teaspoons salt
2 tablespoons shredded
 gingerroot
1/4 cup lightly packed cilantro
 leaves
2 large garlic cloves, chopped
6 cups water
1/4 cup dark soy sauce
Romaine or other lettuce leaves
1 small cucumber, sliced
2 small tomatoes, sliced
6 cilantro sprigs

Rice:
1 cup long-grain rice
Reserved chicken fat
Vegetable oil, if needed
1 large garlic clove, minced
2 teaspoons minced gingerroot
2 large shallots or 1/2 small onion,
 finely chopped
2 cups reserved chicken broth
1/2 teaspoon salt

Red-Chili Dip:
2 small fresh red chilies,
 stemmed, seeded, sliced
6 garlic cloves
3 tablespoons reserved chicken
 broth
1 teaspoon rice vinegar

Ginger Dip:
1 (1-inch-thick) gingerroot piece,
 thinly sliced (rounded 1/4 cup)
2 tablespoons reserved chicken
 broth

Remove any large pieces of fat; wrap and refrigerate for making rice. Sprinkle chicken inside and out with 1 teaspoon salt; let stand 30 minutes. Drain off any juices that accumulate. Place whole chicken in a 4-quart Dutch oven. Add gingerroot, cilantro, garlic, water and remaining 1 teaspoon salt. Bring to a boil. Reduce heat, cover and simmer 45 minutes or until chicken is tender. Let chicken cool in the broth. When cool enough to handle, remove chicken; strip meat from carcass in large chunks. Discard skin and bones. Arrange smallest pieces of meat in center of a small heatproof platter. Slice larger breast chunks crosswise; arrange on top. Pour a little broth over chicken to keep meat from drying out. Cover with foil; refrigerate. Strain broth. Reserve 2 cups for rice, 3 cups for soup and a portion of the remainder for the dips. Make Rice. Make Red-Chili Dip and Ginger Dip. Make Soup. Preheat oven to 250F (120C). To serve, reheat foil-covered chicken in oven until warm; chicken does not need to be hot. Provide 3 tiny sauce bowls, 1 to 2 tablespoons in capacity, for each diner (12 bowls). Or use 3 slightly larger bowls for each 2 diners to share (6 bowls). Divide Red-Chili Dip, Ginger Dip and dark soy sauce among the bowls. Arrange lettuce leaves on a large platter. Slide mound of chicken off its platter into center of lettuce. Arrange cucumber and tomato slices around chicken. Place cilantro sprigs in center. Spoon rice into a serving bowl. Serve soup first or alongside chicken and rice. To eat, dip chicken pieces in desired sauce. Makes 4 servings.

Rice:
Wash rice until water runs clear. Drain well. Render chicken fat in a Dutch oven to produce 2 tablespoons liquid fat; if necessary, add vegetable oil to make the 2 tablespoons. Add garlic, gingerroot and shallots; cook over medium heat until shallots are tender but not browned. Add rice; stir to coat thoroughly with chicken fat. Stir in broth and salt. Bring to a boil. Cover and boil about 5 minutes, or until broth is absorbed. Reduce heat to very low; steam rice 30 minutes or until tender and dry, using a heat diffuser if necessary. Makes 4 servings.

Soup:

3 cups reserved chicken broth
1/2 teaspoon chicken-bouillon
   granules
1/2 teaspoon light soy sauce
Salt, if desired
1 cup finely shredded lettuce
2 green onions, chopped

Red Chili Dip:
Place chilies and garlic in a mortar; pound until reduced to a paste. Place in a small cup. Stir in chicken broth and vinegar.

Ginger Dip:
Place gingerroot in a mortar. Pound until thoroughly crushed. Place in a small cup. Stir in broth.

Soup:
Place broth in a 2-quart saucepan. Stir in chicken-bouillon granules and soy sauce. Bring to a boil. Taste and add salt if needed. Stir in lettuce; remove from heat. Divide among 4 small soup bowls. Sprinkle each serving with green onions. Makes 4 servings.

Chicken Wrapped in Lettuce
Larb Gai
(Thailand)

These savory little bundles will please light eaters.

2 tablespoons soy sauce
1 tablespoon fish sauce
2 teaspoons lemon juice
1 teaspoon water
1-1/2 teaspoons sugar
Scant 1/2 teaspoon black pepper
1/4 cup vegetable oil
2 large garlic cloves, minced
2 whole chicken breasts, boned,
   skinned, cut into 1/2-inch
   chunks
1/2 medium-size onion, thinly
   sliced
1 small or 1/2 large red bell
   pepper, slivered
2 serrano chilies, sliced
   lengthwise
1/4 cup lightly packed mint leaves
8 butter-lettuce or other
   leaf-lettuce leaves

Combine soy sauce, fish sauce, lemon juice, water, sugar and pepper in a small bowl; set aside. Heat wok over high heat. Add oil and heat. Add garlic; stir-fry 30 seconds. Add chicken and onion; stir-fry 1 minute. Add bell pepper and chilies; stir-fry 2 minutes. Add soy-sauce mixture; cook, stirring, 30 seconds. Stir in mint; cook 20 seconds. Spoon onto a heated platter. To eat, tear lettuce leaves into pieces, spoon some of the chicken mixture onto each piece, wrap and eat. Makes 4 servings.

Chicken with Mint & Green Peppers
Gai Pad Kaprow
(Thailand)

Notice that Thais do not follow the Chinese practice of thickening their sauces with cornstarch.

1-1/2 chicken breasts, boned, skinned
1 large garlic clove
1 or 2 serrano chilies, stemmed, seeded, chopped
2 medium-size green bell peppers
1/2 cup chicken broth
1 tablespoon fish sauce
2 teaspoons oyster sauce
2 teaspoons sugar
3 tablespoons vegetable oil
1/2 cup lightly packed mint leaves

Cut chicken into 3/4- to 1-inch chunks; set aside. Pound garlic and chili to a paste in a mortar; set aside. Cut bell peppers lengthwise into 1/2-inch wide strips, removing seeds and any white membrane. Cut strips in half crosswise; set aside. Combine chicken broth, fish sauce, oyster sauce and sugar in a small bowl. Heat a wok over high heat. Add oil and heat. Add chili paste; stir-fry 10 seconds. Add chicken; stir-fry 3 to 4 minutes or until chicken is no longer pink. Add broth mixture; bring to a boil. Boil, stirring, 3 to 4 minutes. Add green peppers and mint. Cook, stirring, 1 minute, or until peppers are heated through. Do not overcook or peppers will soften and loose their bright color. Spoon onto a heated platter; serve at once. Makes 4 small servings.

Chicken & Pork Adobo
Adobong Manok at Baboy
(The Philippines)

Some adobos are dry, but this one includes plenty of coconut-flavored broth.

1 (3-1/2-lb.) chicken
1 lb. boneless lean pork, cut in 1-inch chunks
8 garlic cloves, minced
1 cup water
2 tablespoons distilled white vinegar
2 teaspoons salt
1/4 teaspoon black pepper
1 cup coconut milk
Basic Steamed Rice, page 133

Cut up chicken. Separate thighs from drumsticks. Cut breast in half crosswise. Place chicken and pork in a 4-quart Dutch oven. Add garlic, water, vinegar, salt and pepper. Bring to a boil. Reduce heat, cover and simmer 45 minutes. Add coconut milk. Cover and simmer 10 more minutes or until chicken and pork are tender. For each serving, place some of the chicken and pork on a plate with steamed rice. Spoon broth over meat. Makes 6 servings.

Lemon Grass Chicken
Gà Xào Sẵ Ớt
(Vietnam)

Chicken breast meat is regarded as a delicacy by some, but the dark meat, which is juicier and less expensive, is preferred for this dish.

6 chicken thighs, boned, skinned
  (about 1-1/4 lbs. trimmed meat)
2 lemon grass stalks, minced
1/4 cup soy sauce
1/4 teaspoon salt
2 tablespoons chicken broth
1 teaspoon sugar
1 teaspoon minced fresh red chili
  or serrano chili or 1/4 teaspoon
  hot-pepper flakes
1/2 teaspoon cornstarch
2 teaspoons water
1/2 medium-size onion
1/4 cup vegetable oil
1 teaspoon minced onion
1 teaspoon minced gingerroot
1 teaspoon minced garlic

Cut chicken into 1-inch-square pieces. Place in a medium bowl. Stir in lemon grass, 2 tablespoons of the soy sauce and salt. Mix well. Cover and refrigerate 2 hours or longer. Bring to room temperature before cooking. Combine chicken broth, remaining 2 tablespoons soy sauce, sugar and chili in a small bowl; set aside. Blend cornstarch with water in another small bowl; set aside. Cut onion half lengthwise; cut each piece into 4 wedges; separate layers. Heat wok over medium-high heat. Add oil and heat. Add minced onion, gingerroot and garlic; stir-fry 15 seconds. Do not burn. Increase heat. Add chicken; stir-fry 2 minutes. Add sliced onion; stir-fry 1 minute. Add chicken-broth mixture; cook, stirring, 1 minute. Stir cornstarch mixture to blend in cornstarch that has settled. Add to chicken mixture; cook until sauce is thickened, about 30 seconds. Spoon onto a heated platter; serve at once. Makes 4 servings.

Chicken Adobo
Adobong Manok
(The Philippines)

Filipinos use a great deal of garlic but this recipe, from Robert's Hollywood Grille in Los Angeles, has only a medium amount.

1 (3-1/2-lb.) chicken
1 garlic clove, halved
1/4 teaspoon black pepper
2 tablespoons vegetable oil
2/3 cup water
3 tablespoons soy sauce
2 tablespoons distilled white
  vinegar
2 tablespoons red-wine vinegar
1 teaspoon garlic powder
1 teaspoon black peppercorns
1 bay leaf
1 tablespoon cornstarch
1 tablespoon water
Basic Steamed Rice, page 133

Cut up chicken. Cut off wing tips, excess skin and fat and reserve for another use. Separate drumsticks and thighs. Cut breast in half crosswise. Rub chicken all over with cut garlic. Sprinkle with pepper. Heat oil in a Dutch oven. Add the cut garlic and chicken. Cook chicken slowly 10 minutes, turning to cook all sides. Add 2/3 cup water, soy sauce, vinegars, garlic powder, peppercorns and bay leaf to chicken. Bring to a boil. Reduce heat, cover and simmer 30 minutes or until chicken is tender. Lift out chicken pieces, place on a platter and keep warm. Strain cooking liquid from Dutch oven into a small saucepan. Let stand a few minutes for fat to rise to the surface; spoon off fat. Bring to a boil. Blend cornstarch and 1 tablespoon water in a small bowl. Gradually stir into saucepan. Boil, stirring, until slightly thickened. To serve, spoon sauce over chicken. Serve with rice. Makes 4 servings.

MEAT

In the Philippines, a celebration isn't complete without *lechon*—a whole pig roasted on a pole over open coals. In Malaysia, where Muslims predominate, such a dish would be out of place because Muslims do not eat pork. Thus religious guidelines can be as important as taste and budget in determining the choice of food.

In Malaysia, Brunei and Indonesia, all strongly Muslim, and in Singapore, these restrictions are especially apparent. In markets there, food products are labeled *halal* to guarantee that they do not contain pork or by-products such as lard. To be halal, meat must come from animals slaughtered according to Muslim precepts. Lamb curries, various forms of spiced beef and satay made with mutton or beef are typical meat dishes acceptable to Muslims.

On the other hand, pork is essential to the Chinese, who heavily populate the region. An interesting dish that blends Chinese and local influence is a Singaporean dish, Straits Chinese Satay Babi—*Babi* is the Malay word for pork—a form of satay that is neither cut into kabobs nor grilled but sliced and simmered in coconut milk.

Leading hotels and restaurants in Southeast Asia use beef imported from the United States or Australia, but there is also locally raised meat such as the chewy Batangas beef of the Philippines. In Manila, a popular dish is Bistec Pilipino, which is simply steak and onions with a soy sauce and lime-juice marinade.

Vietnamese beef dishes range from Chinese-style stir-fries to a stew that might be country French except for such Asian ingredients as soy sauce, soybean condiment and lemon grass. The presentation is different too. Mint sprigs and onion rings garnish each serving, and a lemon wedge is served on the side to squeeze over a mixture of salt and pepper. The beef is then dipped in this tangy condiment.

The French influence appears repeatedly in Vietnamese cookery. The beef stew is eaten with French bread, not rice or noodles. Port wine seasons meat for a stir-fry instead of Chinese wine, and the thinly sliced meat used in Lemon Grass Beef is sautéed in butter.

Some recipes will seem comfortably familiar, because they require no specialized ingredients or can be adapted easily to common supermarket products. These include Javanese versions of meatloaf and meatballs, the Filipino steak with onions and two other Filipino dishes, Pork Adobo and Braised Pork with Tomatoes. Brunei's Steak with Hot Tomato Sauce is strikingly similar to Mexican *carne asada* and very easy to make. Those who do Chinese cooking will be at home preparing Beef with Fried Walnuts, a Cantonese recipe from Singapore, and Thai Garlic-Pepper Beef.

Thai and Vietnamese cookery make frequent use of fresh basil, mint and cilantro, which are now carried in many supermarkets and are also easy to grow. Thai dishes that should appeal to home herb growers include broiled pork chops seasoned with garlic and cilantro and ground beef cooked with fresh basil. Both take little time to prepare yet have excellent flavor.

Beef with Fried Walnuts
Hér Tāo Niú Ròu
(Singapore)

Crunchy deep-fried walnuts make an interesting contrast to the tender beef in this Cantonese dish.

1 lb. beef flank steak or any tender steak, partially frozen
1/3 cup chicken broth
1 teaspoon soy sauce
1 teaspoon oyster sauce
1/2 teaspoon sesame oil
1/2 teaspoon salt
Dash white pepper
1 teaspoon cornstarch
2 cups vegetable oil
1 cup walnut halves
3 green onions, white part only, cut into 1-inch lengths
1 (2-inch) piece carrot, thinly sliced
1-1/2 tablespoons thinly sliced gingerroot

Cut steak with the grain into sections 1-1/2 to 2 inches wide, then cut across the grain into slices 1/16 to 1/8 inch thick. Combine chicken broth, soy sauce, oyster sauce, sesame oil, salt, pepper and cornstarch in a small bowl; set aside. Heat a wok over medium-high heat. Add 1 cup of the oil; heat to 360F (180C) or until a 1-inch bread cube turns golden brown in 60 seconds. Add walnuts; fry until nuts start to brown, about 3 minutes. Remove with a slotted spoon; drain on paper towels. Add remaining 1 cup oil to wok; heat to 360F (180C). Add beef; fry, stirring, until browned, about 1 minute. Using a slotted spoon, transfer beef to a bowl or plate. Drain off oil from wok, leaving about 1 tablespoon. Add onions, carrot and gingerroot; stir-fry 30 seconds. Return beef and walnuts to wok; stir-fry 1 minute. Stir cornstarch mixture to blend in cornstarch that has settled. Add to wok; cook, stirring, until mixture thickens and coats meat and vegetables. Makes 4 servings.

Steak with Hot Tomato Sauce
Daging Belador
(Brunei)

The broiled steak is topped with a spicy mixture that resembles a Mexican salsa.

1 lb. tomatoes, peeled, cut into chunks
1 medium-size onion, cut into chunks
1 fresh hot red chili or other hot chili, stemmed, seeded
1 tablespoon vegetable oil
1 teaspoon salt
1/2 teaspoon sugar
1-1/2 lbs. beef top sirloin steak, cut 1/2 inch thick
3/4 teaspoon salt
1/8 teaspoon black pepper

Combine tomatoes, onion and chili in a blender or food processor fitted with the metal blade; process until pureed. Heat oil in a medium-size saucepan over medium heat. Add pureed mixture, 1 teaspoon salt and the sugar. Bring to a boil. Boil, uncovered, until sauce is thickened and reduced to about 1-1/2 cups, stirring occasionally. Sauce may be prepared in advance and reheated at serving time. Bring steak to room temperature. Preheat broiler. Place steak on a rack in broiler pan; sprinkle with remaining 3/4 teaspoon salt and the pepper. Broil 5 inches from heat source 5 minutes. Turn; broil 3 minutes or to medium doneness with a little pink in the center. Cut into 4 portions. Place on heated individual serving plates. Spoon sauce over top. Makes 4 servings.

Coconut Beef
Rendang Daging

(Brunei)

Rendang is a popular dish among Indonesians and Malays. The recipe undergoes regional variations, but coconut milk and spices are always part of it. Unlike curries, which include a large amount of sauce, rendangs are usually cooked until the meat has absorbed the coconut milk and seasonings.

8 shallots
2 lemon grass stalks, coarsely chopped
1 (1-inch-thick) gingerroot piece, sliced
4 small dried red chilies, soaked in hot water until softened, drained
2 teaspoons ground laos
6 tablespoons grated fresh coconut or 1/4 cup unsweetened dried coconut
1 teaspoon water (if using dried coconut)
1 lb. beef top round steak or top sirloin steak (1/2 inch thick)
2-1/2 tablespoons vegetable oil
2-1/2 cups coconut milk
1 teaspoon sugar
1 teaspoon salt

Combine shallots, lemon grass, gingerroot, drained chilies and laos in a blender or food processor fitted with the metal blade; process until finely ground. Spoon into a small bowl; set aside. Place coconut in a small skillet; toast over medium heat, shaking skillet frequently, until coconut is golden brown. Turn into a mortar. Pound coconut to a paste; if using dried coconut, add 1 teaspoon water while pounding. Set aside. Cut meat into slices about 1/2 inch thick and 2 inches square. Heat a wok over medium heat. Add oil and heat. Add ground shallot mixture; stir-fry 5 minutes. Add coconut; stir-fry 1 minute. Increase heat, add meat and cook until browned, about 5 minutes, stirring often to mix with seasonings. Add coconut milk, sugar and salt. Simmer, uncovered, stirring occasionally, until liquid has evaporated and sauce is reduced to a thick coating on the meat, about 1 hour. Toward end of cooking, oil will separate from the coconut milk and the meat will fry in the coconut oil. Makes 4 servings.

Ground Beef with Basil
Nua Pad Bai Kaprow

(Thailand)

When you need a quick, easy dish, try this. To vary the flavor, use pork instead of beef. The texture will be nicer if the meat is finely chopped by hand rather than ground. Fresh basil is essential to this dish. **Photo on page 105.**

1 tablespoon vegetable oil
3 large garlic cloves, minced
1 serrano chili, minced
3/4 lb. coarsely ground lean beef
2 tablespoons fish sauce or soy sauce
1 teaspoon sugar
1 cup lightly packed basil leaves

Heat oil in a medium-size skillet. Add garlic and chili; cook 30 seconds. Add meat; cook 2 minutes or until browned, stirring to break up meat. Add fish sauce and sugar; cook 2 minutes. Add basil; cook, stirring, 1-1/2 more minutes. Spoon onto a heated platter. Makes 4 servings.

Steak with Lime Juice & Onions
Bistec Pilipino
(The Philippines)

This simple dish of steak and onions is very popular in the Philippines where calamansi (calamondin) juice would be used for the marinade. Lime juice is a good substitute.

1-1/2 lbs. beef top sirloin steak,
    cut 1/2 inch thick
1 large onion
1/4 cup soy sauce
1/4 cup lime juice

Trim fat from steak; reserve. Place steak in a shallow glass baking dish. Cut onion in half lengthwise, then cut crosswise into thin slices. Place onion on top of steak. Mix soy sauce and lime juice in a small bowl. Pour over steak and onion. Cover and marinate in refrigerator 1 hour; turn once. Bring to room temperature before cooking. Heat a large heavy skillet over medium-high heat. Place reserved fat in skillet; render to make 1 to 1-1/2 tablespoons liquid fat. Discard solid portion. Drain steak. Place in skillet; cook 2-1/2 minutes. Turn; cook 1-1/2 minutes for medium rare or to desired degree of doneness. Place on a heated platter. Drain onion from marinade, add to skillet and cook about 2 minutes or until crisp-tender. Spoon on top of steak. Makes 4 servings.

Garlic-Pepper Beef
Nua Katim
(Thailand)

The peppery beef has become a standard in Thai restaurants in the United States.

1 lb. beef flank steak, partially
    frozen
4 garlic cloves
1/2 cup lightly packed cilantro
    leaves
1 tablespoon soy sauce
1-1/2 tablespoons water
1-1/4 teaspoons coarsely ground
    black pepper
1/2 teaspoon sugar
1/3 cup water
4 teaspoons fish sauce
1/2 teaspoon cornstarch
1 tablespoon water
3 tablespoons vegetable oil
1 small onion, halved lengthwise,
    cut into 8 wedges

Cut steak on the diagonal into thin slices. Place in a medium-size bowl. In a mortar, pound garlic and 1/4 cup of the cilantro leaves to a paste. Stir in soy sauce, 1-1/2 tablespoons water, pepper and sugar; spoon onto steak. Let stand 30 minutes. Combine 1/3 cup water and fish sauce in a small bowl; set aside. Blend cornstarch and remaining 1 tablespoon water in a separate bowl; set aside. Heat a wok over high heat. Add oil and heat. Add steak; cook, stirring, until no longer pink. Boil until any liquid given off by meat evaporates. Add fish-sauce mixture and onion; cook, stirring, 1 minute. Stir cornstarch mixture to blend in cornstarch that has settled. Add to wok; cook, stirring, until sauce thickens slightly. Spoon onto a heated platter; arrange remaining 1/4 cup cilantro leaves in center. Makes 4 servings.

Stir-Fried Beef & Vegetables
Bò Xào

(Vietnam)

Chinese influence is apparent in the cooking technique and ingredients of this dish. The exception is port wine, a European touch.

1 lb. beef flank steak, partially frozen
1 teaspoon cornstarch
2 tablespoons soy sauce
1 tablespoon port wine
2 garlic cloves, crushed, minced
1 tablespoon finely chopped onion
1/2 teaspoon sugar
1/8 teaspoon black pepper
6 small dried Oriental black mushrooms
1 medium-size green or red bell pepper
1/2 medium-size onion, halved lengthwise
1/4 cup chicken broth
1 teaspoon soy sauce
1/2 teaspoon cornstarch
4 tablespoons vegetable oil
1/4 teaspoon salt

Cut meat with the grain into sections 2 inches wide, then cut across the grain into slices 1/16 to 1/8 inch thick. Place in a medium bowl; mix in 1 teaspoon cornstarch, then add 2 tablespoons soy sauce, the port wine, garlic, chopped onion, sugar and black pepper and stir well. Cover and marinate in refrigerator 1 to 2 hours. Bring to room temperature before cooking. Meanwhile, soak mushrooms in cold water until softened. Remove and discard stems. Cut mushrooms into thin slices. Cut bell pepper into 1" x 1/3" strips. Cut onion halves into wedges 1/3 inch thick at widest point; separate layers. Mix chicken broth, remaining 1 teaspoon soy sauce and 1/2 teaspoon cornstarch in a small bowl; set aside. Heat a wok over high heat. Add 2 tablespoons of the oil and heat. Add mushrooms, bell pepper and onion; stir-fry 1 minute. Season with salt. Transfer from wok to dish. Heat remaining 2 tablespoons oil in wok. Add meat; stir-fry 2 minutes or until browned. Return vegetables to wok; stir-fry 1 minute. Stir cornstarch mixture to blend in cornstarch that has settled. Add to wok; cook, stirring, until sauce thickens, about 45 seconds. Spoon onto a heated platter. Makes 4 servings.

Tip: Partially freezing meat makes it easier to cut into thin slices.

Beef in Ginger-Tomato Sauce
Beef Jaal Frezy
(Malaysia)

Pakistani in origin, this spicy beef dish from Kuala Lumpur resembles a Chinese stir-fry.

1 lb. trimmed beef top sirloin
   steak, 1/2 to 3/4 inch thick,
   partially frozen
1 (1-1/2-inch-thick) gingerroot
   piece, sliced
4 large garlic cloves
3 tablespoons vegetable oil
1 large onion, chopped
2 medium-size tomatoes (1/2 lb.),
   peeled, chopped
1-1/2 teaspoons ground coriander
1 teaspoon sugar
1 teaspoon salt
1/4 teaspoon red (cayenne)
   pepper
1/8 teaspoon black pepper
1/4 cup lightly packed cilantro
   leaves

Cut beef into 1/8-inch-thick slices; set aside. Combine gingerroot and garlic in a food processor fitted with the metal blade; process until finely ground, or mince by hand. Heat oil in a large skillet over medium heat. Add onion; cook, stirring often, until onion starts to brown. Add garlic mixture; cook 3 minutes, stirring to prevent burning. Increase heat, add beef and cook until browned, about 5 minutes, stirring to mix with seasonings. Stir in tomatoes; cook 3 minutes or until blended with sauce. Stir in coriander, sugar, salt, red pepper and black pepper. Reduce heat, cover and simmer 3 minutes. Uncover and stir in cilantro. Makes 4 servings.

Javanese Stewed Beef
Semur Jawa
(Indonesia)

The addition of Indonesian-style soy sauce and cinnamon turns a simple stew into an exotic dish.

2 tablespoons vegetable oil
1 tablespoon butter
1-1/2 lbs. beef stew meat, cut into
   1-inch cubes
1 large onion, chopped
1 garlic clove, minced
1/4 cup Indonesian-style soy sauce
   (kecap)
1 cup water
1 (1-inch) cinnamon stick
2 whole cloves
1 teaspoon salt
1/8 teaspoon black pepper

Heat oil and butter in heavy 3-quart saucepan. Add meat, onion and garlic; cook until meat is no longer red and onion is tender. Add remaining ingredients. Bring to a boil. Reduce heat, cover and simmer 1-1/2 hours or until meat is tender, stirring occasionally. Makes 4 servings.

Beef Stew with Onion Rings & Mint
Bò Kho
(Vietnam)

Tasting this stew, it is hard to detect the Asian seasonings. Van Hoa Restaurant in Los Angeles adds the unusual garnish of raw onion rings and mint sprigs.

2 lbs. trimmed boneless beef
   chuck
2 tablespoons soy sauce
2 tablespoons tomato paste
2 tablespoons finely ground
   lemon grass (1 small stalk)
1 tablespoon soybean condiment
1 teaspoon curry powder
1 teaspoon paprika
1 teaspoon black pepper
3 bay leaves
2 tablespoons vegetable oil
2 large garlic cloves, crushed
3 cups water
1 lb. carrots, diagonally cut into
   1/2-inch slices
1 large (8-oz.) onion, cut into
   1-inch wedges
4 teaspoons salt
1/2 teaspoon coarse-grind black
   pepper
1 medium-size onion, sliced into
   rings
4 large mint sprigs
1 small lemon, cut into 4 wedges
4 French rolls or 1 small loaf
   French bread, heated just before
   serving

Cut beef into 1-1/2-inch chunks. Place in a medium bowl. Stir in soy sauce, tomato paste, lemon grass, soybean condiment, curry powder, paprika, 1 teaspoon pepper and bay leaves. Cover and refrigerate at least 3 hours to blend flavors. Heat oil in a Dutch oven. Add garlic and meat; cook, stirring occasionally, 6 minutes or until meat is lightly browned. Add water; bring to a boil. Cover and simmer 1-1/2 hours, stirring several times. Add carrots and onion wedges. Cover and simmer 1 more hour; discard bay leaves. At serving time, mix salt and coarse pepper. Divide among 4 small containers for dipping. Ladle stew into heated serving bowls. Top each serving with a few onion rings and a mint sprig. Serve with a lemon wedge. To eat, squeeze enough lemon juice over salt and pepper mixture to moisten. Dip meat and carrots as desired in seasoning mixture. Serve with hot French rolls or French bread. Makes 4 servings.

Stir-Fried Steak with Chilies & Bamboo Shoots

Pad Prik Nua

(Thailand)

Simple and quick to make, this spicy-hot dish can be adapted to taste by reducing the amount of chilies. If desired, substitute soy sauce for the fish sauce.

1 lb. beef flank steak, partially
   frozen
1/2 cup chicken broth
1 tablespoon fish sauce
1 teaspoon Maggi seasoning
3 tablespoons vegetable oil
4 garlic cloves, minced
3 serrano chilies, sliced crosswise
1 (8-oz.) can sliced bamboo
   shoots, drained (1 cup)
1/4 cup lightly packed cilantro
   leaves

Cut meat with the grain into sections 1-1/2 to 2 inches wide, then cut across the grain into 1/16- to 1/8-inch-thick slices. Combine broth, fish sauce and Maggi seasoning in a small bowl. Heat a wok over high heat. Add oil and heat. Add garlic and chilies; stir-fry about 10 seconds. Add meat; cook until most of the red color is gone. Stir in bamboo shoots. Add broth mixture; bring to a boil, stirring. Add cilantro, stir and spoon onto a platter. Makes 4 servings.

Thai Barbecued Steak

Kao Neo Nua Yang

(Thailand)

This dish from northeastern Thailand would typically be served with steamed glutinous rice, brought to the table in a rustic basket shaped like an urn. **Photo on page 105.**

1 lb. beef top sirloin steak
3 tablespoons fish sauce
2 tablespoons water
1 tablespoon vegetable oil
1/4 cup packed light-brown sugar
1/2 lb. green cabbage (1/2 small
   head)
12 green beans
8 mint sprigs

Chili Sauce:
5 tablespoons fish sauce
5 tablespoons water
1 tablespoon lime or lemon juice
1-1/2 teaspoons sugar
4 green onions, including a small
   portion of the tops, thinly sliced
3/4 teaspoon crushed dried hot
   chilies

Trim and discard excess fat from steak. Place in a shallow baking dish. Combine fish sauce, water, oil and brown sugar in a small bowl. Add to steak; turn to coat evenly. Cover and marinate in refrigerator 2 to 8 hours; turn once. Make Chili Sauce. Cut cabbage in half; remove core. Loosen leaves but do not detach. Place cabbage and green beans in a large bowl. Cover with ice water; soak about 30 minutes before serving. Bring meat to room temperature before grilling. Prepare barbecue. Drain meat from marinade. Place on grill; cook over hot coals 5 minutes on each side or to desired doneness. (Steak may also be broiled.) Cut steak diagonally into 1/3-inch-thick slices. Arrange on a platter. Drain cabbage and green beans; arrange with mint sprigs on a separate platter. Dip steak slices in Chili Sauce; eat with vegetables and mint as desired. Makes 4 servings.

Chili Sauce:
Combine ingredients. Let stand at least 1 hour before serving to blend flavors. Divide among 4 small sauce dishes.

Lemon Grass Beef
Bò Nướng Ngói

(Vietnam)

This dish is ideal for tabletop cookery. Arrange the beef on a platter, then let guests cook it themselves using an electric skillet or griddle. The dipping sauce is another version of the Nuoc Mam Sauce, page 30, that accompanies many Vietnamese dishes. Select a cut of meat thick enough to yield slices 1 to 2 inches wide.

1 lb. boneless beef round roast, partially frozen, or pre-cut beef for sukiyaki
1 tablespoon fish sauce
1-1/2 teaspoons sugar
2 garlic cloves, crushed, minced
1/4 lb. rice stick noodles
Tops of 4 green onions, chopped
1 tablespoon unsalted Roasted Peanuts, page 31, chopped
8 leaves butter lettuce or other leafy lettuce
5 oz. bean sprouts
8 mint sprigs
1-1/2 tablespoons butter
1 lemon grass stalk, thinly sliced

Dipping Sauce:
1/3 cup lemon juice
1/3 cup distilled white vinegar
1/3 cup fish sauce
1/3 cup water
1/3 cup sugar
1 large garlic clove, crushed, minced
1/2 small serrano chili, sliced, if desired
4 teaspoons shredded carrot

Cut meat in slices 1/16 to 1/8 inch thick. Place in a medium bowl. Stir in fish sauce, sugar and garlic. Cover and marinate in refrigerator 2 to 3 hours. Bring to room temperature before cooking. Make Dipping Sauce. Soak rice sticks in a large saucepan in water to cover 20 minutes; drain. Just before serving, bring 2 quarts water to a boil in a large saucepan. Add drained rice sticks, boil 3 minutes and drain. Arrange on a platter. Top with 1 tablespoon green-onion tops and the chopped peanuts. Arrange lettuce leaves, bean sprouts and mint sprigs on a separate platter. Heat butter in a large non-stick skillet. Add lemon grass; sauté 1 minute. Add meat and remaining green-onion tops; cook until meat is browned on all sides, about 4 minutes. Spoon onto a separate heated platter. To eat, tear off a portion of lettuce leaf. Add some of the meat, bean sprouts and mint leaves. Wrap and dip in bowl of sauce. Serve with rice noodles or wrap some of the noodles in the lettuce with the meat. Makes 4 servings.

Dipping Sauce:
Combine lemon juice, vinegar, fish sauce, water, sugar and garlic in a small saucepan. Bring to a boil. Reduce heat; simmer 1 minute. Remove from heat and add chili, if desired; cool to room temperature. At serving time, divide among 4 small bowls. Add 1 teaspoon carrot shreds to each. Makes 1-1/3 cups sauce.

Spiced Ground Beef
Larb

(Thailand)

Ready-made toasted rice powder is available in some Asian markets. To make your own, toast long-grain rice in a skillet until browned, stirring often to brown evenly and keep from burning. Cool, then grind in an electric spice grinder.

1-1/2 lbs. coarsely ground beef chuck
1 tablespoon fish sauce
1 tablespoon lime juice
1 teaspoon toasted rice powder, if desired
1/2 teaspoon salt
1/4 to 1/2 teaspoon hot chili powder
1/2 cup thinly sliced red onion, cut into thirds or quarters before measuring
2 tablespoons chopped green-onion tops
12 small romaine-lettuce leaves
1/3 cup lightly packed cilantro leaves
1 lime, cut into 6 wedges

In a large non-stick skillet, brown beef without added fat, stirring to break up meat. Drain off drippings. Stir in fish sauce, lime juice, rice powder, if desired, salt and chili powder. Add red onion and green-onion tops; stir until slightly wilted. Line a platter with lettuce leaves. Spoon meat over lettuce; sprinkle with cilantro leaves. Arrange lime wedges at sides. Eat meat with the lettuce and cilantro; season with lime juice as desired. Makes 6 servings.

Variation
In addition to the lettuce and cilantro, accompany the meat with a wedge of raw green cabbage and a few fresh uncooked green beans, cut into 2-inch lengths.

Ann's Indonesian Meat Loaf
Frikadel Bakar

(Indonesia)

A Javanese woman who lived in the United States for several years adds Indonesian seasonings to American-style meat loaf. This is her recipe.

1/3 cup fine dry bread crumbs
1/3 cup warm water
1 tablespoon vegetable oil
1 small onion, finely chopped
1 garlic clove, minced
1/4 teaspoon ground cinnamon
1/8 teaspoon ground cloves
1/8 teaspoon black pepper
1 tablespoon Indonesian-style soy sauce (kecap)
1 egg
1 lb. lean ground beef
1 teaspoon salt

Place bread crumbs in a small bowl; stir in water until crumbs are evenly moistened. Set aside. Heat oil in a small skillet. Add onion and garlic; cook until onion is tender but not browned. Stir in cinnamon, cloves, pepper and soy sauce. Remove from heat. Preheat oven to 350F (175C). Beat egg in a medium-size bowl. Stir in bread crumbs. Add ground beef, onion mixture and salt. Mix well, then knead gently by hand until evenly blended. Lightly pack mixture into an 8"x 4" loaf pan. Bake 45 minutes. Remove from oven; let stand 10 to 15 minutes. With a wide spatula, remove from pan to a heated platter. Makes 4 servings.

Meatballs in Coconut Sauce
Sambal Goreng Daging

A party at a home in Yogyakarta on the island of Java yielded this recipe. **Photo on pages 36-37.**

1 lb. lean ground beef
1 teaspoon salt
1 medium-size tomato, peeled, cut into wedges
1 medium-size onion, cut into wedges
2 garlic cloves
1 serrano chili
1 tablespoon vegetable oil
1 cup water
1 teaspoon salt
1/2 teaspoon ground laos
2 bay leaves
2 cups coconut milk
1/4 lb. Chinese pea pods, ends removed
Basic Steamed Rice, page 133

Form meat into balls 1/2 to 3/4 inch in diameter. Bring 2 quarts water and 1 teaspoon salt to a boil in a 4-quart saucepan. Add meatballs; cook until they rise to the surface. Remove with a slotted spoon; set aside. Discard water. Combine tomato, onion, garlic and chili in a blender or food processor fitted with the metal blade; process until pureed. Heat oil in same 4-quart saucepan over medium heat. Add tomato mixture; cook, stirring frequently, 5 minutes. Add meatballs, the 1 cup water, remaining salt, laos and bay leaves. Bring to a boil. Cover and boil gently 30 minutes. Add coconut milk; boil gently, uncovered, 30 more minutes, adding pea pods during last 2 minutes of cooking time. Remove bay leaves. Spoon into a heated serving bowl. Serve with rice to soak up the sauce. Makes 4 servings.

Javanese Stewed Meatballs
Frikadel

Egg noodles or steamed rice may be served with the meatballs instead of rice stick noodles.

4 (1/2-inch-thick) French-bread slices
1 lb. lean ground beef
3 tablespoons ketchup
1 egg, beaten
1 teaspoon garlic salt
1/8 teaspoon black pepper
1 cup water
2 tablespoons Indonesian-style soy sauce (kecap) or regular soy sauce
1-1/2 teaspoons garlic salt
1/2 medium-size onion, sliced
2 large garlic cloves, sliced
1 (1/2-inch) cinnamon stick
2 whole cloves
1/4 lb. rice stick noodles
Shrimp Chips, page 43

Soak bread in water to cover until thoroughly moistened. Squeeze out water and crumble bread into a medium-size bowl; there will be about 1/2 cup moist crumbs. Add meat, ketchup, egg, 1 teaspoon garlic salt and pepper. Mix well, then knead gently by hand until evenly blended. Form mixture into 24 meatballs; set aside. In a Dutch oven or other pan large enough to hold meatballs in a single layer, combine water, soy sauce and 1-1/2 teaspoons garlic salt. (If using regular soy sauce, no additional garlic salt may be needed.) Add onion, garlic, cinnamon and cloves. Bring to a boil. Add meatballs. Reduce heat, cover and simmer 30 minutes. Meanwhile, soak rice sticks in water to cover about 30 minutes or until softened; drain. Shortly before serving, bring 2 quarts water to a boil in a large saucepan. Add drained rice noodles; boil 3 minutes. Drain; arrange noodles around edge of a large platter. Place meatballs in center. Spoon some of the cooking liquid over the meatballs. Garnish with shrimp chips, if desired. Makes 4 servings.

Raffles Lamb Curry
Kari Kambing

(Singapore)

Serve the curry with rice, mango chutney and assorted curry condiments. See menu on page 14.

2 tablespoons curry powder
2 tablespoons water
2 tablespoons vegetable oil
1 tablespoon minced gingerroot
3 large garlic cloves, minced
2 lbs. boneless lean lamb, cut into
   1-inch chunks
1 cup water
1/2 cup evaporated milk
1/4 cup canned tomato puree
1 (1-inch) cinnamon stick
4 green cardamom pods
4 whole cloves
1-1/2 teaspoons salt
Dash black pepper

Blend curry powder and water in a small bowl to form a soft paste. Heat oil in a Dutch oven over medium heat. Add curry paste, gingerroot and garlic; fry 2 minutes, stirring to keep from burning. Increase heat, add meat and cook until no longer pink, about 8 minutes, stirring often to mix with seasonings. Add remaining ingredients. Bring to a boil. Reduce heat, cover and simmer 45 minutes or until meat is tender. Makes 6 servings.

Malaysian Lamb Curry
Kari Kambing

(Malaysia)

This curry was served in Kuala Lumpur at a buffet dinner ending the daily fast that Muslims observe during the month of Ramadan.

1/4 lb. shallots
3 garlic cloves
1 (1-inch) gingerroot piece
3 tablespoons ground coriander
1-1/2 teaspoons hot chili powder
1 teaspoon ground cumin
2 (14-oz.) cans coconut milk
3 tablespoons vegetable oil
1/4 teaspoon cardamom seeds
8 whole cloves
1 (1-inch) cinnamon stick
2 lbs. boneless lean lamb, cut into
   1-inch chunks
1-1/2 teaspoons salt
3 medium-size tomatoes (3/4 lb.),
   cut into 6 wedges each

Combine shallots, garlic, gingerroot, coriander, chili powder and cumin in a food processor fitted with the metal blade. Process to a fine paste; there will be about 3/4 cup paste. Spoon from processor into a small bowl; set aside. Do not shake cans of coconut milk; open carefully. Spoon off 3/4 cup of the thick coconut milk at the top; set aside. Heat oil in a Dutch oven over medium heat. Add cardamom seeds, cloves and cinnamon stick; fry, stirring, 1 minute. Add ground paste; fry gently 5 minutes, stirring often to keep from burning. Increase heat. Add meat; cook about 8 minutes or until no longer pink, stirring to mix with spices. Add salt and the thinner coconut milk left after removing thick milk. Bring to a boil. Reduce heat, cover and simmer 45 minutes, stirring occasionally. Stir in thick coconut milk and tomatoes. Bring to a boil, reduce heat and simmer, uncovered, stirring occasionally, 30 minutes or until lamb is tender. Makes 6 to 8 servings.

Baked Pork Meatballs with Two Sauces
Nem Nướng
(Vietnam)

Wrap the meatballs in Vietnamese-style rice-paper wrappers along with fresh herbs, lettuce and bean sprouts, then dip the bundle in tangy Nuoc Mam Sauce or Peanut Sauce or both. As an alternative to rice wrappers, serve the meatballs with steamed rice or rice stick noodles and spoon the sauces over the meat.

1 lb. boneless pork butt
1 egg, beaten
2 tablespoons finely chopped
  onion
1 tablespoon soy sauce
2 garlic cloves, minced
1-1/2 tablespoons sugar
1/2 teaspoon salt
1/8 teaspoon white pepper
Nuoc Mam Sauce, page 30
8 romaine-lettuce leaves, cut
  crosswise into slices 1 to 1-1/2
  inches wide
3/4 lb. bean sprouts
8 mint sprigs
8 cilantro sprigs
12 (8-inch) rice paper wrappers

Peanut Sauce:
2/3 cup creamy peanut butter
3/4 cup water
2 tablespoons sugar
1/2 teaspoon salt
1 teaspoon chopped roasted
  peanuts
1 teaspoon chopped fresh parsley

Gingery Sweet-Sour Vegetables:
1 (4-oz.) carrot
1 (8-oz.) cucumber
2 tablespoons rice vinegar
2 teaspoons sugar
1/4 teaspoon salt
1 (1/4-inch-thick) gingerroot slice

Make Gingery Sweet-Sour Vegetables. Put pork through medium blade of a meat grinder twice. Or cut meat into 1-inch cubes and grind in a food processor fitted with the metal blade. Place in a medium-size bowl. Add egg, onion, soy sauce, garlic, sugar, salt and white pepper. Knead gently until well mixed. Cover and let stand in refrigerator 1 hour or longer to blend flavors. Make Nuoc Mam Sauce and Peanut Sauce. Just before cooking meat, arrange lettuce, bean sprouts, mint and cilantro on a platter. Brush rice wrappers on each side with water. Stack on a plate, cover and let stand until softened. Divide Nuoc Mam Sauce among 4 small dipping bowls. Preheat oven to 450F (230C). Divide meat in half. Form each portion into 12 meatballs. Spray a 15" x 10" jelly-roll pan with non-stick coating. Arrange meatballs in pan. Bake without turning 12 minutes. Transfer to a platter. Arrange sweet-sour vegetables in a serving bowl; garnish with reserved cucumber peel. Serve meatballs with rice wrappers, vegetable platter, sauces and sweet-sour vegetables. To eat, tear off a portion of a rice wrapper. Place a meatball on rice wrapper. Add herbs, lettuce and bean sprouts as desired; wrap. Dip in sauces as desired. Serve sweet-sour vegetables alongside. Makes 4 servings.

Peanut Sauce:
Combine peanut butter, water, sugar and salt in a small saucepan. Heat, stirring, until blended. Keep warm or cool to room temperature before serving. If sauce thickens on standing, dilute with additional water. Pour into 4 small dipping bowls. Place some of the chopped peanuts and parsley in center of each bowl. Makes 1-1/3 cups sauce.

Gingery Sweet-Sour Vegetables:
Cut carrot crosswise into thin slices using a fluted cutter. Peel cucumber, reserving a few thin strips of peel for garnish. Cut peeled cucumber crosswise into thin slices with fluted cutter. Place carrot and cucumber in a medium-size bowl. Stir vinegar, sugar and salt in a small bowl until sugar and salt dissolve. Stir into vegetables. Place ginger slice in garlic press; squeeze juice over vegetables. Mix again. Cover and refrigerate 3 hours; stir occasionally. Makes 4 servings.

Pork Adobo
Adobong Baboy
(The Philippines)

This is just one version of this popular Filipino dish. Some cooks boil the pork until the liquid cooks away, then fry the meat in its drippings. Leftover adobo is delicious in sandwiches.

5 tablespoons soy sauce
1/4 cup palm vinegar or rice
    vinegar
3 garlic cloves, crushed
1 bay leaf
1/4 teaspoon black pepper
2 lbs. boneless pork leg, cut into
    1-1/2-inch chunks
Salt, if desired
1 teaspoon cornstarch
1 teaspoon cold water

Combine soy sauce, vinegar, garlic, bay leaf and pepper in a 2-quart stainless steel or glass bowl. Stir in pork. Cover and marinate in refrigerator at least 2 hours, turning pork 2 or 3 times to season evenly. Place pork and marinade in a 3-quart saucepan. Place over medium heat and, without stirring, bring to a full boil. Boil 5 minutes, uncovered, still without stirring. Boil 20 more minutes, uncovered, or until pork is tender, stirring occasionally to keep meat from sticking to the pan. When meat is done, taste and add salt, if desired. Blend cornstarch and cold water in a small bowl. Stir into liquid in pan; boil, stirring, until slightly thickened. Discard bay leaf. Makes 4 servings.

Straits Chinese Pork Satay
Satay Babi
(Singapore)

Satay is not only grilled but also fried and stewed. An example of the latter is this Straits Chinese recipe.

1/2 lb. shallots or mild onions
6 candlenuts
2 small dried hot chilies,
    stemmed, seeded
1/2 teaspoon shrimp paste (terasi)
2 tablespoons vegetable oil
1 lb. pork tenderloin, sliced 1/4
    inch thick
1-1/4 cups coconut milk
2 tablespoons sugar
1 teaspoon salt
Steamed rice

Combine shallots, candlenuts, chilies and shrimp paste in a food processor fitted with the metal blade; process until pureed, stopping processor and stirring down mixture as needed. Heat oil in a 3-quart saucepan over medium-high heat. Add ground mixture; fry about 4 minutes, stirring often to keep from burning. Add pork; cook 5 to 6 minutes or until no longer pink, stirring frequently. Stir in coconut milk, sugar and salt. Bring to a boil. Reduce heat, cover and simmer 30 minutes, stirring occasionally. Serve with rice. Makes 4 servings.

Braised Pork with Tomatoes
Apritadang Baboy

(The Philippines)

Spanish and Oriental influences blend in this dish. Try it for a hearty winter dinner.
Photo on page 105.

5 tablespoons soy sauce
1/4 cup palm vinegar or rice
    vinegar
3 garlic cloves, crushed
1 bay leaf
1/4 teaspoon black pepper
2 lbs. boneless pork leg, cut into
    1-1/2-inch chunks
2 tablespoons vegetable oil
1 medium-size onion, halved,
    sliced
1 (1-lb.) can peeled whole
    tomatoes
2 medium-size russet potatoes
    (3/4 lb.), peeled, quartered
1-1/2 cups water
1 small green bell pepper, cut
    into 1/2-inch strips
2 tablespoons fine dry bread
    crumbs

Combine soy sauce, vinegar, garlic, bay leaf and pepper in a 2-quart stainless steel or glass bowl. Stir in pork. Cover and marinate in refrigerator at least 2 hours, turning pork 2 or 3 times to season evenly. Heat oil in a Dutch oven over medium heat. Add onion; cook until tender but not browned. Add undrained tomatoes. Bring to a boil; boil 3 minutes, mashing tomatoes well. Add pork and marinade. Bring to a full boil without stirring. Boil gently, uncovered, 15 minutes, stirring occasionally. Add potatoes and water. Boil gently, uncovered, 20 minutes. Reduce heat. Add bell-pepper strips; simmer, uncovered, 20 to 25 minutes or until potatoes are tender. Stir in bread crumbs; cook until thickened. Remove bay leaf. Makes 4 to 6 servings.

Broiled Garlic Pork Chops
Mu Katim Prik Thai

(Thailand)

If the chops are seasoned in advance, the final preparation takes only 10 minutes, making this a Thai-style convenience dish.

1/2 cup lightly packed cilantro
2 large garlic cloves
1 teaspoon salt
1/4 teaspoon coarsely ground
    black pepper
4 thin loin pork chops, trimmed
    of fat

Combine cilantro and garlic in a mortar and pound to a paste, or chop together on a board until almost pureed. Spoon mixture into a small bowl; stir in salt and pepper. Spread some of mixture over each side of chops. Place chops on a plate, cover and marinate in refrigerator at least 3 hours. Bring to room temperature before cooking. Preheat broiler. Place chops on rack in a broiler pan; broil 4 to 5 inches from heat source 5 minutes on each side or until no longer pink in center. Makes 4 servings.

SALADS & RELISHES

Asian salads run the gamut from light, fresh vegetable plates to meat and seafood dishes substantial enough for a main course. There are also piquant sweet and sour relishes to go with curries and other spicy dishes. These are most often made with cucumber but also with carrots, green beans, pineapple or a mixture of ingredients. The Indonesian and Malay name for the relishes is *acar* (pronounced ah-char). In Thailand the word is *ajad,* which is pronounced almost the same. In the Philippines, acar becomes *atsara* or *achara.* There the main ingredient is shredded green papaya, and the relish tastes so much like American sauerkraut salad that sauerkraut can be substituted for the papaya.

Shrimp salad with mayonnaise and steak salad tossed with bottled creamy dressing may sound more Western than Asian. However, the recipes come from Bangkok, where supermarkets carry convenience products like those found in western countries. On the other hand, the Thais have a distinctly Asian version of pasta salad, Yum Woon Sen, which is made with bean thread noodles, chicken and shrimp.

Warm meat salads seemed original when introduced by innovative American chefs, but the Thais have made them for years. One of the most popular is composed of broiled steak cut into strips and tossed with a tangy lime or lemon juice dressing spiked with chili. The dressing contains no oil, which makes it ideal for dieters.

Vietnam also has a beef dish that can pass for a salad. This one consists of stir-fried steak and onion served over lettuce and garnished with tomato and cilantro.

Peanut butter lovers can try Indonesian Gado Gado, a stunning platter of vegetables accompanied by a peanut sauce similar to that served with satay. Carrots, potatoes, green beans, cabbage, bean sprouts and hard-cooked egg are arranged in an attractive pattern and garnished with puffy fried shrimp chips.

A Thai peanut dressing contains coconut milk and is served over a mixed salad garnished with unique croutons made by frying cut-up won-ton wrappers until crisp. Not peanut butter but the chopped peanuts are part of another Thai dish whimsically named Galloping Horses. The nuts are mixed with cooked ground pork and sprinkled over sliced fresh pineapple; slivered red chilies and cilantro sprigs add color. Peanuts and pineapple are also part of an Indonesian salad named Asinan, but the dressing and other components make it different from the Thai dish.

Additional recipes in this chapter include Thai cabbage, chicken and fruit salads that are nothing like their western counterparts and a Singaporean vegetable plate enriched with tofu and decorated with lacy lotus root.

Straits Chinese Pickled Vegetables
Nonya Acar

(Singapore)

Spicy with ginger and chilies, this unusual Asian "cole slaw" is sure to be a conversation piece.

1 medium-size cucumber
1/2 pound green cabbage (1/2 small head)
2 tablespoons salt
1 small carrot, shredded
1/4 pound jícama, peeled, shredded
2 to 3 small dried chilies
1/3 cup thinly sliced gingerroot
1/4 cup vegetable oil
1/3 cup sugar
1/4 cup distilled white vinegar
1/2 teaspoon salt
2 tablespoons unsalted Roasted Peanuts, page 31, chopped
2 teaspoons toasted sesame seeds

Peel cucumber, cut in half lengthwise and remove seeds. Shred cucumber into fine strips using a hand grater or julienne blade of a food processor. Cut cabbage in half, remove core, then cut crosswise into thin slices. Combine 6 cups water and 2 tablespoons salt in a large bowl. Stir in cucumber, cabbage, carrot and jícama; cover and let stand at room temperature 1 hour. Meanwhile, soak chilies in hot water until softened. Remove stems and seeds. Combine chilies and gingerroot in a food processor fitted with the metal blade; process until pureed. Heat oil in a small heavy saucepan over medium heat. Add gingerroot mixture; fry 1-1/2 minutes. Add sugar; cook until mixture is bubbly and pale brown, about 3 minutes. Add vinegar; boil 3 minutes or until mixture thickens and separates when spoon is drawn across the pan. Stir in 1/2 teaspoon salt. Cool thoroughly. Drain vegetables. Rinse and drain again. Squeeze a handful at a time to remove as much liquid as possible. Place in a 1-quart bowl. Stir in cooled gingerroot sauce. Cover and refrigerate until chilled. Just before serving, sprinkle top with peanuts and sesame seeds. Toss at the table. Makes 3 cups or about 8 small servings.

Straits Chinese Pineapple Relish
Acar Nenas

(Singapore)

This relish from the Luna Coffee House of the Apollo Hotel combines pineapple with such unexpected companions as garlic, chili and onion.

1 large cucumber
1/2 medium-size onion
3 cups small, thin, fresh pineapple wedges
1-1/2 teaspoons salt
1 large garlic clove
1 fresh small red chili or serrano chili, sliced crosswise
2 tablespoons distilled white vinegar
2 tablespoons sugar

Peel cucumber. Cut in half lengthwise; scoop out seeds. Cut cucumber crosswise into 1/4-inch-thick slices. Cut onion in half lengthwise, then cut crosswise into thin slices. Combine cucumber, onion and pineapple in a medium-size bowl. Stir in salt. Let stand 1 hour. Take small handfuls of mixture at a time; squeeze out as much liquid as possible. Place in another bowl. Let stand 30 minutes. Drain off any liquid that has accumulated. Pound garlic with chili in a mortar to form a paste. Stir garlic paste, vinegar and sugar in a small cup until sugar dissolves. Stir dressing into pineapple mixture. Cover and marinate in refrigerator at least 2 hours before serving. Makes about 2 cups or 6 to 8 small servings.

Cucumber Pickles
Acar Timun

(Malaysia)

Indian and Malay cooking techniques blend in this cucumber relish that is served at Bilal, an Indian restaurant in Kuala Lumpur.

2 medium-size cucumbers
2 tablespoons vegetable oil
1 teaspoon mustard seeds
3 tablespoons sugar
1/2 teaspoon hot chili powder
3/4 teaspoon salt
3 tablespoons distilled white vinegar
1/4 teaspoon red food color

Peel cucumbers. Cut in half lengthwise; scoop out seeds. Cut each half in half crosswise or, if cucumbers are long, into thirds. Cut each section lengthwise into 1/8-inch-thick slices; set aside. Heat oil in a medium-size skillet. Add mustard seeds, sugar, chili powder and salt; fry, stirring, 2 minutes. Add cucumber slices; cook, stirring, 2 minutes. Add vinegar. Push cucumbers to 1 side of skillet. Stir food color into sauce, then mix with cucumbers. Spoon into a bowl. Cover; let stand several hours, or refrigerate overnight before serving. Can be served chilled or at room temperature. Makes 6 to 8 servings.

Green-Papaya Relish
Papayang Atsara

(The Philippines)

Green papayas have very pale, green-white flesh. If you can't find one, try the sauerkraut variation.

1 green (unripe) papaya, about 1-1/4 lbs.
1 tablespoon salt
3 cups boiling water
1/2 cup distilled white vinegar
1/4 cup sugar
3/4 teaspoon salt
Dash white pepper
1/4 red bell pepper, finely shredded
1/4 small onion, finely shredded
1/2 small carrot, finely shredded (1/4 cup)

Quarter papaya lengthwise; peel. Scoop out and discard seeds. Cut papaya into long fine shreds, using shredding or julienne blade of a food processor or hand grater. Place in a medium-size bowl. Add salt; squeeze with your hands until papaya becomes very juicy. Pour boiling water over papaya; let stand 10 minutes. Pour into a sieve, drain and rinse well. Squeeze out as much water as possible from papaya. Place in a medium bowl. Combine vinegar, sugar, salt and white pepper in a small saucepan. Bring to a boil. Add bell pepper, onion and carrot. Remove from heat; stir 30 seconds. Pour over papaya; stir until combined. Cover and refrigerate until chilled. Makes 2 cups.

Variation
Substitute 1 (1-lb.) can sauerkraut for the papaya. Pour sauerkraut into a sieve; rinse thoroughly. Drain well, squeezing out any excess water. Place in a medium bowl. Add vinegar dressing and shredded vegetables, mix well, cover and chill.

Pickled Green Beans
Acar Buncis
(Indonesia)

*These sweet and sour beans would fit an American potluck as easily as an Indonesian dinner. **Photo on pages 36-37.***

1/2 lb. green beans
1/2 cup water
2 tablespoons sugar
3/4 teaspoon salt
1/2 teaspoon garlic salt
3 tablespoons distilled white vinegar
1/4 cup chopped red onion

Cut beans diagonally into 1-inch-long pieces. Place beans, water, sugar, salt and garlic salt in a 1-quart saucepan. Bring to a boil. Reduce heat, cover and simmer 12 minutes or until beans are tender but still slightly crisp. Stir in vinegar. Spoon into a serving bowl. Top with onion. Cover and refrigerate 2 hours or overnight. Makes 2 cups or about 8 small servings.

Cucumber-Yogurt Relish
Raita
(Singapore)

Hot chilies and chili powder spice the relish in South Indian style.

1 medium-size cucumber
1/2 medium-size onion
2 (8-oz.) cartons plain yogurt (2 cups)
1 or 2 serrano chilies, halved, seeded, coarsely chopped
1/2 teaspoon salt
1/4 teaspoon ground cumin
1/4 teaspoon hot chili powder

Peel cucumber, cut in half and remove seeds. Shred cucumber using julienne blade of food processor or hand grater. Squeeze shreds to remove excess liquid. Cut onion into thin slices, then into smaller pieces. Spoon yogurt into a medium-size bowl. Beat lightly. Stir in cucumber, onion, chili and salt. Sprinkle cumin and chili powder over top. Makes about 2-1/2 cups or 6 servings.

Shredded Carrot Relish
Gỏi
(Vietnam)

This relish is a popular attraction at the Vietnamese catering trucks that set up shop at various locations in Los Angeles.

1/2 lb. carrots
2/3 cup water
1/4 cup lemon juice
3 tablespoons sugar
1/2 teaspoon salt
1 small fresh red chili or 1 serrano chili, halved lengthwise
1 large garlic clove, crushed

Peel carrots; cut into fine shreds 1-1/2 to 2 inches long using julienne blade of a food processor or a hand grater. There will be about 2 cups carrot shreds. In a medium-size bowl, stir water, lemon juice, sugar and salt until sugar and salt are dissolved. Add shredded carrots. Lightly pound chili to release flavor. Stir pounded chili and garlic into carrots. Cover and refrigerate 2 hours or longer for flavors to blend. Makes 4 to 6 servings.

Carrot & Green-Bean Relish
Som Tam
(Thailand)

Cooking the beans a short time gives them the bright color that enhances the appearance of the relish.

1/4 cup lemon juice
1 tablespoon fish sauce
2 tablespoons water
1 tablespoon sugar
4 small dried shrimp
2 garlic cloves
1 serrano chili, sliced crosswise
6 green beans
1/2 lb. carrots, shredded

Stir lemon juice, fish sauce, water and sugar in a small bowl until sugar dissolves. Pound shrimp in a mortar until powdered. Add to dressing. Pound garlic until well crushed. Add garlic and chili to dressing. Set aside while preparing beans. Cut beans diagonally into 1-inch-long pieces. Bring 2 cups water to a boil in a small saucepan. Add beans; boil 2 minutes. Drain. Rinse with cold water; drain again. Combine beans, carrots and dressing in a medium-size bowl. Cover and refrigerate at least 2 hours before serving to allow flavors to blend. Makes 4 to 6 servings.

Fruits with Spicy Sweet Sauce
Naum Pla Van
(Thailand)

The unusual dip accompanies a platterful of fruits and cucumber. For a simpler presentation, a single fruit may be used.

2/3 cup sugar
2 tablespoons light corn syrup
1/4 cup fish sauce
1/4 cup water
4 teaspoons finely ground
    unsweetened dried coconut
1 teaspoon ground dried shrimp
1/4 teaspoon hot red-pepper flakes
Assorted fruits and vegetables,
    such as thinly sliced unpeeled
    tart apples, thin jícama wedges,
    thin fresh pineapple wedges,
    thin firm papaya or melon slices
    and thin cucumber slices

Combine sugar, corn syrup, fish sauce and water in a small saucepan. Bring to a full rolling boil. Remove from heat. Stir in coconut, dried shrimp and pepper flakes. Cool to room temperature. If using apples, slice and place in ice water mixed with lemon juice to prevent browning. Use 2 tablespoons lemon juice to 3 cups water for 2 apples. Arrange fruits and vegetables on a large platter. (Without other fruits, 2 apples will make 6 to 8 servings.) Place sauce in a small bowl in center of platter. To eat, dip fruits and vegetables in sauce. Makes 2/3 cup sauce, enough for 6 servings.

Fresh Coconut Chutney
Thengai Chatney

(Singapore)

Fried lentils give a nutty flavor to this unusual chutney. The lentils are called dal by Indian cooks.

2 tablespoons vegetable oil
1/4 cup split orange lentils
1/2 coconut, peeled, chopped
   (1-1/2 cups)
1 (8-oz.) carton plain yogurt (1
   cup)
1/4 teaspoon salt
2 serrano chilies, seeded if
   desired
1 teaspoon vegetable oil
1 teaspoon mustard seeds
1 teaspoon crumbled dried curry
   leaves, if desired

Heat 2 tablespoons oil in a small skillet over medium heat. Add lentils; cook about 7 minutes or until color deepens. Remove with a slotted spoon; drain on paper towels. Grind to a powder in a spice grinder. Process coconut until finely chopped in a food processor fitted with the metal blade. Add ground lentils, yogurt, salt and chilies; process until pureed. Scrape into a medium-size bowl. Heat remaining 1 teaspoon oil in a small skillet. Add mustard seeds; fry until seeds start to pop. Stir in curry leaves, if desired. Immediately stir into coconut mixture. Cover and refrigerate at least 1 hour to soften lentils. Makes 2 cups.

Variation
If spice grinder is not available, grind fried lentils with coconut in food processor. Lentils will remain in a large pieces. Chutney will need to stand several hours for lentils to soften.

Lada's Cucumber Salad
Ajad

(Thailand)

*This spicy relish is served with satay, barbecued chicken and many other Thai dishes. **Photo on page 40.***

3 tablespoons rice vinegar
1 tablespoon sugar
1/2 teaspoon salt
Dash black pepper
1 (8-oz.) cucumber, peeled
1/2 cup thinly sliced red onion
   (cut slices into thirds or
   quarters before measuring)
2 tablespoons cilantro leaves,
   chopped
1 small fresh red chili or serrano
   chili, sliced

In a medium-size bowl, stir vinegar, sugar, salt and pepper until sugar and salt are dissolved. Quarter cucumber lengthwise. Cut quarters crosswise into 1/8-inch-thick slices. Add cucumber, onion, cilantro and chili to vinegar dressing; toss until combined. Cover and marinate in refrigerator 3 hours, stirring occasionally. Makes 4 servings.

Shrimp Salad with Sweet Mayonnaise
Yum Nam Khon
(Thailand)

A beautiful salad to serve for a western-style luncheon with hot rolls or muffins as accompaniment. **Photo on page 106.**

6 cups water
1 teaspoon salt
1/2 lb. medium-size shrimp
2 egg yolks
2 tablespoons sugar
1 tablespoon lemon juice
1/4 teaspoon dry mustard
1/4 teaspoon salt
3/4 cup vegetable oil
5 romaine-lettuce leaves
1 small cucumber
1 medium-size tomato, cut into 12 wedges
1/2 cup thinly sliced red onion (cut slices into thirds or quarters before measuring)

Bring water and salt to a boil in a large saucepan. Add unshelled shrimp; boil 4 minutes or until pink. Shell shrimp, but leave tail and shell attached to section next to tail. Slit backs; remove sand veins. Cover and refrigerate shrimp until chilled. Beat egg yolks, sugar, lemon juice, mustard and salt in a medium-size bowl. Add oil, a drop at a time, beating until mixture thickens. Continue adding remaining oil slowly while beating; set aside. Cut off thick ends of romaine. Cut leaves in half lengthwise, then cut crosswise into 1-inch-wide slices. There should be at least 4 cups romaine slices. Cut 6 thin slices diagonally from cucumber, making slices about the same length as tomato wedges. Cut each slice in half lengthwise. Reserve remaining cucumber for another use. Place romaine in center of a large platter. Top with onion slices. Top onion and romaine with all but 2 tablespoons mayonnaise. Arrange shrimp on mayonnaise; drizzle with remaining mayonnaise. Make a fan-like arrangement of tomato slices around 1 end of platter. Arrange cucumber slices in same way around other end of platter. Makes 4 servings.

Shrimp & Young-Corn Salad
Yum Kao Pode On
(Thailand)

This Bangkok salad is low in calories; the dressing consists solely of vinegar.

1/2 lb. small to medium shrimp, shelled, deveined
1 (15-oz.) can young corn, drained, rinsed
1/2 cup sliced celery
1/4 cup sliced green onions
2 serrano chilies, thinly sliced
3 garlic cloves, minced
1/4 cup distilled white vinegar
1/4 teaspoon salt
Dash white pepper
2 leaves romaine, salad bowl or other leafy lettuce
1 medium-size tomato

Bring 2 cups salted water to a boil in a 1-quart saucepan. Add shrimp; cook 3 minutes or just until pink. Drain; rinse with cold water. Cut corn diagonally into 1/2-inch-wide slices. Combine shrimp, corn, celery, green onions, chilies and garlic in a medium-size bowl. Add vinegar, salt and pepper. Mix lightly but thoroughly. Cover and marinate in refrigerator 2 hours or longer. To serve, place lettuce leaves end to end on platter. Spoon salad into center. Thinly slice tomato and arrange on each side. Makes 4 small servings.

Bean Thread Salad with Chicken & Shrimp
Yum Woon Sen

(Thailand)

Unlike other forms of pasta, bean thread noodles become transparent when cooked. The golden needles and black fungus, added for crunchy texture, are dried ingredients available in Chinese shops.

18 small to medium-size shrimp, shelled, deveined
1 chicken-breast half
1/4 cup dried golden needles
2 small pieces dried black fungus
2-1/2 oz. bean thread noodles
3 tablespoons sliced green-onion tops
1/4 cup lightly packed cilantro leaves
1 teaspoon finely chopped mint
3 or 4 romaine-lettuce leaves
2 tablespoons unsalted Roasted Peanuts, page 31, coarsely chopped
6 cilantro sprigs

Lemon Dressing:
1/3 cup lemon juice
3 tablespoons fish sauce
4 teaspoons sugar
2 garlic cloves, minced
1 serrano chili, sliced crosswise
Dash white pepper

Bring 2 cups salted water to a boil in a 1-quart saucepan. Add shrimp; boil 3 minutes or just until pink. Drain and rinse under cold water. Place in a small bowl, cover and refrigerate until chilled. Place chicken breast in same saucepan. Add water to cover and 1/4 teaspoon salt. Bring to a boil. Reduce heat, cover and simmer 20 minutes. Drain and cool. Discard skin and bones. Shred meat. Cover meat and refrigerate until chilled. Separately soak golden needles, black fungus and bean thread noodles in water to cover about 30 minutes or until soft. Drain, rinse and squeeze golden needles to extract excess water. Drain, rinse and cut black fungus into fine shreds. Bring 2 quarts (8 cups) water to a boil in a large saucepan. Drain bean threads, add to boiling water and boil 3 minutes or until transparent. Drain in sieve. Cut through cooked noodles with kitchen scissors to make shorter lengths. Let cool. Make Lemon Dressing. Combine shrimp, chicken, golden needles, black fungus, green-onion tops, cilantro leaves and mint in a large bowl. Add Lemon Dressing; toss to combine. Add bean threads; toss gently. Cover and refrigerate until chilled. Just before serving, line a platter with lettuce leaves. Set aside 1 teaspoon chopped peanuts. Toss remainder with salad. Arrange salad on lettuce. Sprinkle with reserved peanuts; garnish with cilantro sprigs. Makes 6 servings.

Lemon Dressing:
Combine all ingredients in a small bowl; stir until sugar dissolves.

Top to bottom: Ground Beef with Basil, page 84; Braised Pork with Tomatoes, page 96; Thai Barbecued Steak, page 89

Above: Baluarte Mango Daiquiri, page 170; Aristocrat Barbecued Chicken, page 75; Java Rice, page 134

Opposite: Top to bottom: Galloping Horses, page 116; Hot Beef Salad, page 114; Shrimp Salad with Sweet Mayonnaise, page 103

Following pages: Clockwise from left: Basic Steamed Rice, page 133; Eggplant Curry, page 123; Assorted condiments; Anglo-Indian Chicken Curry, page 74

Above: Clockwise from bottom left: Fried Fish Cakes with Cucumber Relish, page 61; Steamed Fish with Coconut Sauce, page 60; Shrimp in Tomato Sauce, page 65

Opposite: Clockwise from bottom left: Fried Tofu, page 131; Vegetables with Tropical Fruit & Cashews, page 127; South Indian Potatoes, page 126

Vegetable Platter with Peanut Sauce
Gado Gado
(Indonesia)

For a large party, double or triple recipe and serve Gado Gado as a salad bar, arranging each ingredient and the sauce in separate bowls. ***Photo on pages 36-37.***

1 medium-size boiling potato
  (6-oz.), peeled
1/2 lb. carrots (2 small)
1/4 lb. green beans
1/2 lb. cabbage (1/2 small head)
Salt
6 oz. bean sprouts (about 2 cups)
2 hard-cooked eggs, cut in wedges
1 small cucumber, peeled, sliced
Shrimp Chips, page 43, if desired

Peanut Sauce:
1 tablespoon vegetable oil
1/4 medium-size onion, finely
  chopped
1 garlic clove, minced
Dash black pepper
1/2 cup crunchy peanut butter
1/2 cup water
1-1/2 tablespoons Indonesian-style
  soy sauce (kecap)
2 teaspoons lemon juice
1 teaspoon sugar
1/8 teaspoon red (cayenne)
  pepper, if desired

Make Peanut Sauce. Place potato in a small saucepan. Add water to cover, bring to a boil and boil until just tender, about 25 minutes. Drain and cool. Cut into 1/4-inch-thick slices. Meanwhile, quarter carrots lengthwise. Cut crosswise into 1-inch chunks. Cut green beans diagonally into 1-1/2-inch lengths. Cut cabbage in half lengthwise. Remove core, then cut crosswise into slices 1/2 inch wide. Bring 1 quart salted water to a boil in a 3-quart saucepan. Add carrots, cover and cook about 8 minutes or until tender. Drain, rinse with cold water and drain well. Pat dry with paper towels; set aside. Add more salted water to saucepan. Bring to a boil. Add green beans, cover and boil 5 minutes. Drain, rinse with cold water and drain well. Pat dry with paper towels; set aside. Bring 2 quarts salted water to a boil. Add cabbage, cover and boil 4 minutes or until tender. Remove from heat. Lift cabbage from water with a slotted spoon, retaining water. Rinse cabbage with cold water; drain well. Pat dry with paper towels; set aside. Drop bean sprouts into hot water remaining in pan; let stand 1 minute. Drain, rinse with cold water and drain well. Arrange cabbage in center of a large round platter. Arrange cooked vegetables, egg wedges and cucumber slices in separate groups around cabbage, alternating to make a pleasing pattern of colors. Scatter a handful of shrimp chips around edge or over top. Serve Peanut Sauce separately to add as desired. Makes 4 to 6 servings.

Peanut Sauce:
Heat oil in a small saucepan over low heat. Add onion, garlic and black pepper; cook slowly until tender and lightly browned. Add peanut butter; stir until melted. Stir in water, soy sauce, lemon juice, sugar and red pepper. Serve warm. Makes 1 cup sauce.

Top to bottom: Penang Papaya Pudding, page 159; Strawberry Flan, page 148; Coconut Crepes, page 151

Hot Beef Salad
Bò Lúc Lắć

(Vietnam)

Stir-fried beef combines with tomato and lettuce for this main dish salad. Individual metal sizzling platters with wood bases are nice for the presentation.
Photo on page 106.

1 (1-lb.) flank steak, partially
   frozen
2 tablespoons soy sauce
1 tablespoon vegetable oil
1/2 teaspoon sugar
3 garlic cloves, minced
1 medium-size onion
2 small dried chilies
2 tablespoons soy sauce
2 tablespoons beef stock
5 tablespoons vegetable oil
1/2 teaspoon sugar
12 red-leaf-lettuce leaves
2 medium-size tomatoes, each cut
   into 6 slices
16 cilantro sprigs

Cut meat lengthwise in 2 or 3 strips; cut strips diagonally into 1/8-inch-thick slices. Place in a medium-size bowl. Add 2 tablespoons soy sauce, 1 tablespoon oil, 1/2 teaspoon sugar and garlic. Mix well. Cover and marinate in refrigerator at least 2 hours. Mix again and bring to room temperature before cooking. Cut onion in half lengthwise. Cut each half into quarters, making 8 wedges. Separate onion layers; set aside. Soak chilies in warm water about 30 minutes or until softened. Discard seeds and stems; mince chilies. Combine chilies, remaining 2 tablespoons soy sauce and beef stock in a small bowl. Heat wok over high heat. Add 4 tablespoons oil and heat. Add onion; stir-fry 1 minute. Remove onion with a slotted spoon, draining oil back into pan; place onion in a small bowl. Add steak to wok; stir-fry 3 minutes. Remove steak and any liquid in wok; add to onion. Heat remaining 1 tablespoon oil in wok. Add remaining 1/2 teaspoon sugar. As soon as sugar melts, stir in chili mixture. Return steak and onion to wok; stir-fry 1 minute. Remove from heat. Arrange 3 lettuce leaves on each of 4 lightly heated large individual plates or platters. Place 1/4 of beef in center of each serving. Arrange 3 tomato slices around beef. Arrange 4 cilantro sprigs on each serving. Makes 4 servings.

Hot & Sour Beef Salad

Yum Nua

A little meat, a lot of vegetables and an oilless dressing add up to a healthful dish. This salad is widely served in Bangkok and at Thai restaurants in the United States.

1/2 cup lime juice
3 tablespoons sugar
2 tablespoons fish sauce
3 serrano chilies, thinly sliced
6 large romaine-lettuce leaves
1 small cucumber, peeled, sliced
   1/8-inch thick
2 small tomatoes, each cut into 8
   wedges
1 small red onion (1/4 lb.),
   halved, thinly sliced
1 (1- to 1-1/4 lb.) flank steak
1 teaspoon garlic salt
3 large green onions, including
   some of the tops, sliced
1/2 cup cilantro sprigs

Combine lime juice, sugar, fish sauce and chilies in a small bowl. Cover and let stand 1 hour. Cut lettuce crosswise into slices 1/2 inch wide. Arrange lettuce on a platter. Arrange cucumbers at each end and tomatoes at sides. Scatter onion over top. Cover and refrigerate platter until chilled. Sprinkle meat with garlic salt. Let stand 30 to 45 minutes. Preheat broiler. Place steak on rack in a broiler pan. Broil 4 inches from heat source 5 minutes; turn and broil 3 more minutes. Steak will be rare; adjust cooking time according to thickness. Cut steak across the grain into 1/4-inch-thick slices. Cut very long slices in half. Arrange steak slices on lettuce. Top with green onions and cilantro sprigs. Spoon dressing over salad. Makes 4 servings.

Cabbage Salad with Dried Shrimp & Peanuts

Som Tam

This salad would ordinarily be made with shredded green papaya but is also very good with cabbage.

2 garlic cloves
1 serrano chili
2 (1/4-inch) slices from a
   medium-size tomato
2 tablespoons fish sauce
2-1/2 tablespoons lime juice
1-1/2 teaspoons dark-brown sugar
1-1/2 teaspoons granulated sugar
6 cups shredded green cabbage
   (1 small head)
2 tablespoons dried shrimp, finely
   chopped
2 tablespoons finely chopped,
   unsalted Roasted Peanuts,
   page 31

To make dressing, pound garlic and chili in a mortar until well crushed. Cut up tomato slices, add to mortar and pound slightly. Stir in fish sauce, lime juice and sugars. Place cabbage in a large bowl. Add dressing and shrimp. Pound cabbage lightly with pestle. Cover; let stand 30 minutes to 1 hour at room temperature for cabbage to soften slightly and blend with dressing. Stir in peanuts just before serving. Makes 6 servings.

Mixed Salad with Peanut Dressing & Won-Ton Crisps

Yum Yai

(Thailand)

Doubling the amount of hard-cooked eggs will turn this into a vegetarian main-dish salad.

8 square won-ton wrappers
Vegetable oil for deep-frying
8 romaine-lettuce leaves
2 pickling cucumbers, cut
   diagonally in thin slices
2 medium-size tomatoes, halved,
   sliced
2 hard-cooked eggs, each cut into
   6 wedges
1 cup finely shredded red cabbage
1/2 cup coarsely shredded carrot

Peanut Dressing:
2/3 cup creamy peanut butter
1 cup coconut milk
4 teaspoons sugar
1/4 to 1/2 teaspoon salt
2 tablespoons lime juice
1/4 teaspoon hot-pepper sauce

Make Peanut Dressing. Separate won-ton wrappers, then restack loosely but neatly and cut into 3/4-inch squares. Heat 1/2 inch oil in a small skillet until a 1-inch bread cube turns golden brown in 60 seconds. Add won-ton squares a few at a time; fry until lightly browned. Drain on paper towels; set aside. Cut lettuce crosswise into slices 1/2 inch wide. Arrange lettuce in mounds in centers of 4 large salad plates. Arrange cucumber slices around lettuce. Arrange tomato slices on top of or between cucumber slices. Place 3 egg wedges around lettuce on each plate. Top lettuce with cabbage, then carrot shreds. Spoon about 1/4 cup peanut dressing over each salad. Sprinkle with fried won-tons. Pass remaining dressing separately. Makes 4 servings.

Peanut Dressing:
Combine peanut butter, coconut milk, sugar and salt to taste in a small saucepan. Stir over low heat just until blended. Remove from heat; stir in lime juice and hot-pepper sauce. Serve at room temperature. Makes 1-1/2 cups.

Galloping Horses

Ma Ho

(Thailand)

Fresh pineapple is the foundation of this refreshing and unusual salad. As a variation, substitute orange slices for the pineapple. **Photo on page 106.**

1/2 pineapple (halved lengthwise)
2 tablespoons vegetable oil
1 tablespoon raw peanuts
1 garlic clove, minced
1/4 lb. boneless lean pork, finely
   ground
1 tablespoon fish sauce or soy
   sauce
1 tablespoon sugar
1/2 teaspoon distilled white
   vinegar
1/4 cup cilantro leaves
1 small fresh red chili, slivered

Cut pineapple half lengthwise in 2 equal pieces. Remove core; peel and remove eyes. Cut pineapple crosswise into slices 1/4 to 1/3 inch thick. Overlap slices on a platter; set aside. Heat oil in a small skillet. Add peanuts; fry until browned. Set skillet off heat. Remove peanuts, reserving oil. Coarsely crush peanuts in a mortar or with a rolling pin. Reheat oil over medium heat. Add garlic; fry a few seconds. Increase heat, add pork and cook until no longer pink, stirring to break up meat. Stir in peanuts, fish sauce, sugar and vinegar. Cook until most of liquid has boiled away but pork is still moist; do not overcook or meat will be dry. Spoon pork over pineapple slices. Arrange cilantro over pork. Decorate with chili slivers. Serve at room temperature. Makes 4 servings.

Bangkok-Style Steak Salad
Yum Nua

A creamy, herb-flavored ranch-type dressing from the supermarket will produce good results with this recipe.

Roots and small portion of stems
   from 1 bunch cilantro
3 medium-size garlic cloves
1 teaspoon black peppercorns
1 tablespoon soy sauce
1-1/2 teaspoons Worcestershire
   sauce
1 (1-lb.) flank steak
2 tablespoons vegetable oil
6 large butter-lettuce or
   red-leaf-lettuce leaves
1/2 cup thinly sliced red onion
   (cut slices into thirds or
   quarters before measuring)
1/3 cucumber, peeled, thinly
   sliced
1 medium-size tomato, halved,
   cored, sliced
1/3 cup bottled non-sweet,
   creamy, ranch-type dressing

Wash lower portion of cilantro sprigs, then cut off any roots and a small portion of the stems; there should be about 2 tablespoons, loosely packed. Place cilantro roots and stems, garlic and peppercorns in a mortar; pound until reduced to a paste. Stir in soy sauce and Worcestershire sauce. Rub mixture over both sides of steak. Place steak in a shallow dish, cover and marinate in refrigerator 4 to 6 hours. Heat oil in a medium-size, preferably non-stick, skillet over medium-high heat. Skillet should be large enough to hold steak flat. Add steak. Cover and cook 4 minutes. Turn, cover and cook second side 4 minutes. Steak will be medium rare. Remove to a cutting board. Cool slightly, then cut across the grain into slices about 1/3 inch thick and 1-1/2 to 2 inches long, reserving juices. Cool to room temperature. Meanwhile, wash lettuce; tear into bite-size pieces. Place in a salad bowl. Add onion, cucumber and tomato; toss lightly with dressing. Add sliced steak and steak juices; toss to mix. Makes 4 servings.

Pineapple Salad
Asinan

(Indonesia)

"Sweet and hot" describes this mixture of pineapple and vegetables with brown-sugar dressing. To control the spiciness, the chili sauce is placed on the side of the plate to mix in as desired.

1 (8-1/4-oz.) can sliced pineapple (juice pack), drained
1 medium-size cucumber, peeled, cut into 1/8-inch-thick rounds
1 small carrot, cut into very thin slices
1/4 lb. bean sprouts
1/3 cup packed dark-brown sugar
3 tablespoons distilled white vinegar
3/4 teaspoon salt
1/4 cup unsalted Roasted Peanuts, page 31, coarsely ground or finely crushed
Mr. Lee's Red-Chili Sauce, page 29

Cut pineapple into small wedges; place in a medium-size bowl. Add cucumber. Combine carrot slices and bean sprouts in a separate bowl. Bring 3 cups water to a boil in a medium-size saucepan. Pour over carrot and bean sprouts. Pour at once into a colander and drain. Rinse with cold water; drain thoroughly. Add to pineapple and cucumber. Stir brown sugar, vinegar and salt in a small bowl until sugar dissolves. Pour over salad; toss gently. Cover and refrigerate until chilled. At serving time, drain salad, discarding dressing. Divide among 4 salad plates. Top each serving with 1 tablespoon peanuts. Place a small amount of chili sauce at edge of salad. Makes 4 servings.

Festival Chicken Salad
Naum Gai

(Thailand)

The Thai cook who prepared this salad for a temple festival suggested steamed glutinous rice as an accompaniment.

2 whole chicken breasts, boned, skinned
1/2 teaspoon salt
3 green onions, including a little of the tops, chopped
1/4 cup lightly packed cilantro leaves, coarsely chopped
Romaine or other leafy lettuce
4 whole green onions
4 cherry tomatoes
1 cup bean sprouts

Put chicken through medium blade of a meat grinder or process in a food processor fitted with the metal blade. Bring 6 cups water and salt to a boil in a 3-quart saucepan. Add chicken, stirring to break up. Boil 2 minutes or until chicken is white and cooked through. Drain thoroughly; cool. Make Festival Dressing. Place chicken in a medium-size bowl. Add dressing, chopped green onions and cilantro. Toss to combine. Cover and refrigerate until chilled. Line a platter or individual plates with lettuce leaves. Spoon salad over lettuce. Garnish with whole green onions, cherry tomatoes and bean sprouts. Makes 4 servings.

Festival Dressing:
1/3 cup lemon juice
4 teaspoons fish sauce
1 garlic clove, minced
3/4 teaspoon salt
1/2 teaspoon hot red-pepper flakes

Festival Dressing:
Stir ingredients in a small bowl until salt dissolves.

Bean Sprouts & Lotus Root with Tofu (Singapore)

For a complete vegetarian meal, serve this salad with toasted nut bread and a fruit dessert. The recipe was created not by an Asian but by a European chef working at the Hilton in Singapore. The dressing can also be used with other salads.

1/3 cup corn oil
3 tablespoons sesame oil
3 tablespoons soy sauce
3 tablespoons rice vinegar
1 tablespoon distilled white
   vinegar
1/4 lb. Chinese long beans
1/2 lb. bean sprouts
1/4 cup lightly packed cilantro
   leaves
1 tablespoon finely shredded
   gingerroot
1 (1-lb.) carton tofu
1-1/2 cups vegetable oil
1/4 lb. lotus root
4 red-leaf-lettuce or other leafy
   lettuce leaves, cut crosswise into
   slices 1 inch wide
8 cilantro sprigs
1 small fresh red chili, if desired,
   stemmed, seeded, slivered
8 radishes, thinly sliced

Combine corn oil, sesame oil, soy sauce and vinegars in a small jar with a tight-fitting lid. Shake well to blend; set aside. Cut beans into 1-inch pieces. Bring a small saucepan of water to a boil. Add beans; boil 2 minutes. Drain; rinse with cold water. Drain and cool. Combine beans, bean sprouts, cilantro leaves and gingerroot in a large bowl. Shake dressing again. Add 1/3 cup dressing to vegetables; toss lightly to mix. Cover and refrigerate 1 to 2 hours. Drain tofu; pat dry. Cut into slices 3/4 to 1 inch thick. Heat vegetable oil in a wok to 360F (180C) or until a 1-inch bread cube turns golden brown in 60 seconds. Carefully lower tofu slices into oil; fry until lightly browned on each side, about 8 minutes total, turning once. Fry in batches if necessary to avoid overcrowding. Drain on paper towels and cool. Cut into 1/2-inch-thick slices. Peel lotus root with a potato peeler; cut into very thin slices. There should be at least 16 slices. For each serving, place 1/4 of the lettuce on the lower half of a large plate. Fan 1/4 of the tofu slices on lettuce. Arrange cilantro sprigs on either side. Drain the vegetable mixture. If desired, add chili to vegetables just before serving. Spoon 1/4 of the vegetables above the lettuce. Surround with 4 lotus root slices and 1/4 of the radish slices. Spoon some of the remaining dressing over each salad. Makes 4 servings.

Variation
Instead of red chili, add 2 tablespoons finely slivered red bell pepper. Substitute cucumber slices for the lotus root.

VEGETABLES

Wonderful things happen to vegetables in the hands of inventive Asian cooks. Often-dull staples such as cabbage, carrots and potatoes take on fresh new life in an Indian curry or in a soupy Indonesian *sayur* rich with coconut milk. Thai curry paste adds excitement to asparagus or green beans, and eggplant changes its personality according to the origin of the cook. In a Manila restaurant, slender Oriental eggplants might appear with a coconut and vinegar sauce while a Javanese would stew them with sweet Indonesian-style soy sauce, and an Anglo-Indian recipe from Singapore mixes in curry sauce and mango chutney.

Many Indians are vegetarians for religious reasons, and restaurants catering to their needs are found in cities with large Indian communities. In Singapore's Little India, where South Indian food predominates, vegetarian meals are served on a banana leaf or in little metal bowls on a tray. The food is eaten with the fingers, which makes wash basins as essential to the dining rooms as tables and chairs. Rice or bread aid in scooping up the ingredients.

The recipes in this chapter for Spiced Garbanzo Beans and South Indian Potatoes would be part of such a meal. Other components might include Fresh Coconut Chutney and Cucumber-Yogurt Relish, both in the chapter on salads, and Rice & Vegetable Pilaf on page 136. All are from the Madras New Woodlands Restaurant, a typical vegetarian eating place in Singapore.

Yogurt appears in many Indian dishes. One example is a North Indian curry from Singapore that blends mushrooms, tomatoes and peas. Another, from Kuala Lumpur, is Vegetables with Tropical Fruits & Cashews (Navaratnam Korma), a concoction as ornate as a tapestry. If the korma is served to important guests, it might be decorated with glittery, edible silver leaf.

The Indonesian sayur is a vegetable dish that incorporates a large amount of broth. Sayur Lodeh, made with coconut milk, is presented here in a Sumatran version that includes shrimp and shrimp stock. Sayur Asam has a clear broth lightly soured with tamarind and employs peanuts to increase the nutritional value. Sayur Lemak is a Straits Chinese dish from Singapore that contains another important nutritional extender, tofu.

In a region where meat may be scarce and expensive or avoided for religious reasons, tofu is a valuable source of protein. Traditional open air markets and modern supermarkets alike stock it, and contemporary chefs experiment with it, producing dishes such as Bean Sprouts & Lotus Root with Tofu in the chapter on salads.

Tofu dishes can be as simple as a block of soft tofu topped with fried shallots, soy sauce and cilantro or complex enough for a main course. An example of the latter is Fried Tofu (Tahu Goreng), an Indonesian dish of browned tofu squares propped against a mound of lettuce and bean sprouts, sprinkled with a sweet soy sauce dressing and decorated with crushed peanuts.

In Singapore, a Cantonese restaurant serves triangles of fried tofu with a dip of soy sauce laced with fiery red chilies. Such assertive seasoning is not typical of Cantonese cooking, but Southeast Asian people like spicy flavors, and Chinese restaurateurs oblige, often providing their customers with a bowl of chilies to add zest to the meal.

Asparagus with Red Curry Paste
Pad Prik King
(Thailand)

Thinly sliced asparagus cooks in record time. Green beans are a year-round alternative.

3/4 lb. asparagus or green beans
1 tablespoon vegetable oil
1-1/2 teaspoons Red Curry Paste, page 30
1 tablespoon fish sauce
1 tablespoon water
1/4 teaspoon black pepper

Snap off tough ends of asparagus stalks. Cut asparagus diagonally into slices about 1/8 inch thick. If using green beans, snap off ends. Cut diagonally into 1-inch pieces. Cook green beans in boiling salted water in a medium-size saucepan 3 minutes or until crisp-tender; drain. Do not precook asparagus. Heat a wok over medium-high heat. Add oil and heat. Stir in curry paste. Add asparagus or green beans; stir-fry 1 minute. Add fish sauce, water and pepper; stir-fry 1 minute. Spoon onto a platter. Makes 4 servings.

Variation
Vegetables will be very spicy. For a milder flavor, use 1/2 to 1 teaspoon curry paste and 1/8 teaspoon black pepper.

Coconut Curried Vegetables
Gaeng Keo Wan
(Thailand)

Substitute any combination of cooked vegetables in this sauce. Meat may also be added.

1 (14-oz.) can coconut milk (1-3/4 cups)
1 tablespoon Green Curry Paste, page 29
1 tablespoon fish sauce
1 teaspoon lemon juice
1/4 to 1/2 teaspoon salt
1 (10-oz.) pkg. frozen green peas, thawed
1 (15-oz.) can straw mushrooms, drained

Combine coconut milk, curry paste, fish sauce, lemon juice and salt in a large saucepan. Bring to a boil. Add peas and mushrooms. Bring to a boil again. Reduce heat, cover and simmer 5 minutes or until vegetables are heated through. Makes 6 servings.

Eggplant with Coconut-Vinegar Sauce
Paksiw na Latong

(The Philippines)

Slender Oriental eggplants topped with snowy coconut sauce make an unusual meat accompaniment.

1 lb. Oriental eggplants (4 small)
3/4 cup water
1 tablespoon distilled white
    vinegar
2 garlic cloves, crushed
1/2 teaspoon salt
1-1/2 tablespoons chopped parsley

Coconut-Vinegar Sauce:
3/4 cup coconut milk
1/3 cup water
1-1/2 tablespoons distilled white
    vinegar
1 large garlic clove, crushed
1/2 teaspoon salt
1/2 teaspoon cornstarch blended
    with 1/2 teaspoon cold water

Prepare Coconut-Vinegar Sauce; keep warm. Cut off stem ends of eggplants. Cut eggplants into halves lengthwise. Place remaining ingredients except parsley and the sauce in a skillet large enough to hold eggplants in a single layer. Bring to a boil. Lay eggplants cut-sides down in skillet. Cover and simmer 5 minutes; turn. Simmer 5 to 10 more minutes or until tender. Remove eggplants from skillet; carefully pat dry with paper towels. For each serving, place 2 eggplant halves cut-side up on a dinner plate; top with some of the sauce. Sprinkle with chopped parsley. Makes 4 servings.

Coconut-Vinegar Sauce:
Place all ingredients except cornstarch mixture in a small heavy saucepan. Bring to a boil; boil gently 3 minutes, stirring occasionally. Stir cornstarch mixture to blend in cornstarch that has settled; stir into sauce. Boil, stirring, 2 minutes or until slightly thickened. Makes 1 cup.

Javanese Eggplant
Semur Terung

(Indonesia)

Indonesian-style soy sauce adds a special flavor to this dish. Serve it with plain meats such as roast chicken or grilled pork chops.

1 lb. Oriental eggplants (4 small)
    or 1 lb. regular eggplant (1
    small)
5 tablespoons vegetable oil
1/2 medium-size onion, finely
    chopped
1 large garlic clove, minced
1/2 lb. tomatoes (2 medium),
    peeled, chopped
2 tablespoons Indonesian-style
    soy sauce (kecap)
2 tablespoons water
Salt, if desired

Cut off stem ends of Oriental eggplants but do not peel. If using regular eggplant, quarter lengthwise and peel. Cut eggplant diagonally into slices 1/2 inch thick. Heat 4 tablespoons oil in a large non-stick skillet over medium heat. Add eggplant; sauté about 10 minutes or until softened, turning occasionally. Remove from skillet. Add remaining 1 tablespoon oil to skillet. Add onion and garlic; cook until onion is tender. Add tomatoes; cook about 2 minutes or until softened. Return eggplant to pan. Stir in soy sauce and water. Simmer, stirring frequently, 4 to 5 minutes or until eggplant is very soft. Taste and add salt if desired. Makes 4 servings.

Eggplant Curry
Kari Terung

(Singapore)

The secret of the flavor is mango chutney. Make Anglo-Indian Chicken Curry, page 74, at the same time so you'll have the sauce, or reserve the sauce to make this dish later. **Photo on pages 108-109.**

1 small eggplant (about 1 lb.)
1-1/2 cups vegetable oil
1 cup sauce from Anglo-Indian
    Chicken Curry, page 74
3 tablespoons mango chutney,
    chopped
Salt, if desired

Cut off stem and remove a thin slice from bottom end of eggplant. Cut eggplant crosswise into 1/2-inch-thick slices. Cut slices into strips 1/3 to 1/2 inch thick. Heat oil in a wok to 375F (190C). Add 1/3 of the eggplant at a time; fry until soft and lightly browned, about 8 minutes. Drain on paper towels. Eggplant may be prepared in advance to this point. When ready to serve, place eggplant in a 1-quart saucepan. Stir in curry sauce and mango chutney. Bring to a boil. Taste and add salt, if desired. Makes 4 servings.

Variation
Instead of deep-frying eggplant, place in a microwave-safe casserole dish. Toss with 1/4 cup oil. Cover with plastic wrap; microwave on high power (100%) 8 to 10 minutes or until eggplant is soft.

Mixed Vegetables with Tamarind & Peanuts
Sayur Asam

(Indonesia)

An inn in Yogyakarta, the cultural center of Java, prepares vegetables this way.

1/4 teaspoon shrimp paste (terasi),
    if desired
1/2 cup coarsely chopped red
    onion
1 large garlic clove
2 candlenuts
1 teaspoon ground laos
3/4 lb. green beans
1 ear corn
1 Oriental eggplant (about 1/4 lb.)
1 cup chicken broth and 1 cup
    water or 2 cups water
1 serrano chili, sliced crosswise
3/4 teaspoon salt
1/4 cup unsalted Roasted Peanuts,
    page 31
1/2 cup Tamarind Liquid, page 32

If using, wrap shrimp paste in foil; roast on top of range over medium heat 3 minutes. Combine shrimp paste, onion, garlic and candlenuts in a blender or food processor fitted with the metal blade; process until pureed. Stir in laos; set aside. Cut beans diagonally into 1-inch pieces. Cut corn kernels from cob; there should be about 1 cup. Cut eggplant in half lengthwise. Cut each half into thirds lengthwise, then cut crosswise into 1-inch chunks; set aside. Combine green beans, corn and chicken broth in a 3-quart saucepan. Bring to a boil. Add onion mixture, chili and salt. Reduce heat, cover and simmer 10 minutes. Add eggplant and peanuts; simmer, covered, 10 minutes. Add tamarind liquid; simmer, covered, 10 more minutes. Serve vegetables in bowls with cooking liquid. Makes 6 to 8 servings.

Sumatra-Style Vegetables in Coconut Milk
Sayur Lodeh
(Indonesia)

Spoon the sayur onto steamed rice to capture the fragrant sauce.

1/2 lb. medium-size shrimp, shelled, shells reserved, deveined
2 cups water
1-1/2 cups coconut milk
1 lemon grass stalk, pounded
4 (1/8-inch-thick) slices thawed frozen laos root or 1 teaspoon ground laos
2 teaspoons salt
1/8 teaspoon ground turmeric
1/2 lb. green cabbage (1/2 small head)
1 medium-size carrot
8 green beans
1/2 medium-size chayote, peeled, cut into 1-inch chunks (1 cup chunks)
1/2 cup (1/4-inch-thick pieces) canned young corn
1/2 cup cooked tiny shrimp
Basic Steamed Rice, page 133

Wash shrimp shells. Package and freeze shrimp for another use. Place shells and water in a 1-quart saucepan. Bring to a boil. Reduce heat, cover and simmer 30 minutes. Strain stock. Measure and add water to make 2 cups. Place shrimp stock, coconut milk, lemon grass, laos, salt and turmeric in a 3-quart saucepan. Cut cabbage half in half again; remove core. Cut crosswise into 1-inch slices. Quarter carrot lengthwise. Cut crosswise into 1-inch pieces. Cut green beans diagonally into 1-inch pieces. Add cabbage, carrot, green beans, chayote and corn to saucepan. Bring to a boil. Reduce heat, cover and simmer 20 to 30 minutes or until all vegetables are tender. Add shrimp; cook 1 minute to heat. Remove lemon grass. Spoon into a serving bowl. Serve with steamed rice. Makes 6 servings.

Vegetables & Tofu in Coconut Milk
Sayur Lemak

(Singapore)

The word lemak indicates that the ingredients are cooked in coconut milk.

1-1/2 tofu slices (about 7 oz.) from
    a 19-oz. carton packed in slices
1/2 cup vegetable oil
1 tablespoon dried shrimp
2 lemon grass stalks, sliced
6 candlenuts
1 small fresh red chili
1 small dried red chili, soaked
    until softened, drained
1/2 teaspoon shrimp paste (terasi)
1 teaspoon ground laos
3/4 teaspoon ground turmeric
1 small head green cabbage
    (about 1 lb.), quartered, cored
1/2 lb. green beans
1 large carrot (about 6 oz.)
1 qt. coconut milk (4 cups)
1-1/2 teaspoons salt

Cut tofu slice in half. Slit each half (including the extra half slice) from 1 side to the other to make thinner pieces of the same size. Heat oil in a small skillet to 375F (190C) or until a 1-inch bread cube turns golden brown in 50 seconds. Add tofu; fry, in batches, until lightly browned and firm. Drain on paper towels, reserving 3 tablespoons oil. Cool slightly. Cut tofu lengthwise into 1/4-inch-wide strips, then cut strips in half. Soak shrimp in hot water until softened, about 30 minutes. Drain and mince. Combine lemon grass, candlenuts, fresh and dried chilies and shrimp paste in a food processor fitted with the metal blade; process until pureed. Scrape into a small bowl; stir in laos and turmeric. Set aside. Cut cabbage crosswise into slices about 1/2 inch wide. Cut beans diagonally into thin slices 1-1/2 inches long. Cut carrots crosswise into 1-1/2-inch chunks. Cut chunks lengthwise into 1/4-inch-thick slices; cut slices into thin sticks. Heat reserved oil in a Dutch oven over medium heat. Add lemon grass mixture; fry, stirring, 1-1/2 minutes or until fragrant, being careful not to burn. Stir in cabbage, beans, carrot, shrimp, coconut milk and salt. Bring to a boil. Reduce heat, cover and simmer 45 minutes or until vegetables are tender, stirring occasionally; do not boil vigorously as this will curdle coconut milk. Vegetables should be soupy; if sauce cooks down too much, add water as needed. Add tofu slices; heat through. Serve vegetables in bowls with sauce. Makes 8 servings.

Tip: Tofu comes packed in solid blocks and in slices. The sliced tofu is convenient to use when only a small amount is needed. Place the unused portion in a clean container, cover with water and store, covered, in the refrigerator. Change the water every day or two to keep the tofu fresh. It will keep up to a week.

North Indian Vegetable Curry with Yogurt
Shabnam Curry   (Singapore)

Imaginative seasoning turns creamed vegetables into an exotic dish for company. The recipe is from the Oberoi Imperial Hotel.

1 large onion, cut into chunks
3 large garlic cloves
1 (2-inch) gingerroot piece, peeled, sliced
3 tablespoons vegetable oil
3/4 lb. mushrooms, sliced
1 lb. tomatoes (4 medium), unpeeled, coarsely chopped
1 (8-oz.) carton plain yogurt (1 cup)
1 teaspoon ground coriander
1/4 teaspoon red (cayenne) pepper
1/2 teaspoon ground cumin
1/2 teaspoon ground turmeric
1/4 teaspoon white pepper
1/4 cup whipping cream
1/4 cup water
1-1/2 teaspoons salt
1-1/2 cups thawed frozen green peas
1 tablespoon butter

Combine onion, garlic and gingerroot in a blender or food processor fitted with the metal blade; process until pureed. Heat oil in a Dutch oven over medium heat. Add onion mixture; sauté, stirring frequently, 8 to 10 minutes or until onion is tender, being careful not to burn. Add mushrooms; cook about 3 minutes or until slightly wilted. Add tomatoes, yogurt, coriander, red pepper, cumin, turmeric and white pepper; cook 5 minutes, stirring occasionally. Stir in cream, water and salt. Simmer, covered, 5 minutes. Add peas; simmer, covered, 5 minutes. Add butter; heat until melted. Serve in bowls. Makes 8 servings.

South Indian Potatoes
Alu Bhaji   (Singapore)

Southern Indian dishes are often very hot. Reduce the chili powder for a milder flavor. Garnish with cilantro, if desired. **Photo on page 110.**

2 tablespoons vegetable oil
1 large onion, chopped
1/2 to 1 teaspoon hot chili powder
1 teaspoon ground turmeric
1 teaspoon ground coriander
1 teaspoon salt
1 lb. russet potatoes, peeled, cut into 1/2-inch cubes, in cold water
1 cup water
1 teaspoon garam masala

Heat oil in a medium-size saucepan over medium heat. Add onion; cook until tender, stirring frequently. Stir in chili powder, turmeric, coriander and salt. Add potatoes and the 1 cup water. Bring to a boil. Reduce heat, cover and simmer 30 minutes or until potatoes are tender. Stir in garam masala. Makes 4 servings.

Vegetables with Tropical Fruits & Cashews
Navaratnam Korma

(Malaysia)

This North Indian dish from Jothy's restaurant in Kuala Lumpur will have the best flavor if prepared a day or two in advance and reheated. When selecting the fruits, choose the large Mexican-style papaya, if available, rather than the smaller Hawaiian papaya. **Photo on page 110.**

3 tablespoons vegetable oil
1 (2-inch) cinnamon stick
Seeds from 1 green cardamom pod
1 large onion (8 oz.), finely chopped
2 large garlic cloves, minced
1 (1/2-inch-thick) gingerroot slice, minced
6 to 8 oz. tomatoes (2 small tomatoes), unpeeled, diced
1/2 cup water
1/2 cup plain yogurt
1 large carrot (6 oz.), peeled, cut into 1/2-inch cubes
1/2 cup cubed cauliflowerets (1/2-inch cubes)
7 to 8 green beans, cut into 1/2-inch slices (1/2 cup)
3 tablespoons fresh or thawed frozen green peas
1 teaspoon salt
2 tablespoons whipping cream
3/4 cup cubed fresh pineapple (1/2-inch cubes)
3/4 cup cubed papaya (1/2-inch cubes)
1/2 teaspoon ground turmeric
1/4 teaspoon white pepper
12 unsalted roasted cashews, chopped
1 tablespoon plus 1 teaspoon golden raisins, soaked in warm water to plump, drained

Heat oil in a 3-quart saucepan over medium heat. Add cinnamon stick and cardamom seeds; stir to coat with oil. Add onion; cook until lightly browned. Add garlic and gingerroot. Cook 2 minutes, stirring to prevent burning. Increase heat to medium; add tomatoes. Cook, stirring, 5 minutes. Add water and yogurt; bring to a boil. Add carrot, cauliflowerets, green beans, peas and salt. Reduce heat, cover and simmer 25 minutes. Stir in cream, pineapple, papaya, turmeric and white pepper. Cover and simmer 20 minutes, stirring occasionally. Spoon into a heated serving bowl. Sprinkle with cashews and raisins. Makes 6 servings.

Spiced Garbanzo Beans

Kabli Channa

(Singapore)

Think of this South Indian dish as chili beans with a change of seasonings.

1-1/3 cups dried garbanzo beans
6 cups water
1-1/2 teaspoons salt
2 tablespoons vegetable oil
2 small to medium onions, chopped
2 garlic cloves, minced
1 teaspoon minced gingerroot
1 teaspoon ground turmeric
1 teaspoon ground cumin
1 teaspoon ground coriander
1 teaspoon mango powder (amchur) or lemon juice
1 teaspoon garam masala
1 tablespoon chopped cilantro
4 small serrano chilies

Place beans in a 3-quart saucepan. Add enough water to cover; let stand overnight. The next day, drain and rinse beans. Return to saucepan. Add the 6 cups water and salt. Bring to a boil. Reduce heat, cover loosely and simmer about 2 hours or until tender. Drain beans, reserving 1-1/2 cups cooking liquid. Wash and dry saucepan. Heat oil in saucepan over medium heat. Add onions, garlic and gingerroot; cook, stirring, until onions are tender but not browned. Stir in turmeric, cumin, coriander, mango powder and garam masala. Stir in garbanzo beans and reserved cooking liquid. Bring to a boil. Reduce heat, cover and simmer 10 minutes. Turn into a heated serving bowl. Sprinkle with cilantro. Garnish with chilies. Makes 6 to 8 servings.

Stir-Fried Cabbage & Eggs

Kobis Dan Telur

(Malaysia)

This Chinese-style dish was demonstrated during a cooking class at the Kuala Lumpur YWCA.

1 head green cabbage, about 22 oz., quartered, cored
4 eggs
1-1/2 tablespoons vegetable oil
1-1/2 teaspoons butter
2 garlic cloves, minced
1/4 lb. medium-size shrimp, shelled, deveined, minced or finely ground
1/4 lb. lean pork, minced or finely ground
1 (6-oz.) red onion, halved lengthwise, thinly sliced
1 teaspoon salt
1/4 teaspoon black pepper
1/2 teaspoon MSG, if desired

Cut cabbage quarters crosswise into thin slices; set aside. Break eggs into a small bowl; do not beat. Set aside. Heat oil and butter in a wok or large non-stick skillet. Add garlic; cook until garlic starts to brown. Add shrimp and pork; cook, stirring, until mixture is lightly browned. Add onion and cabbage; stir until cabbage starts to wilt. Add eggs, salt, pepper and MSG, if desired. Stir to break up eggs and combine with cabbage. Cook until eggs are set and mixture is dry. Makes 6 large servings.

Dry Vegetable Curry with Cilantro

Nentara

(Singapore)

Think vegetables are boring? Not when prepared with ginger and spices as in this recipe from Omar Khayyam, a restaurant in Singapore.

2 fresh mild green
   (Anaheim-type) chilies
1/2 lb. small whole boiling onions
   (10 to 12), peeled
1/4 cup Clarified Butter, page 32
1 teaspoon cumin seeds
1/2 teaspoon ground turmeric
Dash red (cayenne) pepper
1-1/4 teaspoons salt
2 tablespoons shredded
   gingerroot
1 lb. cauliflower (1/2 large head),
   trimmed, cut into small
   flowerets
1 large russet potato, peeled, cut
   into 1-inch chunks, in cold
   water
1/4 teaspoon garam masala
1-1/2 cups thawed frozen green
   peas
1 large tomato, unpeeled, cut into
   1-inch chunks
2 cups lightly packed cilantro
   leaves, finely chopped

To peel chilies, place in a single layer on a baking sheet; broil until blistered all over. Place in a paper bag 15 minutes to steam. Remove peel; discard stems and seeds. Cut chilies into thin strips 1-1/2 to 2 inches long; there will be about 1/2 cup strips. Set aside. Drop onions into a small saucepan of boiling water. Boil 5 minutes; drain. Heat butter in a Dutch oven over medium heat. Add cumin seeds; fry 30 seconds, stirring. Stir in turmeric, red pepper and salt. Add ginger-root, chilies, onions, cauliflowerets and potato. Sprinkle with garam masala. Reduce heat, cover and simmer 20 minutes, stirring occasionally. Add peas and tomato; cook 5 more minutes. Just before serving, stir in cilantro. Turn into a heated large serving bowl. Makes 6 servings.

Corn Pancakes
Begedel Jagung

Javanese-style corn cakes go equally well with American fried chicken or Broiled Chicken Dewi, page 76.

1 egg
1 (8-3/4-oz.) can cream-style corn
1/4 cup canned shrimp, coarsely chopped
2 large green onions, white part only, finely chopped
1 tablespoon celery leaves, minced
1 small garlic clove, minced
1/2 teaspoon salt
1/8 teaspoon black pepper
2-1/2 tablespoons all-purpose flour
1 tablespoon butter

Beat egg in a medium-size bowl. Stir in corn, shrimp, green onions, celery leaves, garlic, salt and pepper. Stir in flour. Heat a griddle or large skillet over medium-high heat. Melt 1/2 the butter on griddle. For each pancake, spoon 2 tablespoons batter onto griddle. Cook until browned on bottom. Turn and cook other side until browned. Add remaining butter to griddle as needed. Makes 8 to 9 fritters or 4 servings.

Fried Tofu with Soy Sauce & Chili Dip
Tahu Goreng Canton

Bland tofu goes well with a dip that is sweet, salty and spicy.

1 (19-oz.) carton tofu, packed in 4 slices
1/2 cup soy sauce
1/4 cup packed dark-brown sugar
2 teaspoons Mr. Lee's Red-Chili Sauce, page 29
Vegetable oil for deep-frying

Drain tofu. Cut each slice in half crosswise to make 8 thinner slices of the same size. Cut slices in half diagonally to make 16 triangles. Stir soy sauce and sugar in a small bowl until sugar dissolves. Divide among 4 small sauce dishes. Place 1/2 teaspoon chili sauce in center of each. Heat 1/2 inch oil in a medium-size skillet until a 1-inch bread cube turns golden brown in 50 seconds. Add tofu triangles a few at a time; fry until lightly browned, 1-1/2 to 2 minutes on each side. Drain on paper towels. Serve at once with sauce for dipping. Makes 4 servings.

Tofu with Shallots & Cilantro
Tahu Cina

(Malaysia)

A Chinese resident of Kuala Lumpur suggested serving tofu this way as an appetizer or side dish.

1 (1-lb.) carton soft tofu, in 1 piece
2 tablespoons vegetable oil
5 large shallots, minced
3 tablespoons soy sauce
1/4 cup lightly packed cilantro leaves

Remove tofu from carton 1 hour before serving; drain well. Place on a platter. Bring to room temperature. Drain off any liquid from platter; pat tofu dry with a paper towel. Heat oil in a small, heavy saucepan. Add shallots; fry until tender but not browned. Spoon oil and shallots onto tofu. Pour soy sauce over tofu. Sprinkle with cilantro. Makes 6 servings.

Fried Tofu
Tahu Goreng

(Indonesia)

Hot tofu, crunchy cold bean sprouts and lettuce make an interesting combination. Photo on page 110.

3 large iceberg-lettuce leaves
1/4 lb. bean sprouts
1/2 cup vegetable oil
2 tablespoons raw peanuts
2 tofu slices (about 9-1/2 oz.) from a 19-oz. carton packed in slices

Soy-Sauce Dressing:
3 tablespoons mushroom soy sauce or regular soy sauce
2 tablespoons rice vinegar
2 tablespoons sugar
1 small garlic clove, minced
1/8 to 1/4 teaspoon hot red-pepper flakes

Cut lettuce crosswise into 1/4-inch slices; there should be 2 cups. Wash bean sprouts; drain thoroughly. Mix bean sprouts and lettuce in a medium-size bowl. Cover and refrigerate. Prepare Soy-Sauce Dressing. Heat oil in a small saucepan to 375F (190C) or until a 1-inch bread cube turns golden brown in 50 seconds. Add peanuts; fry until browned, being careful not to burn. Remove with a slotted spoon; drain on paper towels. Cool; reserve oil. Crush peanuts in a mortar or with a rolling pin; set aside. Just before serving, remove tofu from container. Cut each slice in half through the side to make 4 thinner slices of the same size. Cut these slices in half crosswise, making 8 tofu slices. Reheat oil in saucepan. Fry tofu slices 2 or 3 at a time until lightly browned and puffy. Drain on paper towels; keep warm. To serve, mound lettuce mixture on a round platter. Sprinkle evenly with Soy-Sauce Dressing. Place fried tofu around edges of salad. Sprinkle crushed peanuts over all. Makes 4 servings.

Soy-Sauce Dressing:
Combine all ingredients in a small bowl; let stand 30 minutes or longer to blend flavors. Makes 1/3 cup.

RICE & NOODLES

Rice is the perfect companion to foods with spicy seasonings and generous amounts of sauce. It is so important to the Asian diet—"Asia" here meaning the region in its broader sense, not just the southeast portion—that 90 percent of the world's rice is grown and consumed there. This figure comes from the International Rice Research Institute located at Los Baños in the Philippines. There scientists have developed rice varieties that will produce abundant harvests in areas diverse in altitude, climate and rainfall.

Rice is the center of a meal in Thailand, a neutral background for the exquisite range of flavors involved in Thai cookery. Indonesia has its rijsttafel (rice table), a parade of dishes designed to go with rice. In Bali, woodcarvers fashion graceful images of *Dewi Seri,* the goddess of rice. Eaten at every economic level, rice may be the main component of a meal for a poor family, supplemented by a bit of fish or vegetables when available.

Premium grades of rice include the long-grain variety that the Thais call jasmine in honor of its aromatic qualities and the refined *basmati* rice favored by Indian cooks. In the Philippines, rice with a shorter grain is common. In Indonesia, long- and medium-grain rices are sometimes cooked together.

Throughout the region, desserts and dumplings are made with glutinous rice, a short-grain rice that becomes sticky and compact when cooked. A black variety of glutinous rice appears in certain dishes including a sweet porridge made with coconut milk (see page 156).

The most efficient way to cook rice is with an electric rice cooker. These are manufactured in sizes appropriate for small households as well as larger ones. Rice can also be cooked successfully in an ordinary pan following the method described in Basic Steamed Rice.

Like rice, noodles often form the bulk of an Asian meal, serving as an extender for meat and other ingredients that are too expensive to eat in quantity. The variety of noodles produced in Southeast Asia is amazing. Rice and wheat flour noodles come fresh or dried, thick or thin. There are also bean thread noodles, produced from mung bean starch.

Dried rice noodles and bean thread noodles require a different mode of preparation from wheat noodles. They are usually soaked until soft, then boiled until tender. In some cases, they are added to a dish without prior boiling.

Many types of Asian noodles are available in the United States. In areas where the choice is limited, common domestic forms of pasta can be substituted. For example, ordinary spaghetti works well in a recipe for the noodle dish known in the Philippines as *pancit,* which is usually made with pancit Canton, a dry noodle processed so that it cooks quickly.

In Southeast Asia, noodles are rarely served plain but come dressed up with meat, seafood, vegetables, tofu and sauces or broth. A clever idea for entertaining, observed at a party in Bangkok, was a noodle bar. Guests were given a bowl of plain noodles. They then chose from an assortment of toppings and condiments set out buffet-style to compose a dish suited to their taste.

Basic Steamed Rice

For best results, use a heavy pan for slow, even heating. To measure the amount of water needed, Asian cooks place the tip of a forefinger on the rice, then add water up to the first joint. **Photo on pages 108-109.**

1 cup long-grain rice
2 cups water

Place rice in a heavy 3-quart saucepan. Add water to cover; swish through rice with your hand. Drain off any chaff that floats to the surface. Turn rice into a sieve, rinse well and drain. Return to pan. Add 2 cups water. Cover and bring to a boil. Boil gently 5 to 10 minutes, until water is absorbed. The time required for this step will vary according to the utensil used and intensity of heat. Reduce heat to very low; steam, without stirring, 20 to 30 minutes or until rice is tender. Use a heat diffuser if necessary to prevent the rice from burning and sticking. Fluff with a fork before serving. Makes 4 servings.

Variations
(Indonesia)
For a slightly stickier version of steamed rice, combine 1/3 cup medium-grain rice with 2/3 cup long-grain rice. Cook as directed.
Coconut Rice (Singapore, Malaysia)
Substitute 1/2 cup coconut milk for 1/2 cup of the water. Add 1/2 teaspoon salt.

Garlic Rice
Sinangag
(The Philippines)

This rice, served with dried fish, sausage or other meats, is a breakfast staple in the Philippines. Some cooks fry the garlic just long enough to flavor the oil. Others like it golden brown and crisp.

1 tablespoon vegetable oil
1 large garlic clove, minced
1 teaspoon salt
1 cup long-grain rice, cooked, refrigerated overnight

Heat a wok over medium heat. Add oil and heat. Add garlic and salt; fry until fragrant and oil is flavored, being careful not to burn garlic. Add rice; toss until rice is heated through. Makes 4 servings.

Fried Rice

(The Philippines)

The Filipino touch in this basically Chinese dish is the addition of Maggi seasoning.

2 tablespoons vegetable oil
1 garlic clove, minced
1-1/2 teaspoons chicken-bouillon
  granules
1 cup long-grain rice, cooked,
  refrigerated overnight
2 green onions, minced
2 tablespoons shredded carrot
1 teaspoon Maggi seasoning

Heat a wok over medium heat. Add oil and heat. Add garlic; fry a few seconds. Stir in bouillon granules. Immediately add rice; stir to break up rice and mix with seasonings. Add onions, carrot and Maggi seasoning; cook, stirring, until rice is hot and evenly colored. Makes 4 servings.

Java Rice

(The Philippines)

The Aristocrat Restaurant in Manila accompanies its barbecued chicken with rice that acquires its bright color from orange annatto seeds. **Photo on page 107.**

2 tablespoons vegetable oil
2 teaspoons annatto seeds
1 cup long-grain rice, washed,
  drained
1/3 cup canned tomato sauce
1-2/3 cups water
1 teaspoon salt

Combine oil and annatto seeds in a small skillet. Heat gently over low heat until oil turns a golden orange, about 5 minutes, swirling seeds in skillet several times. Strain oil; discard seeds. Pour oil into a Dutch oven and heat. Add rice; sauté 2 minutes. Add tomato sauce, water and salt. Cover and boil until liquid is absorbed, 5 to 10 minutes. Reduce heat to very low; steam, without stirring, 30 minutes or until rice is tender. Use a heat diffuser if necessary to prevent rice from burning and sticking. Fluff with a fork before serving. Makes 4 servings.

Rice Pilaf

(The Philippines)

Unlike Chinese fried rice, this pilaf is prepared without prior cooking of the rice.

2 tablespoons vegetable oil
1 cup long-grain rice, washed,
  drained
1/2 medium-size onion, finely
  chopped
1 large garlic clove, minced
1-3/4 cups chicken broth
3 tablespoons soy sauce
1/4 teaspoon salt
1/4 cup chopped green-onion tops
  (3 onions)
2 tablespoons coarsely shredded
  carrot

Heat oil in a Dutch oven over medium heat. Add rice; fry until rice starts to change color, about 5 minutes. Add onion and garlic; fry until tender but not browned. Stir in remaining ingredients. Cover and boil until broth is absorbed, 5 to 10 minutes. Reduce heat to very low; steam, without stirring, 30 minutes or until rice is tender. Use a heat diffuser if necessary to prevent rice from burning and sticking. Fluff with a fork before serving. Makes 4 servings.

Yellow Rice
Nasi Kuning

(Indonesia)

Indonesians serve this colorful rice on special occasions. The recipe comes from Jakarta. **Photo on page 38.**

2 cups coconut milk
1 (1/4-inch-thick) gingerroot slice
1 (2-inch) lemon grass piece, crushed
1/2 teaspoon ground turmeric
1 teaspoon salt
1 cup long-grain rice, washed, drained
Crisp-Fried Onion Shreds, page 31
1 medium-size tomato, thinly sliced
1/2 cucumber, thinly sliced

Place coconut milk, gingerroot and lemon grass in a heavy 3-quart saucepan; bring to a boil. Reduce heat; simmer 15 minutes. Strain, discarding gingerroot and lemon grass; return coconut milk to saucepan. Stir in turmeric, salt and rice. Bring to a boil. Reduce heat, cover and simmer until liquid is absorbed, 5 to 10 minutes. Reduce heat to very low; steam, without stirring, 30 minutes or until rice is tender. Use a heat diffuser if necessary to prevent rice from burning and sticking. Mound rice in center of a large round platter. Sprinkle with fried onions. Alternate tomato and cucumber slices around edge. Makes 4 to 6 servings.

Pineapple Rice
Kao Pad Supparod

(Thailand)

Buy a large pineapple, cut it in half lengthwise and scoop out the fruit. Then use the shells as serving containers for the rice.

1 Chinese sausage
1/2 cup water
12 medium-size shrimp, shelled, deveined
1 tablespoon vegetable oil
1/4 medium-size onion, finely chopped
1 garlic clove, minced
1-1/2 teaspoons salt
1 cup long-grain rice, cooked, refrigerated overnight
2 tablespoons golden raisins, soaked in hot water until soft, drained
1 egg
1/2 cup diced fresh pineapple
2 green onions, chopped

Place sausage and 1/2 cup water in a small skillet; bring to a boil. Reduce heat, cover and simmer 10 minutes, turning sausage after 5 minutes. Drain sausage; cut diagonally into thin slices. Set aside. Cook shrimp in boiling salted water 3 minutes or just until pink. Drain; set aside. Heat a wok over medium-high heat. Add oil and heat. Add onion; cook until tender but not browned. Add garlic; cook a few seconds to flavor oil. Add salt, then rice; toss until rice is heated. Push rice to 1 side of wok. Add sausage, shrimp and drained raisins. Stir until heated, then toss to mix with rice. Make a well in center. Break egg into well, stir until scrambled, then mix with rice. Make well again, pushing rice mixture up side of wok. Add pineapple. Cook until heated, then mix with rice. Stir in green onions. Spoon into a serving dish or pineapple shells. Makes 4 to 6 servings.

Celebration Rice
Nasi Beraini

(Brunei)

Golden rice, accented with almonds and cashews, is a banquet dish from the palace of the sultan in Brunei. The seasonings show Indian influence.

5 tablespoons ghee, vegetable oil
  or Clarified Butter, page 32
1/3 cup sliced shallots
1 small garlic clove, minced
1 (1/4-inch-thick) gingerroot slice,
  minced
1-1/2 teaspoons salt
1/2 teaspoon ground turmeric
2-1/2 cups water
1-1/4 cups long-grain rice, washed,
  drained
2 tablespoons plain yogurt
1/2 small tomato, sliced
1/2 small fresh red chili, in 1
  piece
1 cilantro sprig, chopped
1-1/2 teaspoons chopped blanched
  almonds
1-1/2 teaspoons chopped raw
  cashews

Heat 2 tablespoons ghee or oil in a small skillet. Add 1/2 the shallots; fry until golden brown. Drain on paper towels; set aside. Mince remaining shallots as finely as possible. Heat remaining 3 tablespoons ghee or oil in a Dutch oven. Add minced shallots, garlic and gingerroot; sauté gently 2 minutes. Stir in salt and turmeric. Add water; bring to a boil. Add rice, yogurt, tomato, chili, cilantro and nuts. Cover and simmer over low heat about 40 minutes or until water is absorbed and rice is tender. Discard chili. Spoon into a serving dish; garnish with fried shallots. Makes 6 servings.

Rice & Vegetable Pilaf
Pullao

(Singapore)

This vegetarian rice dish from Singapore originated in southern India.

2-1/3 cups basmati rice
3 tablespoons vegetable oil
4 green cardamom pods
4 whole cloves
1 (2-inch) cinnamon stick
1/4 cup chopped onion
1/4 cup finely diced carrot
1/4 cup finely diced cauliflowerets
1/4 cup thawed frozen green peas
  or drained canned green peas
1 teaspoon cumin seeds
1 teaspoon chili powder
2 teaspoons salt
2-1/3 cups water

Wash rice thoroughly. Soak 1 hour in water to cover. Drain well. Heat oil in a heavy 3-quart saucepan over medium heat. Add cardamom pods, cloves and cinnamon; fry 1 minute. Add onion; fry until golden brown, about 4 minutes. Add carrot, cauliflowerets, peas, cumin seeds, chili powder and salt, then stir in rice. Add water. Cover, bring to a boil and boil until liquid is absorbed, about 10 minutes. Reduce heat to low; steam, without stirring, about 30 minutes or until rice is tender. Use a heat diffuser if necessary to prevent rice from burning and sticking. Fluff with a fork before serving. Makes 6 servings.

Aromatic Rice
Nasi Briyani

(Malaysia)

The Omar Khayam restaurant in Kuala Lumpur serves rice that is fragrant with sweet spices.

1 cup basmati rice
6 tablespoons ghee, vegetable oil
   or Clarified Butter, page 32
1 (2-inch) cinnamon stick
4 whole cloves
4 green cardamom pods
6 black peppercorns
1 garlic clove, minced
1 medium onion, halved through
   stem end, thinly sliced
1-3/4 cups chicken broth
1 teaspoon salt
1 teaspoon ground turmeric
1-1/2 teaspoons water

Wash rice thoroughly. Soak 1 hour in water to cover. Drain well. Heat 2 tablespoons ghee or oil in a heavy 3-quart saucepan. Add cinnamon stick, cloves, cardamom pods and peppercorns; fry 30 seconds. Add garlic and 1/2 the onion; fry until onion is tender. Add rice; fry 2 minutes, stirring frequently. Add broth and salt. Cover and boil until broth is absorbed, 5 to 10 minutes. Reduce heat to very low; steam, without stirring, 30 minutes or until rice is tender. Use a heat diffuser if necessary to prevent rice from burning and sticking. Meanwhile, heat 3 tablespoons of remaining ghee in a small skillet; add remaining onion. Fry until onion is brown and crisp. Remove with a slotted spoon. Drain onion on paper towels; set aside. Pour remaining 1 tablespoon ghee or butter over top of cooked rice. Blend turmeric with water in a small cup; drizzle over rice. Cover and steam 10 more minutes. Spoon into a serving dish; sprinkle with fried onion. Makes 4 to 6 servings.

Rice E & O Style
Nasi Minyak

(Malaysia)

Ginger juice gives a delicate flavor to this rice dish from the Eastern & Oriental Hotel, a British structure that brings to mind colonial days in Penang.

1 (1-inch-thick) gingerroot piece,
   sliced
3 tablespoons Clarified Butter,
   page 32
1 large shallot, sliced
1 large garlic clove, minced
1 (1-inch) cinnamon stick
2 whole cloves
1 whole star anise
3 tablespoons raw cashew pieces
1 tablespoon golden raisins
1 cup long-grain rice, washed,
   drained
3 tablespoons canned tomato
   sauce
1-3/4 cups water
1 teaspoon salt

Pound gingerroot slices in a mortar until thoroughly crushed. Place 1/3 of the gingerroot at a time in palm of your hand; squeeze out as much juice as possible into a small dish. Discard pulp; there should be 1- to 1-1/2 tablespoons juice. Heat clarified butter in a Dutch oven. Add shallot, garlic, cinnamon stick, cloves and star anise. Fry, stirring, 2 minutes. Add cashews and raisins; fry, stirring, 2 minutes. Add rice; cook, stirring, 30 seconds. Stir in tomato sauce, ginger juice, water and salt. Bring to a boil, cover and boil until liquid is absorbed, 5 to 10 minutes. Reduce heat to very low; steam, without stirring, 30 minutes or until rice is tender. Use a heat diffuser if necessary to prevent rice from burning and sticking. Fluff with a fork before serving. Makes 4 to 6 servings.

Pot-Roasted Rice with Chicken & Mushrooms
Com Tay Cam
(Vietnam)

Advance preparation makes this a convenient dish for entertaining. The rice is cooked the day before, then baked with the chicken and mushrooms.

1 medium-size onion, quartered
    lengthwise
2 tablespoons vegetable oil
1 cup long-grain rice, washed,
    drained
1 garlic clove, minced
2 cups chicken broth
1/4 teaspoon salt, or to taste
1 tablespoon vegetable oil
1/2 chicken breast, boned,
    skinned, cut into 1/2-inch cubes
1/4 lb. mushrooms, cut into
    1/2-inch cubes
2 tablespoons soy sauce

Mince 1 of the onion quarters; wrap and refrigerate remaining onion. Heat 2 tablespoons oil in a Dutch oven over medium heat. Add rice; fry until rice starts to change color. Add minced onion and garlic; cook until onion is almost tender but not browned. Add 1 cup of the broth and salt. Cover and boil until broth is absorbed, about 3 minutes. Add remaining 1 cup broth. Cover and boil about 3 minutes or until broth is absorbed. Reduce heat to very low; steam, without stirring, 30 minutes. Use a heat diffuser if necessary to prevent rice from sticking and burning. Cool rice. Spoon into a bowl, cover and refrigerate overnight. The next day, bring rice to room temperature. Preheat oven to 350F (175C). Heat 1 tablespoon oil in a medium-size skillet. Add chicken; stir-fry over medium heat about 3 minutes. Add mushrooms; cook until wilted. Add soy sauce; simmer until most of liquid cooks away. Toss chicken mixture with rice. Turn into a 1-1/2-quart baking dish. Cover and bake rice 30 minutes or until heated through. Meanwhile, cut reserved onion quarters into thin slices; fry as directed for Crisp-Fried Onion Shreds, page 31. Serve rice sprinkled with fried onions. Makes 6 servings.

Lemony Yellow Rice
Kao Man
(Thailand)

Lime leaves and lemon grass give a wonderful aromatic flavor to the rice. If they are not available, substitute two bay leaves and two strips of lemon peel, each 1/2 inch wide and 2 to 3 inches long.

1 cup long-grain rice, washed,
    drained
1 cup chicken broth
1 cup coconut milk
1 teaspoon salt
1/2 teaspoon ground turmeric
1 lemon grass stalk, pounded
4 kaffir lime leaves, finely
    shredded

Place rice in a heavy 3-quart saucepan. Stir in chicken broth, coconut milk, salt and turmeric. Add lemon grass and lime leaves. Cover, bring to a boil and boil until liquid is absorbed, 5 to 10 minutes. Reduce heat to very low; steam, without stirring, 30 minutes or until rice is tender. Use a heat diffuser if necessary to prevent rice from burning and sticking. Remove lemon grass and fluff rice with a fork before serving. Makes 4 servings.

Baked Yellow Rice
Nasi Kuning

(Singapore)

Adapted from traditional recipes, this is an easy way to prepare rice.

1 cup long-grain rice, washed,
   drained
1 tablespoon butter
1 teaspoon salt
1/2 teaspoon curry powder
1/4 teaspoon ground turmeric
2 cups boiling water

Preheat oven to 400F (205C). Place rice in an ungreased 1-1/2-quart baking dish with a tight-fitting lid. Add butter, salt, curry powder and turmeric. Add boiling water; stir until butter melts. Cover; bake 25 minutes or until water is absorbed and rice is tender. Let stand, covered, 5 minutes before serving. Fluff with a fork before serving. Makes 4 servings.

Stir-Fried Rice Noodles
Pad Thai

(Thailand)

Sweet-sour seasonings, crisp bean sprouts and crunchy peanuts stirred into the noodles make this a memorable dish.

8 oz. (1/8-inch-wide) rice noodles
1 whole chicken breast, boned,
   skinned
8 medium-size shrimp, shelled,
   deveined
1/2 cup water
1/4 cup fish sauce
3 tablespoons sugar
1 tablespoon lime juice
1 teaspoon paprika
1/8 teaspoon red (cayenne)
   pepper
1/2 lb. bean sprouts
3 green onions, white part only,
   cut into 1-inch shreds
3 tablespoons vegetable oil
4 large garlic cloves, finely
   chopped
1 egg
4 tablespoons finely crushed
   Roasted Peanuts, page 31

Place rice noodles in a large bowl. Cover with water; soak 45 minutes. Cut chicken into 1-1/2" x 1/3" strips. Cut shrimp in half lengthwise; set aside. Combine water, fish sauce, sugar, lime juice, paprika and red pepper in a small bowl; set aside. Reserve 1/4 of bean sprouts for topping; combine remaining bean sprouts and green onions. Drain noodles. Heat a wok over medium-high heat. Add oil and heat. Add garlic; fry until garlic starts to brown. Increase heat. Add chicken; stir-fry until almost cooked, about 2 minutes. Push chicken to 1 side. Break egg into wok. Stir quickly to break up yolk and scramble egg. When egg is set, mix with chicken. Add drained noodles, shrimp, fish-sauce mixture and 3 tablespoons peanuts. Cook and stir over high heat 2 to 3 minutes or until noodles are soft and most of liquid is absorbed. Add green-onion mixture; cook, stirring, 1 more minute. Spoon onto a heated platter. Sprinkle with reserved bean sprouts, then with remaining peanuts. Makes 6 servings.

Sweet Sticky Noodles

Mee Krob

(Thailand)

Crisp and syrupy sweet, these noodles are hard to resist. The crucial step is to boil the sauce down to a thick glaze. If the sauce has too much liquid, the noodles will be soggy. **Photo on page 38.**

1/2 cup sugar
1/4 cup water
1-1/2 tablespoons ketchup
1 tablespoon tomato paste
1 tablespoon lemon juice
1 tablespoon fish sauce
2 tablespoons shredded carrot
1/2 egg, beaten (2 tablespoons)
1/4 teaspoon all-purpose flour
1-1/2 cups vegetable oil
4 oz. thin rice stick noodles
6 small shallots or 1/2
   medium-size onion, finely
   chopped
3 large garlic cloves, finely
   chopped
16 medium-size shrimp, shelled,
   deveined
1 teaspoon fish sauce
Dash black pepper
1/4 lb. bean sprouts
1/2 cup lightly packed cilantro
   sprigs

Combine sugar, water, ketchup, tomato paste, lemon juice and 1 tablespoon fish sauce in a measuring cup; set aside. Half fill a small saucepan with water; bring to a boil. Add carrot; boil 1 minute. Drain and set aside. Combine egg and flour in a small bowl; set aside. Heat oil in a wok to 375F (190C) or until a 1-inch bread cube turns golden brown in 50 seconds. Take a small handful of rice sticks, break up and drop into oil. Press with spatula to submerge completely. Almost instantly, rice sticks will puff up. Drain on paper towels. Continue until all rice sticks are fried. Remove any noodle scraps from oil. Whisk egg mixture to lighten, then pour into oil. Egg will puff up. Fry until lightly browned. Remove and drain on paper towels. Set aside for garnish. Drain oil from wok, reserving oil; clean wok. Reheat 1-1/2 tablespoons oil in wok over medium heat. Add shallots and garlic; cook over medium heat until limp and lightly browned, 1-1/2 to 2 minutes. Add shrimp; cook 2 to 3 minutes or until pink. Stir in 1 teaspoon fish sauce and pepper. Remove shrimp mixture from wok to a plate. Add sugar mixture to wok; boil until reduced to a thick, syrupy glaze, about 5 minutes. Mixture must be almost dry or it will wilt noodles. Stir shrimp mixture into glaze. Turn off heat. Add rice sticks to wok; stir until coated with glaze, breaking up noodles slightly while stirring. Arrange on a large platter; press into a mound. Arrange bean sprouts around edge. Sprinkle noodles with reserved carrots, then with cilantro sprigs. Arrange fried egg in center of noodles, or tear into pieces and arrange with bean sprouts. Serve at once. Makes 6 to 8 servings.

Tip: Small amounts of leftover meat and vegetables may be transformed into a new dish by adding them to noodles.

Fresh Rice Noodles with Beef
Beef Kway Teow

(Singapore)

Many food stalls, or hawker stalls as they are called in Singapore, serve this dish. The fresh rice noodles are surprisingly sturdy and do not break up when stir-fried. If they are not available, try substituting an equal amount of cooked wide egg noodles.

1 lb. boneless lean beef steak (top sirloin, round steak or flank steak), sliced 1/8 inch thick
2 tablespoons soy sauce
1 teaspoon vegetable oil
1/2 teaspoon salt
1/2 teaspoon sugar
1/4 cup vegetable oil
1 large shallot, thinly sliced
1 lb. fresh rice noodles
2 garlic cloves, minced
1/4 lb. bean sprouts
1/2 teaspoon cornstarch
2 tablespoons water
1 tablespoon oyster sauce
3 green onions, chopped
8 cilantro sprigs

Place steak in a medium-size bowl. Add 1 tablespoon of the soy sauce, 1 teaspoon oil, the salt and sugar. Mix well. Cover and marinate in refrigerator 1 hour or longer. Heat remaining 1/4 cup oil in a small skillet. Add shallot; fry until browned and crisp. Drain on paper towels; set aside for garnish. Reserve 3 tablespoons oil. If rice noodles are not pre-cut, cut into strips 1/2 inch wide. Heat a wok over medium-high heat. Add 2 tablespoons reserved oil and heat. Add 1/2 of the garlic; fry a few seconds. Add bean sprouts, then noodles and remaining 1 tablespoon soy sauce. Stir-fry 2 minutes. Spoon noodles onto a heated platter; keep warm. Remove any noodle scraps from wok but do not wash. Mix cornstarch and water in a small cup. Add remaining 1 tablespoon reserved oil to wok and heat. Add remaining garlic; fry a few seconds. Add steak; stir-fry 1-1/2 minutes. Add oyster sauce; stir-fry 30 seconds. Stir cornstarch mixture to blend in cornstarch that has settled; stir into wok. Stir 30 seconds or until sauce is thickened. Place steak on top of noodles. Sprinkle with green onions, then fried shallot. Arrange cilantro sprigs around edge. Makes 4 servings.

Tip: *To make a noodle dish substantial enough for a main course, increase the amount of meat, add a few cooked or canned shrimp if not included in the basic recipe and decorate with hard-cooked egg wedges.*

Deluxe Fried Noodles
Bami Goreng Istimewa
(Indonesia)

These Javanese noodles can be a side dish or a main course. If Chinese dry noodles are hard to find, try substituting fine spaghetti cooked al dente. Regular soy sauce may be substituted for the Indonesian soy sauce.

1 egg
2 teaspoons water
1 teaspoon vegetable oil
6 oz. Chinese-style dry noodles
1 tablespoon vegetable oil
1/2 small onion, finely chopped
6 oz. boneless lean pork, cut into 1/2-inch cubes
1 teaspoon chicken-bouillon granules
1/8 teaspoon coarsely ground black pepper
2 garlic cloves
12 medium-size shrimp, shelled, deveined
1/4 cup shredded carrot
1/4 lb. green cabbage (1/4 small head), cored, finely sliced
1/4 lb. bean sprouts
1/2 teaspoon salt
2 tablespoons Indonesian-style soy sauce (kecap)
Crisp-Fried Onion Shreds, page 31, prepared with 1/2 medium-size onion
1 small cucumber, peeled, sliced
6 Shrimp Chips, page 43

Beat egg with water in a small bowl. Heat a medium-size skillet, preferably non-stick, over medium heat. Brush with 1 teaspoon oil. Pour in egg; swirl to coat bottom of pan. Cook, without stirring, until underside is set. Lift edges, turn over and cook 20 seconds or until second side is firmly set. Remove to a flat surface. Cut in half. Stack halves; cut into thin strips. Set aside for garnish. Cook noodles in boiling salted water to cover in a large saucepan 7 minutes or until tender but not soft. Drain, rinse with cold water and drain again. Heat a wok over medium-high heat. Add 1 tablespoon oil and heat. Add chopped onion; stir-fry until onion starts to soften. Add pork, chicken-bouillon granules and pepper. Squeeze garlic through garlic press into wok. Stir-fry over medium heat 5 minutes or until pork is cooked. Add shrimp; stir-fry 2 minutes. Add carrot and cabbage; stir-fry 1 minute. Add bean sprouts; stir-fry 1 minute. Sprinkle with salt. Turn off heat. Add noodles and soy sauce. Stir to combine. Taste and add more salt if needed. Spoon onto a heated platter. Top with shredded egg, then sprinkle with fried onion. Arrange cucumber slices around edge. Garnish with shrimp chips. Makes 4 to 6 servings.

Noodles with Pork, Shrimp & Vegetables
Pancit

(The Philippines)

In this recipe, spaghetti has been substituted for Filipino-style dried noodles called pancit Canton. The name Canton indicates the Chinese background of the dish. **Photo on page 38.**

3 tablespoons vegetable oil
8 oz. spaghetti
1/2 medium-size onion, thinly sliced
2 garlic cloves, chopped
1/4 lb. boneless lean pork, cut into thin strips
1/2 cup water
1/2 lb. green cabbage (1/4 medium-size), shredded
1/4 lb. Chinese pea pods, ends snapped off, strings removed
1/4 lb. shrimp, shelled, deveined
3 tablespoons soy sauce
1 teaspoon salt
1/8 teaspoon black pepper
1 hard-cooked egg, sliced
Tops of 2 green onions, sliced

Bring 3 quarts salted water to a boil in a large pot. Add 1 tablespoon oil, then add spaghetti. Boil, uncovered, 8 minutes. Drain; rinse with cold water. Heat a wok over medium-high heat. Add 2 tablespoons oil and heat. Add onion and garlic; stir-fry 45 seconds. Add pork; stir-fry until no longer pink. Add water, cover and cook 2 minutes. Uncover, add cabbage and stir until cabbage starts to wilt. Add pea pods and shrimp; cook, stirring, 2 minutes. Stir in soy sauce, salt and pepper. Add spaghetti; cook, stirring, 2 minutes. Arrange on a heated platter; garnish with egg slices and green-onion tops. Makes 6 servings.

Steamed Bean Threads with Fish
Pla Noang

(Thailand)

Crab and other seafood are also prepared in this fashion. The Sichuan peppercorns add a subtle camphor-like flavor that is quite pleasant.

6 oz. bean thread noodles
3/4 lb. lean white fish fillets
3 tablespoons soy sauce
3 teaspoons Chinese wine or dry sherry
2 oz. solid pork fat
1/3 cup chicken broth
1 teaspoon Worcestershire sauce
1/2 teaspoon Sichuan peppercorns, crushed
1/4 teaspoon salt
1 tablespoon finely shredded gingerroot
1/2 cup cilantro sprigs

Place bean threads in a large bowl, cover with cold water and soak until softened, about 20 minutes. Cut fish into 8 pieces. Place in a shallow dish. Add 1 tablespoon of the soy sauce and 1 teaspoon of the wine. Let marinate while preparing remaining ingredients. Bring 2-1/2 quarts water to a rapid boil in a large saucepan. Drain bean threads. Add to boiling water; boil 2 minutes. Drain well. In a heavy 3-quart saucepan, heat pork fat until it yields 1-1/2 to 2 tablespoons liquid fat; discard solid portion. Add chicken broth, remaining 2 tablespoons soy sauce and 2 teaspoons wine, Worcestershire sauce, Sichuan peppercorns, salt, gingerroot, noodles and cilantro; toss to combine. Place fish and marinade on top of noodles. Cover; steam over low heat until fish is cooked through, about 20 minutes. Use a heat diffuser if necessary to keep noodles from burning. Makes 4 servings.

Pork & Noodle Bowl
Mì Quảng

(Vietnam)

A meal in a Vietnamese restaurant often consists of a large bowl of soup or a noodle dish such as this.

1- to 1-1/4 lbs. pork tenderloin
2 tablespoons vegetable oil
1 cup water
1/4 cup soy sauce
1 1/2 teaspoons sugar
1/8 teaspoon red (cayenne) pepper
6 oz. egg noodles, 3/8 inch wide
4 romaine-lettuce leaves, cut crosswise into 1/2-inch slices
6 oz. bean sprouts
4 thin onion slices, halved
24 large mint leaves
8 cilantro sprigs
1/4 cup chopped roasted peanuts

If the tenderloin is thick, cut it in half lengthwise, then cut crosswise into 1/4-inch-thick slices. Heat a wok over high heat. Add oil and heat. Add pork; stir-fry until any liquid that emerges evaporates, 6 to 7 minutes. Add water and soy sauce; bring to a boil. Reduce heat, cover and simmer 10 minutes. Remove pork with a slotted spoon, place in a bowl and keep warm. Strain sauce into a 1-cup measure; add water to make 1 cup. Stir in sugar and red pepper. Pour into a small saucepan; keep hot. In a 3-quart saucepan, cook noodles in boiling salted water to cover 10 minutes or just until tender. Drain well. Divide lettuce among 4 large bowls. Add 1/4 of the bean sprouts and onion slices to each bowl. Divide noodles among bowls. Top with mint leaves and cilantro. Add pork to each bowl; sprinkle with peanuts. Pour 1/4 cup of the hot sauce into each bowl; serve at once. Mix ingredients before eating. Season with additional soy sauce if needed. Makes 4 servings.

Stir-Fried Rice Noodles with Pork
Pancit Bihon

(The Philippines)

A cook in the town of Magdalena prepared these noodles for the late afternoon snack called merienda.

6 oz. rice stick noodles
2 tablespoons vegetable oil
2 garlic cloves, minced
1/4 lb. lean pork, cut into thin strips
4 tablespoons soy sauce
1/2 cup chicken broth
1/4 lb. green cabbage (1/4 small head), cored, finely sliced
1/4 cup finely shredded carrot
1/4 cup finely chopped onion
1/4 teaspoon freshly ground black pepper
2 green onions, chopped
1 small lime, cut into 4 wedges

Soak rice sticks in a medium-size bowl in water to cover 30 minutes. Drain well. Heat a wok over high heat. Add oil and heat. Add garlic, then pork; stir-fry 2 minutes. Add 1 tablespoon soy sauce; stir-fry 2 more minutes or until pork has absorbed soy sauce. Add broth and 1 tablespoon more soy sauce. Stir in cabbage, carrot and onion. Cover; cook 2 minutes. Add noodles, remaining 2 tablespoons soy sauce and pepper. Cook, stirring, 2 minutes or until noodles have absorbed liquid in wok. Spoon onto a heated platter. Sprinkle green onions over top. Serve with lime wedges to squeeze onto noodles as desired. Makes 4 servings.

Lacy Crepes
Roti Jala

The crepes look and taste like homemade fresh egg noodles but are much easier to prepare. Try them with creamed chicken or tuna as well as with Asian curries.

3/4 cup all-purpose flour
1/4 teaspoon salt
1 egg
1-1/4 cups water
6 drops yellow food color
Vegetable oil

Mix flour and salt in a medium-size bowl. Add egg, water and food color. Beat until smooth. Pour batter into a large plastic squeeze bottle. Heat a large non-stick skillet with a bottom diameter of 9 inches over medium-high heat. Brush 1/2 teaspoon oil over skillet. Squeeze batter into skillet in a thin stream, swirling to make lacy circles and crossing circles with batter to hold them together. Cook crepe 1 minute without turning. With spatula, fold crepe in half, then in quarters. Remove to a plate. Cover to keep warm. Continue making crepes in this fashion until batter is used, brushing skillet with additional oil if crepes start to stick. Serve at once. If desired, crepes may be prepared in advance and reheated in a microwave oven. To reheat in the microwave, place crepes in a glass pie plate, cover with plastic wrap or a paper towel and heat at medium-high power (70%) until hot to the touch. Makes about 14 crepes.

Tip: When selecting bean sprouts, look for firm, plump white sprouts. Do not buy sprouts that are brown.

DESSERTS

Lovers of luscious desserts can indulge themselves to the full in Southeast Asia where sweets can be as exotic as Water Chestnut Pudding or as western as a meringue torte filled with buttercream frosting and sprinkled with toasted cashews.

The Water Chestnut Pudding is a Chinese dessert from Singapore. The meringue torte is a specialty of the Philippines. Its French name, Le Gateau Sans Rival, means cake without rival, a title that is justified by the torte's popularity. Even bakery counters in fast food centers sell it.

If any dessert rivals the peerless torte, it is flan, which was brought to the Philippines by the Spaniards. In an especially pretty presentation, cubes of flan are arranged in a dish with strawberries and splashed with vanilla custard sauce.

Other desserts that show European influence include dainty coconut tarts from Singapore and a fresh ginger mousse from Bangkok. Crepes have Asian interpretations, too. An idea from Bangkok is to serve them in a coconut-amaretto sauce with a sprinkling of almonds. In Indonesia, Malaysia and Brunei, crepes are tinted green and stuffed with sweetened coconut. The coloring comes from the pandan plant, but green food color will do as well. Serve the stuffed crepes with coconut sauce or with chocolate sauce and whipped cream, as in Brunei.

When the occasion calls for a handsome cake, it would be hard to surpass a delicate green Pandan Chiffon Cake swirled with whipped cream frosting, a recipe from Malaysia. If pandan flavoring is not available, substitute coconut extract for an equally delightful dessert.

In this hot part of the world, ice is often an integral part of desserts. And ice cream is a necessity. The Thais make wonderful coconut ice cream, which they often top with corn kernels. The use of corn in desserts may surprise some, but it is an old Southeast Asian practice. Another example is a corn-and-coconut-milk porridge from Kuala Lumpur.

A classic dessert of the Philippines is *bibingka,* a cake baked in banana leaves in an earthenware cooker fueled with charcoal. Bibingka variations in this chapter include one made with fresh cassava root and another with glutinous rice, neither requiring the banana leaves or charcoal cooker.

Fruit, of course, is the most common dessert, available for the picking. No Asian fruit has drawn more attention than the durian. Expensive and highly prized, it gives off such a powerful, and to some, unpleasant aroma that it is banned from hotels and airplanes.

Along with such distinctive regional fruits as the jackfruit, starfruit, mangosteen and rambutan, there are bananas, papayas, pineapples, melons and citrus in profusion. And who hasn't heard of the honey-sweet, melt-in-your-mouth mangoes of the Philippines? Despite the outstanding qualities of the Philippine fruit, Indonesians insist that their country produces the sweetest and tastiest varieties.

Even strawberries are native to the region. They grow in high, cool Baguio in the Philippines. And in Bangkok during the season, sarong-clad vendors squat along the sidewalks with huge baskets of berries. What do the Thais do with them? A soda fountain in Bangkok heaps the berries and other fruits in a tall glass with strawberry ice cream and cubes of red gelatin, then drowns the concoction with milk and tops it with whipped cream.

Mocha Meringue Torte
Le Gateau Sans Rival

For a spectacular party dessert, double the recipe and make a six-layer torte. In the Philippines, plain buttercream is commonly used. The mocha flavoring and chocolate topping are a dressier variation.

4 egg whites
1/2 cup sugar
3/4 cup cashews, toasted, finely chopped
1-1/2 teaspoons chocolate shot

Mocha Buttercream Frosting:
4 egg yolks
3/4 cup sugar
6 tablespoons water
3/4 cup butter, softened (12 tablespoons)
1 oz. semisweet chocolate, melted, slightly cooled
1-1/2 teaspoons instant coffee powder

Preheat oven to 300F (150C). Place a 9-inch round cake pan bottom down on waxed paper; trace 3 circles. Cut around tracings to make 3 circles. Invert 3 (9-inch) round cake pans. Grease bottom (now the top) of each. Place waxed-paper circle on bottom. Set aside. Beat egg whites in a large bowl until soft peaks form. Beat in sugar 1 tablespoon at a time, beating until stiff and glossy. Gently fold in 1/2 cup cashews. Spoon 1/3 of meringue onto each prepared cake pan; spread evenly with a spatula. Place in oven at 5 minute intervals. Bake 50 to 60 minutes, until browned and thoroughly dry. As each layer is done, remove from oven; invert onto a large dinner plate. Carefully peel off waxed paper. Place on rack to cool. Make Mocha Buttercream Frosting. To assemble, place 1 meringue layer flat-side up on a platter. With a spatula, spread slightly less than 1/3 of the frosting over meringue. Add a second meringue layer, flat-side down. Press down, then spread with another scant 1/3 of the frosting. Press remaining meringue layer, flat-side down, over frosting. Spread remaining frosting over top and sides. Sprinkle remaining 1/4 cup chopped cashews over top, then sprinkle with chocolate shot. Cover torte loosely with waxed paper; chill until frosting is firm, about 1 hour. Cut in wedges to serve. Store any leftover torte in refrigerator. Makes 6 to 8 servings.

Mocha Buttercream Frosting:
Place egg yolks in a small bowl. Beat with an electric mixer at high speed until pale and thick. Combine sugar and water in a small saucepan. Boil until syrup forms a soft ball when a small amount is dropped into a cup of cold water (234-240F, 112-115C on a candy thermometer). With mixer at high speed, pour syrup in a very thin stream into egg yolks. After syrup is incorporated, continue to beat until outside of bowl feels cool. Set mixer at medium or creaming speed. Add butter 1 tablespoon at a time, beating until each is incorporated. When all butter is added, beat in chocolate and coffee powder. (If ingredients are slightly warm and make frosting too liquid to spread, refrigerate to firm slightly, then beat thoroughly.)

Strawberry Flan

(The Philippines)

A pretty springtime dessert. **Photo on page 112.**

1/3 cup sugar
1 (1-pint) carton half and half
    (2 cups)
3 eggs
1/2 cup sugar
1/2 teaspoon vanilla extract
24 to 32 strawberries (4 berries
    per serving), hulled, thinly
    sliced

Custard Sauce:
2 eggs
3 tablespoons sugar
1-3/4 cups milk
1/2 teaspoon vanilla extract

Preheat oven to 325F (165C). Heat 1/3 cup sugar in a small skillet over medium heat until melted, clear and golden in color. Spoon over bottom and partway up sides of an 8" x 4" loaf pan. Combine half and half, eggs, 1/2 cup sugar and vanilla in a blender. Blend at high speed 20 seconds. Pour into prepared pan. Set in a larger baking pan. Add hot water to come halfway up sides of loaf pan. Bake 1 hour or until a knife inserted slightly off-center comes out clean. Cool, then cover and refrigerate until thoroughly chilled. Flan may be made a day ahead of serving. Make Custard Sauce. To assemble, run a sharp knife around edges of flan. Turn out onto a platter. Cut flan crosswise into 6 slices for 6 servings or 8 slices for 8 servings. Cut each slice into 4 cubes. In each individual dessert dish, arrange 4 flan cubes. Top with 4 sliced strawberries. Spoon custard sauce over top. Makes 6 to 8 servings.

Custard Sauce:
Beat eggs with sugar in top of a double boiler. Scald milk in a small saucepan. Gradually beat milk into egg mixture. Place over simmering water; cook, stirring constantly, until mixture thickens slightly, 20 to 25 minutes. Remove from heat; stir in vanilla. Pour into a bowl, cover and refrigerate until chilled. Makes about 1-3/4 cups.

Flan Kamayan Style
Leche Flan Kamayan

(The Philippines)

Flan is usually baked but this version, from a restaurant in Manila, is steamed.

2/3 cup sugar
6 egg yolks
1 (12-oz.) can evaporated milk
1 (14-oz.) can sweetened
    condensed milk
1 teaspoon vanilla extract

Heat sugar in a medium-size skillet over medium heat until melted, clear and golden. Spoon syrup over bottoms of 8 (4-oz.) custard cups. Beat egg yolks with a small amount of evaporated milk in a medium-size bowl. Beat in remaining evaporated milk, condensed milk and vanilla. Divide mixture among prepared custard cups. Cover each with foil. Place on a rack in a steamer over simmering water. Cover and steam 30 minutes or until a knife inserted slightly off-center comes out clean. If steamer is small, flan may be steamed in batches. Remove custard cups, cool, then refrigerate until chilled. To serve, run a sharp knife around edges. Place an individual serving plate on top of each, invert and let flan slide out onto plate. Makes 8 servings.

Ginger Mousse

Fresh gingerroot gives special flavor to this mousse, which is served at the Regent Hotel in Bangkok. A Japanese ginger grater will reduce the ginger almost to a puree. For best consistency, prepare the dessert no more than 1 hour before serving.

1 (8-oz.) carton whipping cream
(1 cup)
3 egg yolks
1/3 cup sugar
Dash salt
1 tablespoon very finely grated
gingerroot with juice
4 teaspoons chopped crystallized
ginger

Whip cream in a medium-size bowl until stiff. Scrape off and add cream clinging to beater. Remove 1/3 cup whipped cream, place in a small bowl, cover and refrigerate. Without cleaning beater, beat egg yolks, sugar, salt, gingerroot and juice in a small bowl. Lightly fold into whipped cream. Cover and refrigerate. At serving time, divide mixture among 4 dessert glasses. Top each with some of the reserved whipped cream and 1 teaspoon chopped ginger. Makes 4 servings.

Coconut Tarts

It's easy to make tarts when you don't have to roll out the dough. In this recipe, the pastry is pressed into the tart tins.

1/4 cup butter, softened
1 tablespoon sugar
1 egg yolk
1 cup all-purpose flour
2 tablespoons ice water

Coconut Filling:
2 eggs
1/2 cup sugar
1-1/2 cups flaked coconut
1/4 cup butter, melted
1/2 teaspoon vanilla extract

Preheat oven to 350F (175C). Cream butter and sugar in a medium-size bowl. Beat in egg yolk. Stir in flour. Mixture will be dry. Add enough ice water to make a dough that is soft but not sticky. Knead lightly; form into a ball. Divide dough into quarters. Divide each quarter into thirds, making 12 pieces of dough. Place each in center of a 2-1/2-inch fluted tart pan. With your thumbs, press dough evenly over bottom and up sides to top. Place tart pans on a baking sheet. Make Coconut Filling. Divide filling evenly among tart shells. Bake 10 minutes. Reduce heat to 325F (165C); bake 15 more minutes or until golden brown. With aid of a spatula, remove tarts from baking sheet to a rack to cool. When cooled, remove from pans, prying gently at edges with a sharp knife to loosen if necessary. Makes 12.

Coconut Filling:
Beat eggs in a medium bowl. Add sugar; beat until mixture is pale yellow. Mix in coconut, then butter. Stir in vanilla.

Crepes with Coconut-Amaretto Sauce
Khanom Baeng
(Thailand)

When you need a dessert that is both easy and elegant, try this. The crepes and sauce can be prepared ahead of time and assembled just before serving.

2 eggs
1 tablespoon vegetable oil
1 tablespoon sugar
1/4 teaspoon salt
2/3 cup all-purpose flour
1 cup water
Vegetable shortening
1 tablespoon amaretto liqueur
4 to 6 tablespoons toasted
   slivered almonds

Coconut Sauce:
1/3 cup sugar
2 tablespoons cornstarch
1/8 teaspoon salt
2 cups coconut milk

Beat eggs in a medium-size bowl. Beat in oil, sugar and salt. Alternately add flour and water, beginning and ending with flour; beat until batter is smooth. Let stand at room temperature 1 hour before using. Heat a 6- to 7-inch skillet over medium-high heat. Lightly grease with shortening. For each crepe, spoon 2-1/2 to 2-3/4 tablespoons batter into skillet, swirling quickly to coat bottom evenly. Cook until crepe is lightly browned on bottom. Turn and cook until second side is lightly browned. Remove and stack on a plate. (There should be 12 crepes.) Prepare Coconut Sauce. Reheat sauce if prepared ahead. Stir in amaretto. Allow 2 or 3 crepes for each serving. Roll or fold crepes; place on warmed dessert plates. Top each serving with 1/3 cup sauce. Sprinkle each serving with 1 tablespoon almonds. Makes 4 to 6 servings.

Coconut Sauce:
Combine sugar, cornstarch and salt in a small saucepan. Gradually stir in coconut milk. Cook and stir over medium heat until mixture boils and thickens slightly. Serve warm. Makes about 2 cups.

Variation
If coconut milk is not available, make sauce with 2 cups cow's milk and 1/2 teaspoon coconut extract.

Mango Jubilee
(The Philippines)

This dessert is so popular in Manila that one constantly sees bursts of flame as the mangoes and their sauce are ignited at tableside.

3 tablespoons butter
1/3 cup sugar
1/2 cup orange juice
1 teaspoon lime juice
1/4 teaspoon grated lime peel
1 cup packed diced fresh mango
   (1/2- to 3/4-inch dice)
2 tablespoons triple sec or other
   orange-flavored liqueur
1 tablespoon brandy
1 pint vanilla ice cream

Melt butter and sugar in a large skillet or the blazer pan of a chafing dish. Stir in orange juice, lime juice and lime peel. Boil, stirring occasionally, until mixture reduces and becomes syrupy. Add mango; cook 1-1/2 minutes or until mango is heated through. Add triple sec and brandy. Ignite with a long-handled match. Stir until flames subside. Place 2 small scoops ice cream in each dessert bowl. Spoon mango mixture over ice cream. Serve at once. Makes 4 servings.

Coconut Crepes
Kueh Gulong

*Translucent white sauce over bright green crepes makes an eye-catching dessert. If coconut milk is not available, the crepes can be prepared with water. **Photo on page 112.***

2 eggs
3/4 cup coconut milk or water
1/2 cup all-purpose flour
Dash salt
1/8 teaspoon green food color
Vegetable shortening
Coconut Sauce, opposite
Toasted coconut, if desired

Coconut Filling:
1/2 cup packed dark-brown sugar
1/3 cup water
1-1/2 cups flaked coconut

Beat eggs in a medium-size bowl. Beat in coconut milk, flour and salt. Blend in food color. Batter should be bright green. Cover and let stand at room temperature 1 hour before using. Heat a 6-inch skillet over medium-high heat. Grease lightly with shortening. Pour scant 1/4 cup batter into skillet, swirling quickly to coat bottom evenly. Cook until top of crepe appears dry, about 30 seconds depending on heat. Turn and cook 20 to 25 seconds on other side. Remove crepe; stack on a plate. When all are prepared, cover and let stand until cooled. (There should be 8 crepes.) Prepare Coconut Filling. When filling crepes, keep the smoother side (the side cooked last) on the outside. Place 1 slightly rounded tablespoon filling in a strip across crepe 1/3 of the way from 1 edge. Roll up tightly. Continue until all crepes are filled. Allow 2 crepes for each serving. Serve at room temperature topped with Coconut Sauce. Sprinkle with toasted coconut. Makes 4 servings.

Coconut Filling:
Combine brown sugar and water in a small saucepan. Bring to a boil. Add coconut. Cook, stirring, until blended and liquid has almost disappeared. Cool thoroughly, stirring occasionally.

Variation (Brunei)
Spoon a layer of homemade or prepared dark chocolate sauce over each dessert plate. Set crepes on sauce. Garnish with a dollop of whipped cream and a maraschino cherry.

Pandan Chiffon Cake
(Malaysia)

This cake is also popular in Singapore and Brunei. Bakeries sell it whole or by the slice, often without frosting. Pandan flavoring is available in stores that specialize in Southeast Asian products.

2 cups cake flour
1-1/2 cups sugar
1 tablespoon baking powder
1/8 teaspoon salt
7 eggs, separated
3/4 cup coconut milk
1/2 cup vegetable oil
1 teaspoon pandan flavoring
1/4 teaspoon green food color
1/4 teaspoon yellow food color
1 egg white
1/2 teaspoon cream of tartar
4 drops green food color
4 drops yellow food color

Whipped-Cream Frosting:
1 (8-oz.) carton whipping cream
    (1 cup)
1/4 teaspoon pandan flavoring
1/4 teaspoon green food color
1/4 teaspoon yellow food color
3 tablespoons sugar

Preheat oven to 325F (165C). Combine cake flour, sugar, baking powder and salt in a sifter; sift 3 times. Sift last time into a large bowl. Make hollow in center; add egg yolks, coconut milk, oil, pandan flavoring and 1/4 teaspoons of food colors. Beat with an electric mixer at low speed until dry ingredients are moistened, then at high speed until thoroughly blended. Combine 8 egg whites, cream of tartar and drops of food colors in a large bowl. Beat egg whites slowly at first to incorporate cream of tartar and food colors, then beat until stiff but not dry. Gently fold 1/4 to 1/3 of the egg whites into batter to lighten it. Gently but thoroughly fold in remaining egg whites. Turn into ungreased 10-inch tube pan. Bake 55 to 60 minutes or until cake tester comes out clean and top springs back when lightly touched. Invert pan; let cake stand until thoroughly cooled, 4 hours or overnight. Run a thin sharp knife around outer edge of cake and tube of cake pan. If using pan with removable bottom, lift out cake, run knife under cake to loosen and turn out. Otherwise, tap bottom of pan sharply, invert and turn out cake. Make Whipped Cream Frosting. Use a spatula to frost top and sides of cake. Makes 10 to 12 servings.

Whipped-Cream Frosting:
Combine whipping cream, pandan flavoring and food colors in a medium-size bowl. Beat until thick. Gradually beat in sugar until very stiff.

Variation
If pandan flavoring is not available, omit from the cake batter. Substitute 1/4 teaspoon coconut extract for pandan flavoring in the frosting.

Tip: To crack or crush ice without an ice crusher, place it in a heavy plastic bag, set the bag on a sturdy surface and pound with a hammer.

Mixed Fruits with Grass Jelly & Ice
Es Shanghai
(Indonesia)

This hot weather cooler is a cross between a dessert and a drink. As the ice melts, it turns into a beverage. After eating the fruits and jelly, drink or spoon up the remaining liquid.

1 cup water
2/3 cup sugar
1 teaspoon vanilla extract
1/2 teaspoon red food color
1/2 cup diced fresh or canned
    mango, drained
1/2 cup diced canned pineapple,
    drained
2 cups diced Chinese grass jelly
24 canned palm seeds
4 cups finely crushed ice
1/2 cup whipping cream
1/2 cup milk

Combine water and sugar in a small saucepan. Bring to a boil, stirring just until sugar is dissolved. Boil 1 minute. Remove from heat. Stir in vanilla and food color. Cool slightly, cover and refrigerate until chilled. In each of 4 large wine glasses or other large stemmed glasses, place 2 tablespoons mango, 2 tablespoons pineapple, 1/2 cup grass jelly and 6 palm seeds. Top with 1 cup crushed ice. Mix whipping cream and milk. Pour 1/4 cup mixture over each serving. Top with 1/4 cup vanilla syrup. Serve at once. Makes 4 servings.

Variation
Instead of grass jelly, use cubes of firm gelatin in any fruit flavor. Canned longans, lychees or other fruit may be substituted for palm seeds. Since lychees are large, reduce quantity to 3 per serving.

Thai Halo Halo
(Thailand)

Halo halo is a Philippine dessert that includes sweetened beans, coconut shreds and other ingredients topped with crushed ice, milk, ice cream and a spoonful of flan. This is a Thai interpretation of that dessert.

1 (3-oz.) pkg. strawberry gelatin
1 cup boiling water
3/4 cup cold water
1/2 cup sliced strawberries
1 (8-oz.) can pineapple chunks,
    drained, cut into small wedges
1 banana, sliced
1/2 cup seedless green grapes
1 pint strawberry ice cream
1/2 cup evaporated milk
1/2 cup whipping cream
2 strawberries, halved
4 mint sprigs

Place gelatin in a medium-size bowl. Add boiling water; stir until gelatin is completely dissolved. Stir in cold water. Pour into an 8" x 4" loaf pan. Cover and refrigerate until firm. Slice through gelatin in loaf pan to make 1-inch squares. Divide gelatin squares among 4 very large dessert glasses or bowls. Combine strawberries, pineapple, banana and grapes. Place 1/4 cup mixed fruits on top of gelatin in each glass. Add 1/2 cup ice cream to each glass. Place another 1/4 cup fruit on top of ice cream. Spoon 2 tablespoons evaporated milk over each serving. Whip cream in a small bowl until soft peaks form; spoon whipped cream over each serving. Decorate with a strawberry half and mint sprig. Makes 4 servings.

Almond Ice Cream

Kulfi

(Malaysia)

Pakistani and Indian restaurants in Malaysia and Singapore serve kulfi in various flavors. The ice cream is frozen in individual cone-shaped metal molds, which are either imported from India or made to order locally. Custard cups or muffin pans lined with paper baking cups may be substituted.

1/2 gallon milk (2 qts.)
1/4 cup whipping cream
6 tablespoons sugar
1/3 cup unblanched almonds, finely ground

Place milk in a 3-quart saucepan; boil until reduced to 3-1/2 cups, stirring often to prevent burning and to keep skin from forming on top. When milk is reduced, add cream, sugar and almonds. Boil gently 20 minutes. Spoon into 6 (1/2-cup) kulfi molds, custard cups or other individual molds. Cover and freeze. To unmold, run cool water over kulfi mold or dip custard cup quickly into warm water. Loosen with knife; turn out. If using kulfi molds, slice ice cream into large chunks. Makes 6 servings.

Ginger Ice Cream

Ice Krem Khing

(Thailand)

Thai restaurants in the United States often serve ginger-flavored ice cream. This is an easy way to make it.

1 pint vanilla ice cream
1/3 cup finely chopped, preserved ginger packed in syrup
1 tablespoon syrup from preserved ginger
1 teaspoon ground ginger

Soften ice cream. Stir in chopped ginger, ginger syrup and ground ginger. Refreeze. Makes 4 servings.

Coconut Ice Cream

Ice Krem Kati

(Thailand)

To serve the ice cream Thai-style, top it with cooked or canned corn kernels, roasted peanuts or both.

1 (1-pint) carton whipping cream (2 cups)
1 (14-oz.) can coconut milk (1-3/4 cups)
1/2 cup sugar
1 teaspoon coconut extract
1/8 teaspoon salt

Combine ingredients in an ice cream freezer container. Process according to manufacturer's instructions. Makes about 5 cups.

154 *Desserts*

Corn Topping for Ice Cream

Kao Pode Wan

(Thailand)

Corn is naturally sweet and so makes an appropriate sauce for ice cream.

2 tablespoons sugar
2 teaspoons cornstarch
1/4 teaspoon salt
1 cup milk
1 cup corn kernels cut from 1
  large ear cooked corn or 1 cup
  drained canned whole-kernel
  corn

Stir together sugar, cornstarch and salt in 1-quart saucepan. Stir in milk. Add corn. Bring to a boil; cook, stirring, until very thick. Pour into a small bowl; cool slightly. Cover and refrigerate until chilled. Serve as a topping for vanilla or coconut ice cream. Makes 1-1/2 cups.

Frozen Lychees

Lynchee Loy Kao

(Thailand)

It is never too much trouble to prepare dessert when the recipe is as simple as this.

1 (20-oz.) can lychees in heavy
  syrup

Place can in freezer; freeze until solid, several hours or overnight. Open can and let lychees soften slightly before serving. Spoon into 4 dessert bowls. Makes 4 servings.

Lychee-Pineapple Dessert

Raum Mit

(Thailand)

Crunchy bits of ice give welcome relief from the heat and humidity prevalent in Thailand.

1 (20-oz.) can lychees in heavy
  syrup, chilled
1/2 cup coconut milk
3 tablespoons sugar
1/2 cup canned nata de pina
  (pineapple gel) or canned
  pineapple chunks, cut into
  halves, chilled
1 cup coarsely cracked ice

Drain lychees, reserving syrup. Combine syrup, coconut milk and sugar in a small bowl; stir to dissolve sugar. Cover and refrigerate until chilled. There will be about 1-2/3 cups sauce. Divide lychees and nata de pina among 4 large dessert bowls. Divide sauce among bowls. Top each serving with some of the ice. Serve at once. Makes 4 servings.

Cracked-Wheat & Coconut Milk Porridge
Bubur Terigu
(Malaysia)

Cracked wheat is a substitute for a soft white wheat that is available in Malaysia. The recipe comes from Penang.

1/2 cup cracked wheat
3 cups coconut milk
2 cups water
1/2 teaspoon salt
3/4 cup packed dark-brown sugar
1/2 teaspoon pandan flavoring, if desired

Place wheat in a small bowl. Cover generously with water; soak overnight. The next day drain wheat. Place in a 3-quart saucepan. Add 1-1/2 cups coconut milk, the 2 cups water and salt. Bring to a boil. Reduce heat; simmer very gently, uncovered, 45 minutes, stirring occasionally to prevent sticking. (Mixture will be moderately thick and should barely bubble; use a heat diffuser if necessary.) Add brown sugar and pandan flavoring; stir until sugar is melted and blended. Simmer, uncovered, 5 minutes. Porridge may be prepared in advance to this point. Just before serving, add remaining 1-1/2 cups coconut milk. Bring to a boil. Ladle into warmed bowls. Makes 6 to 8 servings.

Corn & Coconut Porridge
Bubur Jagung
(Malaysia)

Corn and coconut milk make good partners. The idea was suggested by a Muslim cook during a Ramadan dinner.

1 (17-oz.) can cream-style corn
1-1/2 cups coconut milk
1/4 cup packed dark-brown sugar
1 tablespoon granulated sugar

Combine ingredients in a 1-1/2-quart saucepan. Bring to a boil, stirring to dissolve sugars. Remove from heat. Serve warm or chilled. Spoon into bowls. Makes 6 servings.

Black-Rice Porridge
Pulot Hitam
(Singapore)

Black glutinous rice can be found in Asian markets that stock Indonesian supplies. For the true salty flavor use a rounded 1/4 teaspoon salt in the coconut milk.

1 cup black glutinous rice
1 qt. water (4 cups)
1 cup sugar
1/4 teaspoon salt
1-1/2 cups coconut milk

Place rice in a strainer; rinse well. Place rice in a large heavy saucepan. Add water. Bring to a boil. Reduce heat, cover and simmer 30 minutes, stirring occasionally. Add sugar; cook, uncovered, 20 to 30 more minutes or until mixture has consistency of a thick porridge. Keep warm. Stir salt into coconut milk. To serve, ladle porridge into individual bowls. Spoon 4 to 6 tablespoons salted coconut milk over each serving. Makes 4 to 6 servings.

Water Chestnut Pudding
Pīng Huā Mǎ Tí Lù

(Singapore)

A pudding in name only, this dessert is more accurately described as a lightly thickened sweet soup.

2-2/3 cups water
1/2 cup sugar
3/4 cup canned water chestnuts (about 24), cut in very small dice
2 tablespoons cornstarch
2 tablespoons cold water
1 egg, beaten

Combine 2-2/3 cups water and sugar in a 1-quart saucepan. Bring to a boil, stirring until sugar has dissolved. Add water chestnuts; bring to a boil again. Blend cornstarch and 2 tablespoons cold water in a small bowl. Stir into boiling mixture; cook until slightly thickened, stirring frequently. Remove from heat. Add egg; stir to form shreds. Serve in soup bowls. Makes 4 servings.

Coconut Pudding
Puding Kelapa

(Indonesia)

The pudding will remain soft like a porridge rather than firmly set.

3 tablespoons cornstarch
2 cups coconut milk
1/2 cup packed dark-brown sugar
1/8 teaspoon salt
1/2 teaspoon vanilla extract

Place cornstarch in a medium saucepan. Gradually stir in coconut milk. Stir in brown sugar and salt. Cook, whisking, over medium heat until mixture thickens and comes to a boil. Boil 1 minute. Remove from heat; stir in vanilla. Spoon mixture into 4 custard cups. Serve warm or chilled. Makes 4 servings.

Cantonese Coconut Pudding
Ya Tze Bo Din

(Malaysia)

Serve the pudding plain or garnish it with a fan of strawberry slices or mandarin-orange segments.

1/3 cup sugar
3 tablespoons cornstarch
2 cups coconut milk

Combine sugar and cornstarch in a medium saucepan. Gradually stir in coconut milk. Cook, stirring, over medium heat until mixture thickens and comes to a boil. Boil 1 minute. Spoon mixture into 4 custard cups or small ramekins. Serve warm or chilled. Makes 4 servings.

Tapioca Pudding with Two Sauces
Gula Melaka
(Singapore)

Gula Melaka means palm sugar, which is traditionally used for one of the sauces. Dark-brown sugar is an excellent substitute.

1/3 cup quick-cooking tapioca
2 cups water
1 (14-oz.) can coconut milk (1-3/4 cups)
1 cup packed dark-brown sugar
1/2 cup water
1 (1/8-inch-thick) gingerroot slice

Combine tapioca, water and 1/4 cup coconut milk in a 1-quart saucepan; let stand 5 minutes. Chill remaining 1-1/2 cups coconut milk. Bring tapioca mixture to a boil over medium heat, stirring frequently; boil 1-1/2 minutes or until thickened. Divide among 6 (4-oz.) custard cups. Cool, then cover and refrigerate until chilled. Combine brown sugar, water and gingerroot in a small saucepan. Bring to a boil, stirring until sugar is dissolved; continue to boil 1 minute. Remove gingerroot. Cool syrup to room temperature. Unmold tapioca into small dessert bowls. Place sugar syrup and chilled coconut milk in separate pitchers. Pass with pudding to add as desired. Makes 6 servings.

Sticky Rice Cake
Bibingkang Malagkit
(The Philippines)

This rich dessert keeps well. Wrap leftovers in foil and refrigerate. Reheat, covered with foil, in a preheated moderate oven. Or place in a microwave-safe dish, cover with plastic wrap and microwave at medium-high power (70%) until warm.

2 cups white glutinous rice
5 cups coconut milk
1/2 teaspoon salt
1-1/4 cups packed light-brown sugar

Wash rice; place in a medium-size bowl. Cover generously with cold water; soak 4 to 6 hours. Drain well. Bring coconut milk to a boil in a 3-quart saucepan. Add rice and salt. Reduce heat to low. Cook, stirring constantly, until rice is almost tender and mixture is very thick, about 15 minutes. Stir in brown sugar until blended. Cover and cook over very low heat 10 minutes; use a heat diffuser if necessary to prevent rice from burning and sticking. Cool, covered, 1 hour. Generously butter an 8-inch square baking pan. Pack rice into pan, making sure surface is even. Preheat broiler. Place pan about 4 inches from heat source. Broil until top is browned, 5 to 7 minutes. Cool slightly. Cut into small squares; serve warm or at room temperature. Makes 12 to 16 servings.

Penang Papaya Pudding
Puding Betik

(Malaysia)

This papaya-orange dessert makes a light and elegant ending to a meal no matter what its nationality. **Photo on page 112.**

1 (1-1/2-lb.) papaya
1/2 cup sugar
3 tablespoons cornstarch
Dash salt
1 cup orange juice
2 tablespoons lemon juice
2 strawberries, halved, or 4
　raspberries
4 mint leaves

Cut papaya in half; scoop out seeds. Cut papaya into wedges; peel. Process papaya until pureed in a blender or food processor fitted with the metal blade; there should be about 1-1/4 cups. Combine sugar, cornstarch and salt in a 1-quart saucepan. Gradually stir in orange juice. Add papaya puree and lemon juice. Cook over medium heat, stirring constantly, until mixture boils and thickens enough to separate slightly when spoon is drawn across the pan. Spoon into a bowl, cover and refrigerate until chilled. Just before serving, stir well. Spoon into stemmed dessert glasses. Garnish each serving with a strawberry half or a raspberry and a mint leaf. Makes 4 servings.

Mangoes & Sticky Rice
Kaoneo Mamoung

(Thailand)

A wonderful dessert that makes mango season worth waiting for. The Thais sprinkle the rice with crunchy roasted mung beans. Toasted sesame seeds are just as good.

1 cup white glutinous rice
1 (14-oz.) can coconut milk (1-3/4
　cups)
1/3 cup sugar
3/4 teaspoon salt
2 medium to large mangoes
1 teaspoon toasted sesame seeds

Wash rice; place in a medium-size bowl. Cover generously with cold water; soak 4 to 6 hours. Drain well. Place in a colander or sieve with fine holes. Set colander on rack over water in a large pot; water must not touch rice. Cover pot; bring water to a boil. Reduce heat slightly; steam rice 25 minutes. Meanwhile, open can of coconut milk carefully without shaking. Spoon off 1/4 cup of any thick milk that has accumulated at the top. Place in a small bowl, cover and refrigerate. Stir remaining coconut milk to blend. Measure 1/2 cup; reserve remainder for another use. Stir coconut milk, sugar and salt in a small bowl until sugar is dissolved. Remove rice from steamer. Spoon into a 1-1/2-quart baking dish. Stir sugar mixture into rice. Cover, return to steamer and steam 10 more minutes. Remove baking dish to a rack. Let rice cool, covered, to room temperature. Peel mangoes. Remove pulp from seeds; slice. Divide the rice among 4 large dessert plates. Top each serving with 1 tablespoon reserved thick coconut milk. Sprinkle with 1/4 teaspoon sesame seeds. Arrange some of the mango slices beside the rice on each plate. Makes 4 servings.

Cassava Cake with Caramel Topping
Bibingkang Casaba
(The Philippines)

A thin layer of caramel sauce adds an appealing finish.

8 oz. fresh cassava root
3 eggs
3/4 cup sugar
1/4 teaspoon salt
1-1/2 cups coconut milk
2 tablespoons butter, melted

Caramel Topping:
1/2 cup coconut milk
1/2 cup packed dark-brown sugar

Cut cassava root into chunks; peel with a potato peeler. Coarsely chop chunks. Process cassava as finely as possible in a food processor fitted with the metal blade; there should be 1 cup ground cassava. Preheat oven to 350F (175C). Butter an 8-inch square baking pan. Beat eggs, sugar and salt in a large bowl. Stir in coconut milk, cassava and melted butter. Pour mixture into buttered pan. Bake 25 to 30 minutes or until dessert feels set when top is pressed. While cake bakes, prepare Caramel Topping. Spread topping evenly over top of cake. Bake 15 more minutes. Place pan on a rack to cool. Cut into squares or bars. Serve bibingka warm or at room temperature. Makes 6 to 8 servings.

Caramel Topping:
Combine coconut milk and brown sugar in a small heavy saucepan. Bring to a boil. Boil, stirring occasionally, until mixture forms a thick syrup that measures between 1/3 and 1/2 cup.

Bananas in Coconut Milk
Klouy Buaod Chee
(Thailand)

This dessert is as good as it is easy.

2 cups coconut milk
1/4 cup sugar
1/2 teaspoon salt
4 medium-ripe bananas, peeled,
   cut into 1-1/2-inch chunks

Combine coconut milk, sugar and salt in a 1-quart saucepan. Bring to a boil. Add bananas. Reduce heat; simmer, uncovered, 5 minutes, or until bananas are partially softened. Cool to room temperature. Serve bananas in bowls with the sauce. Makes 6 servings.

Sweet-Potato Custard with Fried Shallots
Khanom Mo Ken
(Thailand)

The idea may sound odd, but the crisp-fried shallots scattered over the top are a wonderful complement to this dessert.

1-1/2 cups coconut milk
3 eggs
1/3 cup packed dark-brown sugar
1/3 cup packed light-brown sugar
1/2 cup mashed boiled sweet
  potato
1/8 teaspoon salt
1/4 cup vegetable oil
6 small shallots, very thinly sliced

Preheat oven to 350F (175C). Combine coconut milk, eggs, brown sugars, sweet potato and salt in a blender; blend thoroughly. Butter a 1-quart flameproof baking dish. Pour mixture into dish. Set in a large baking pan; add hot water to come halfway up sides of dish. Bake 50 minutes or until knife inserted off-center of custard comes out clean. Remove from hot water. Preheat broiler. Place top of custard about 4 inches from heat source. Broil custard 1-1/2 to 2 minutes or until top is browned; set aside. Heat oil in a small skillet. Add shallots; fry until browned and crisp. Drain on paper towels. Scatter shallots over top of pudding. Serve warm or at room temperature. Makes 6 servings.

Variation
Substitute mashed boiled taro or pumpkin for the sweet potato.

Pineapple-Palm Seed Dessert
Polarmai Loy Gaeow
(Thailand)

Light, refreshing desserts like this are ideal after a spicy meal.

1 cup water
1/2 cup sugar
1/4 teaspoon pandan flavoring
2 cups diced fresh pineapple
1/2 cup canned palm seeds
1 cup coarsely cracked ice

Combine water and sugar in a small saucepan. Bring to a boil, stirring until sugar is dissolved. Remove from heat. Stir in pandan flavoring. Cover and refrigerate until chilled. Divide pineapple and palm seeds among 4 dessert bowls. Divide pandan syrup among bowls. Add 1/4 cup ice to each bowl. Makes 4 servings.

Tip: Palm seeds are imported canned from Thailand and the Philippines. Add them to fruit for an unusual salad or quick dessert.

Fruit With Rice Dumplings in Ginger Syrup
Troi Nước
(Vietnam)

If glutinous rice flour is not available, eliminate the dumplings and increase the amount of fruit.

3 cups water
2/3 cup sugar
1 tablespoon thinly sliced
   gingerroot
1 (11-oz.) can mandarin orange
   segments
1 (8-oz.) can pineapple chunks
1/3 cup glutinous rice flour
3 tablespoons warm water
1 teaspoon toasted sesame seeds

Combine 3 cups water, sugar and gingerroot in a large saucepan. Bring to a boil. Continue to boil until reduced to 2 cups. Cool, then cover and refrigerate until chilled, retaining gingerroot in syrup. Chill cans of fruit. Just before serving, drain fruits, discarding liquid; divide among 4 dessert bowls. In a small bowl, blend rice flour with warm water to make a soft dough. Add more water if needed. Divide dough into 16 pieces. Roll each into a ball. Bring 3 cups water to a boil in a 1-quart saucepan. Add dumplings. Cook at a medium boil, uncovered, until dumplings rise to surface. Cook 1 more minute. Lift from water with a slotted spoon. Rinse with cold water. Place 4 dumplings in each bowl with fruit. Strain gingerroot from syrup. Add 1/2 cup ginger syrup to each bowl. Sprinkle each with 1/4 teaspoon sesame seeds. Makes 4 servings.

Fried Bananas
Klouy Tod
(Thailand)

This recipe comes from the Mae Sa Valley Resort in Chiang Mai province, but fried bananas are popular everywhere in Thailand. You can watch street vendors cooking these in Bangkok.

1/4 cup all-purpose flour
1 teaspoon baking powder
1/4 teaspoon salt
1/2 cup water
1 teaspoon vegetable oil
4 large medium-ripe bananas
1-1/2 cups vegetable oil

Syrup:
1/2 cup sugar
1 cup boiling water
1 (2" x 3/4") lemon-peel strip,
   yellow part only

Make Syrup; set aside. Sift flour, baking powder and salt into a medium-size bowl. Beat in water and oil until smooth. Peel bananas. Cut each crosswise into 4 chunks. Heat oil in a wok or medium-size skillet to 360F (180C) or until a 1-inch bread cube turns golden brown in 60 seconds. Dip each banana chunk in batter, then place in oil. Spoon a little batter over top. Fry until golden on each side, 3 to 4 minutes, turning as needed. Drain on paper towels. Serve at once, passing syrup to spoon over as desired. Makes 4 servings.

Syrup:
Heat sugar in a small saucepan over medium heat until sugar is melted, clear and golden in color. Slowly stir in boiling water; sugar will bubble up and thicken but will dissolve again. Stir until smooth. Bring to a boil, add lemon peel and boil 10 minutes or until syrup is reduced to 3/4 cup. Let cool to room temperature.

BEVERAGES

Cool, refreshing drinks abound in Southeast Asia, where heat and thirst are constant companions. The variety is great. Fresh fruit ades, sweet sugar cane juice, frothy mango shakes, iced coconut water and many more make thirst a pleasure because relieving it is so delightful.

It may seem unconventional, but the Thais stir salt into their lemonade, which intensifies the flavor and makes the drink more satisfying. And those who link avocados with salads will be surprised to learn that the Balinese blend them with ice and condensed milk to make a pale green shake. In the Philippines, tart green mangoes are whipped with ice and syrup for a beverage that is sometimes turned into a cocktail by adding liquor. The unripe mangoes are so much a part of Filipino cuisine that they are displayed in the markets alongside the ripe fruit.

Shredded cantaloupe combined with water, sugar and ice is another popular Filipino cooler. This same drink is also made with the soft flesh of the young coconut, both in the Philippines and in Indonesia. Rose syrup, as pretty as a valentine, is diluted for a bright pink drink favored by Muslim Malays, who drink no alcohol. Sometimes milk or coconut milk is added for a richer, creamy effect. Pineapple, papaya, watermelon, star fruit and others are juiced for drinks at food stalls in Singapore and Malaysia. These same stalls dispense the sugar cane juice and coconut water.

One beverage that has become popular in the United States is Thai iced tea. Tall, sweet and creamy, it is made with tea leaves that have been specially treated to give them a distinctive flavor and deep orange color when brewed. The tea can also be made with regular tea leaves, and a recipe for that version is included along with the authentic one.

Not all Southeast Asian drinks are cold. The Vietnamese favor small glasses of coffee made with strong, full-flavored French-roast beans and sweetened with condensed milk. Sometimes a thermos of hot water is placed on the table for diluting the concentrated coffee to taste. In the Philippines, *salabat,* a spicy tea made with fresh gingerroot, is a stimulating pick-me-up when energy flags. A similar drink is found in Indonesia.

The most famous cocktail of the region is the gin sling of Singapore, often called the Singapore sling. And the most famous version is that dispensed by the Long Bar of the Raffles Hotel. The Raffles opened in 1887, and the sling dates back to 1915, when it was created by a Chinese bartender named Ngiam Tong Boon.

Other cocktails developed more recently appeal to an international range of residents and visitors. Many of these are based on fresh fruits or fruit juices, while some capitalize on the worldwide popularity of Southeast Asia's prime ingredient, the coconut.

Thai Lemonade
Nam Manao
(Thailand)

Limes are often used for this drink in Thailand, but lemons work equally well. In very hot weather, this lightly salted lemonade is sometimes served as a refreshing meal accompaniment.

3/4 cup water
1/4 cup lemon juice
3 tablespoons sugar
1/8 teaspoon salt
Ice cubes

Combine all ingredients except ice in a tall glass. Stir until sugar and salt are dissolved. Fill glass with ice. Makes 1 serving.

Nagasari Avocado Cooler
(Indonesia)

This thick, frappé-like drink is a specialty of a tiny restaurant at Kuta Beach on the island of Bali. **Photo on page 39.**

1 small, very ripe avocado
1/3 cup sweetened condensed milk
2 teaspoons sugar or to taste
2 cups cracked ice
Lemon slice, if desired, for garnish

Combine ingredients in a blender; blend until avocado is pureed and ice is reduced to fine granules. Garnish with lemon slice. Makes 2 servings.

Pineapple Water
(Singapore)

A typical drink that is served at juice stands in Singapore's hawker centers. For the best flavor, use only fresh pineapple for this drink.

1/2 cup fresh pineapple chunks
1/2 cup water
5 ice cubes
1 tablespoon sugar or to taste

Combine ingredients in a blender container; blend until mixture is foamy and only a little ice remains in chunks, stopping and starting blender several times. Vary the amount of sugar according to the sweetness of the pineapple. Makes 1 serving.

Tip: When using only a small amount of canned sweetened condensed milk or evaporated milk in a drink recipe, store the remainder in a tightly covered jar in the refrigerator. The milk will keep for several days.

Cantaloupe Cooler

Melón

(The Philippines)

*Filipinos press the juices from the seedy portion of the cantaloupe through a sieve and add them to the drink. **Photo on page 39**.*

1 cup water
1-1/2 tablespoons sugar
1/3 cup shredded cantaloupe
Ice cubes
Cantaloupe wedge for garnish

Combine water and sugar in a tall glass. Stir until sugar dissolves. Stir in cantaloupe. Add ice cubes. Serve with a spoon to scoop out cantaloupe shreds. Garnish with cantaloupe wedge. Makes 1 serving.

Green-Mango Shake

Katas ng Berdeng Mangga

(The Philippines)

Ripe mangoes can also be used, but the sharper flavor of the unripe green mango adds interesting character to the drink.

1 medium-size green (unripe)
  mango
1 cup cracked ice
3 tablespoons Simple Syrup,
  page 32

Cut mango pulp away from the seed. Peel. Place mango, ice and syrup in a blender; blend at high speed until pureed. Pour into 1 tall glass or 2 smaller glasses. Makes 1 or 2 servings.

Variation
Combine ingredients for Green-Mango Shake and 2 ounces vodka in a blender. Blend until pureed. Makes 2 servings.

Kampong Air

(Brunei)

Thirst-quenching non-alcoholic drinks are popular in Muslim Brunei. This one is named for the large water village at Bandar Seri Begawan, the capital city.

3 oz. (6 tablespoons) canned
  mango nectar
1/2 oz. (1 tablespoon) lemon-lime
  soda or lemonade
1/2 oz. (1 tablespoon) grenadine
1/2 oz. (1 tablespoon) lime juice
Crushed ice
3 oz. (6 tablespoons) lemon-lime
  soda
Ice cubes

Combine all ingredients except 3 ounces soda and the ice cubes in a cocktail shaker. Shake well. Strain into a tall glass. Add remaining soda; stir. Add ice cubes. Makes 1 serving.

Preserved Plum Drink
Xí Muôi

Jars of preserved plums are stocked in Chinese markets. For this salty-sweet drink, use those preserved in water and salt, not vinegar.

3/4 cup water
2 tablespoons sugar
2 teaspoons liquid from Chinese
 preserved plums
2 Chinese preserved plums
Ice cubes

Combine water and sugar in a tall glass; stir until sugar dissolves. Stir in plum liquid. Add plums and ice cubes. Makes 1 serving.

Rosy Milk

Ayer Batu Bandong

Bilal, an Indian restaurant in Kuala Lumpur, serves this pretty beverage with its spicy curries. The variation adds coconut milk. **Photo on page 39.**

6 tablespoons Rose Syrup
1/4 cup evaporated milk
1/4 cup water
1 cup coarsely cracked ice
Mint sprig, if desired, for garnish

Rose Syrup:
1/2 cup water
1/2 cup sugar
2 tablespoons rose water
1/8 teaspoon red food color

Make Rose Syrup. Combine syrup, milk and water in a tall glass. Stir in ice. Makes 1 serving.

Rose Syrup:
Stir water and sugar in a small saucepan over medium heat until sugar dissolves. Bring to a full boil without stirring; boil 5 minutes or until slightly thickened. Remove from heat. Stir in rose water and food color. Cool. Store in a covered jar. Makes about 2/3 cup.

Variation (Singapore)
Reduce Rose Syrup to 1/4 cup. Substitute 2 tablespoons coconut milk for 2 tablespoons of the evaporated milk. Prepare as directed.

Thai Iced Tea Overseas-Style

Cha Yen
(Thailand)

If specially treated Thai tea leaves are not available, regular tea leaves from the supermarket will also make a good drink.

2 tablespoons plus 2 teaspoons tea leaves
1 qt. boiling water
2 tablespoons powdered non-dairy coffee creamer
2/3 cup sweetened condensed milk
1 cup evaporated milk
2 tablespoons sugar
About 6 cups crushed ice

Place tea leaves in a 1-1/2-quart heatproof glass container; add boiling water. Let stand 5 minutes. Strain out tea leaves. Stir coffee creamer into hot tea until blended. Stir in condensed milk, evaporated milk and sugar. Cover and refrigerate until chilled. For each serving, place 1 cup ice in a tall glass. Add tea mixture. Makes 5 to 6 servings.

Thai Iced Tea

Cha Yen
(Thailand)

Proper brewing of the tea requires pouring it several times through a cloth coffee bag. The bags can be found in Latin markets as well as Thai groceries. A very fine strainer would be your best substitute.

3-1/2 cups water
1/3 cup imported Thai tea leaves
1/3 cup sugar
1/3 cup sweetened condensed milk
1/2 cup half and half
About 4 cups crushed ice

Place water in a large saucepan; bring to a boil. Place tea leaves in cloth coffee bag. Pour water through tea into another large container. Pour back through leaves into pan. Repeat pouring 4 more times. Stir sugar, condensed milk and half and half into tea. Pour into a 1-quart jar. Cover and refrigerate until chilled. For each serving, place 1 cup or more crushed ice in a tall glass. Pour 1 cup tea mixture over ice. Serve with straws. Makes 1 quart or 4 servings.

Hot Ginger Tea
Salabat
(The Philippines)

This sweet and spicy tea might be served at merienda, which is the Philippine equivalent of afternoon tea.

2 oz. gingerroot
6 cups water
1/2 cup packed light-brown sugar

Wash gingerroot thoroughly; do not peel. Thinly slice gingerroot; there should be a scant 1/2 cup. Combine gingerroot and water in a 2-quart saucepan. Bring to a boil. Boil gently, uncovered, 30 to 35 minutes or until reduced to 4 cups. Strain to remove gingerroot. Stir in sugar until dissolved. Serve hot. Makes 1 quart or 4 to 6 servings.

French-Style Filter Coffee
Cà Phê Sữa Đá
(Vietnam)

A legacy of French rule in Vietnam, the coffee is very strong and usually served in a heavy glass.

1-1/2 tablespoons finely ground,
    French-roast coffee
3/4 cup boiling water
1 tablespoon sweetened
    condensed milk

Place coffee in a 1-cup coffee filter. Place filter on top of cup or heatproof heavy glass. Gradually add water to coffee. When coffee has dripped through, stir in milk. Makes 1 serving.

Variation
Prepare coffee as directed. Cool. Serve over ice.

Mango Daiquiri
(The Philippines)

This drink can be made with light or dark rum or equal parts of both. The recipe is from the Manila Peninsula Hotel.

1-1/2 oz. (3 tablespoons) rum
1-1/2 oz. (3 tablespoons) canned
    mango nectar
1/2 oz. (1 tablespoon) triple sec
1/2 oz. (1 tablespoon) lime juice
Ice cubes
Orange slice and maraschino
    cherry for garnish

Combine all liquid ingredients and 3 or 4 ice cubes in a cocktail shaker. Shake thoroughly. Strain into a cocktail glass; add ice cubes. Insert a wooden pick through orange slice and cherry; use to garnish drink. Makes 1 serving.

Singapore Gin Sling

(Singapore)

This is the original recipe from the Raffles Hotel, where the drink was created.

2 oz. (1/4 cup) gin
1 oz. (2 tablespoons) Cherry
  Heering or cherry brandy
1/3 oz. (2 teaspoons) orange juice
1/3 oz. (2 teaspoons) pineapple
  juice
1/3 oz. (2 teaspoons) lime juice
1/4 teaspoon Benedictine liqueur
1/4 teaspoon triple sec or other
  orange liqueur
4 drops aromatic bitters
Ice cubes
Pineapple wedge and maraschino
  cherry for garnish

Combine all liquid ingredients and 3 or 4 ice cubes in a cocktail shaker. Shake thoroughly. Strain into a tall cocktail glass. Add ice cubes, if desired. Insert a wooden pick through pineapple wedge and cherry; use to garnish drink. Makes 1 serving.

Singapore Cricket Club's Singapore Sling

(Singapore)

The venerable club with its large playing field was founded in 1852, when Singapore was a British colony. **Photo on page 39**.

1 oz. (2 tablespoons) gin
1 oz. (2 tablespoons) cherry
  brandy
2 teaspoons lemon juice
1-1/2 teaspoons grenadine
2 oz. (1/4 cup) club soda
Ice cubes
Pineapple chunk and maraschino
  cherry for garnish

Combine gin, cherry brandy, lemon juice and grenadine in a cocktail glass. Stir in soda. Add ice cubes. Insert a wooden pick through pineapple and cherry; use to garnish drink. Makes 1 serving.

Siamese Kiss

(Thailand)

This drink was created at Bussaracum, a restaurant in Bangkok that specializes in aristocratic Thai cuisine.

1/2 oz. (1 tablespoon) light rum
1/2 oz. (1 tablespoon) tequila
1/2 oz. (1 tablespoon) cherry
   brandy
1/2 oz. (1 tablespoon) Grand
   Marnier
1-1/2 oz. (3 tablespoons) orange
   juice
2 teaspoons lemon juice
1/2 teaspoon Simple Syrup,
   page 32
Ice cubes
Lime slice and maraschino cherry
   for garnish

In a large cocktail glass, stir all ingredients except ice cubes and garnishes. Add ice cubes. Insert a wooden pick through lime slice and cherry; use to garnish drink. Makes 1 serving.

Baluarte Mango Daiquiri

(The Philippines)

Sweet Philippine mangoes make wonderful daiquiries, as in this recipe from Punta Baluarte, a beach resort outside of Manila. **Photo on page 107.**

1/2 very ripe mango (1/4 to 1/3
   cup pulp)
1-1/2 oz. (3 tablespoons) light or
   golden rum
1 oz. (2 tablespoons) lime juice
2 teaspoons sugar
3 ice cubes
Lime slice for garnish

Combine ingredients in a blender; blend until no large chunks of ice remain. Serve in a stemmed glass. Garnish with lime slice. Makes 1 serving.

Coconut Orchid

(Singapore)

To capture the atmosphere of Singapore, garnish this drink with a small orchid. **Photo on page 39.**

1-1/2 oz. (3 tablespoons) vodka
1/2 oz. (1 tablespoon) Galliano
   liqueur
2 oz. (1/4 cup) pineapple juice
1 oz. (2 tablespoons) cream of
   coconut
3 or 4 ice cubes

Combine all ingredients in a cocktail shaker. Shake thoroughly. Strain into a stemmed glass. Decorate with a small orchid, if desired. Makes 1 serving.

Coconut Lace

(Thailand)

Bangkok's legendary Oriental Hotel offers guests a variety of tall sweet drinks. This one blends fruit flavors with coconut.

3/4 oz. (1-1/2 tablespoons) light rum
3/4 oz. (1-1/2 tablespoons) gin
3/4 oz. (1-1/2 tablespoons) cream of coconut
1/2 oz. (1 tablespoon) pineapple juice
1/2 oz. (1 tablespoon) orange juice
1/2 oz. (1 tablespoon) lemon juice
Ice cubes

Combine all ingredients and 3 or 4 ice cubes in a cocktail shaker. Shake thoroughly. Strain into a slim tumbler or large cocktail glass. Add ice cubes if desired. Makes 1 serving.

Borneo Dream

(Brunei)

A long, cool, light drink that will be welcome in hot weather anywhere.

1 oz. (2 tablespoons) vodka
1 oz. (2 tablespoons) crème de cassis
1 oz. (2 tablespoons) triple sec
2 oz. (1/4 cup) orange juice
2 oz. (1/4 cup) pineapple juice
Ice cubes

Combine all ingredients except ice cubes in a cocktail shaker. Shake thoroughly. Strain into a large glass. Add ice cubes. Makes 1 serving.

Gong Hee Fat Choy

(Singapore)

The traditional Chinese New Year salutation serves as the title of this drink from the Hilton in Singapore.

1 oz. (2 tablespoons) gin
3/4 oz. (1-1/2 tablespoons) Napoleon Mandarine Liqueur
1 oz. (2 tablespoons) orange juice
3/4 oz. (1-1/2 tablespoons) lime juice
1/2 teaspoon Simple Syrup, page 32
1/4 teaspoon grenadine
3 or 4 ice cubes

Combine all ingredients in a cocktail shaker. Shake thoroughly. Strain into a stemmed glass. Makes 1 serving.

Oriental Sling

Bourbon is a substitute for Mekong, the strong Thai whisky that would be used in Bangkok.

1 oz. (2 tablespoons) bourbon
1/2 oz. (1 tablespoon) green
  crème de menthe
1/2 oz. (1 tablespoon) Kahlua
1-1/2 oz. (3 tablespoons)
  pineapple juice
1-1/2 oz. (3 tablespoons) orange
  juice
1 oz. (2 tablespoons) lemon juice
1/2 oz. (1 tablespoon) Simple
  Syrup, page 32
1/2 teaspoon egg white
3 or 4 ice cubes

Combine all ingredients in a cocktail shaker. Shake thoroughly. Pour into a tall glass. Makes 1 serving.

Ramayana Clover Club

(Indonesia)

Lush greenery makes Bali a beautiful vacation spot. This drink comes from a small resort hotel there.

1-1/2 oz. (3 tablespoons) dark rum
1-1/2 oz. (3 tablespoons)
  pineapple juice
3/4 oz. (1-1/2 tablespoons) orange
  juice
3/4 oz. (1-1/2 tablespoons) lime
  juice
2 teaspoons grenadine
1/2 teaspoon Simple Syrup,
  page 32
Ice cubes
2 oz. (1/4 cup) club soda

Combine rum, pineapple juice, orange juice, lime juice, grenadine, syrup and 3 or 4 ice cubes in a cocktail shaker. Shake thoroughly. Strain into a tall glass. Stir in soda. Fill with ice cubes. Makes 1 serving.

Mail Order Sources

Conte di Savoia
555 W. Roosevelt Rd.
Chicago, IL 60607
(312) 666-3471

Carries mostly Malaysian and Indonesian products, including Indonesian-style soy sauce.

Dewi
211 Alpine Street No. 4
Los Angeles, CA 90012
Telephone (213) 625-0914

Source for Indonesian ingredients, including shrimp paste (terasi), Indonesian-style soy sauce, ground laos, sambal oelek, candlenuts, black glutinous rice, rose syrup, krupuk, etc.

De Wildt Imports
RD #3
Bangor, PA 18013
(215) 588-1042

Indonesian and other Southeast Asian ingredients. Extensive catalog available.

Hollinda Company
9544 Las Tunas Drive
Temple City, CA 91780
(818) 286-9981

Indonesian and Malaysian ingredients.

Lorenzana Food Corp.
627 N. Vermont Avenue
Los Angeles, CA 90004
Attention: Sammy Lorenzana
Telephone (213) 665-5155

Filipino ingredients, including palm seeds, palm vinegar, fish sauce, seasoning mixes, etc. Lorenzana also stocks some Thai products.

Vietnam House
242 Farmington Avenue
Hartford, CT 06105
(203) 524-0010

Specializes in Vietnamese ingredients, but also carries other Southeast Asian products.

Metric Chart

Comparison to Metric Measure

When You Know	Symbol	Multiply By	To Find	Symbol
teaspoons	tsp	5.0	milliliters	ml
tablespoons	tbsp	15.0	milliliters	ml
fluid ounces	fl. oz.	30.0	milliliters	ml
cups	c	0.24	liters	l
pints	pt.	0.47	liters	l

When You Know	Symbol	Multiply By	To Find	Symbol
quarts	qt.	0.95	liters	l
ounces	oz.	28.0	grams	g
pounds	lb.	0.45	kilograms	kg
Fahrenheit	F	5/9 (after subtracting 32)	Celsius	C

Fahrenheit to Celsius

F	C
200—205	95
220—225	105
245—250	120
275	135
300—305	150
325—330	165
345—350	175
370—375	190
400—405	205
425—430	220
445—450	230
470—475	245
500	260

Liquid Measure to Milliliters

1/4 teaspoon	=	1.25 milliliters
1/2 teaspoon	=	2.5 milliliters
3/4 teaspoon	=	3.75 milliliters
1 teaspoon	=	5.0 milliliters
1-1/4 teaspoons	=	6.25 milliliters
1-1/2 teaspoons	=	7.5 milliliters
1-3/4 teaspoons	=	8.75 milliliters
2 teaspoons	=	10.0 milliliters
1 tablespoon	=	15.0 milliliters
2 tablespoons	=	30.0 milliliters

Liquid Measure to Liters

1/4 cup	=	0.06 liters
1/2 cup	=	0.12 liters
3/4 cup	=	0.18 liters
1 cup	=	0.24 liters
1-1/4 cups	=	0.3 liters
1-1/2 cups	=	0.36 liters
2 cups	=	0.48 liters
2-1/2 cups	=	0.6 liters
3 cups	=	0.72 liters
3-1/2 cups	=	0.84 liters
4 cups	=	0.96 liters
4-1/2 cups	=	1.08 liters
5 cups	=	1.2 liters
5-1/2 cups	=	1.32 liters

Index